ECONOMIC TRANSITIONS WITH CHINESE CHARACTERISTICS

ECONOMIC TRANSITIONS WITH CHINESE CHARACTERISTICS

SOCIAL CHANGE DURING THIRTY YEARS OF REFORM

Edited by

Arthur Sweetman and Jun Zhang

School of Policy Studies, Queen's University
McGill-Queen's University Press
Montreal & Kingston • London • Ithaca

SCHOOL OF
Policy Studies

Publications Unit
Policy Studies Building
138 Union Street
Kingston, ON, Canada
K7L 3N6
www.queensu.ca/sps/

Library and Archives Canada Cataloguing in Publication

Economic transitions with Chinese characteristics : social change during thirty years of reform / edited by Arthur Sweetman and Jun Zhang.

Includes bibliographical references.
ISBN 978-1-55339-235-4 (bound).—ISBN 978-1-55339-234-7 (pbk.)

1. China—Economic conditions—1976-2000. 2. China—Economic conditions—2000-. 3. China—Economic policy—1976-2000. 4. China—Economic policy—2000-. 5. China—Politics and government—1976-2002. 6. China—Politics and government—2002-. 7. China—Social conditions—1976-2000. 8. China—Social conditions—2000-. I. Sweetman, Arthur II. Zhang, Jun, 1963 Jan. 26-

HC427.95.E263 2008 330.951 C2008-907608-7

Contents for this Volume

Contents for the Related Volume

Economic Transitions with Chinese Characteristics: Thirty Years of Reform and Opening Up

Acknowledgements

The two volumes *Economic Transitions with Chinese Characteristics: Thirty Years of Reform and Opening Up*, and *Economic Transitions with Chinese Characteristics: Social Change During Thirty Years of Reform* grew out of the partnership between Fudan University and Queen's University. We are grateful to those who built this partnership.

We would like to thank staff at the School of Policy Studies Publication Unit, Mark Howes and Valerie Jarus for their many efforts, copyeditor Nancy Mucklow, research associate Hilary Sirman for her proofreading and Marilyn Redmond for keeping track of various people and files. Also, many thanks go to referee Jeff Nankivell who read the manuscript with great care and provided many very useful comments, and to those other referees who contributed anonymous reviews and helped improve the manuscripts.

Jun Zhang would like to acknowledge the Shanghai Education Committee for allowing him to conduct the "Sunshine Project" (Shuguang Jihua, 2006–2009). He also gives special thanks for the assistance provided by research grant "985 Project," to the Chinese Ministry of Education for the key research project grant #05JJD790076, and to his wife and son for their love and encouragement.

Arthur Sweetman would like to acknowledge funding from the Stauffer-Dunning Chair. He would also like to thank Prof. John Dixon for his encouragement of this project, and his wife and daughter for their love and support.

Arthur Sweetman

Director
School of Policy Studies
Queen's University at Kingston
Canada

Jun Zhang

Director
China Centre for Economic Studies
Fudan University, Shanghai
China

Crossing the River by Touching the Stones: An Introduction to Social Change in China during "Reform and Opening"

ARTHUR SWEETMAN AND JUN ZHANG

China's policy of "reform and opening," formalized in 1978, has had wide-ranging ramifications on the structure of Chinese society and the nature of its social programs. Economic perspectives on the impact of the reform on land tenure and migration are first explored, and social issues including education, the labour market, health care, poverty programs, and demographics are then addressed. Finally, the ongoing reform process, as articulated at the 2007 Chinese Communist Party Plenary, is analyzed, and criteria for future growth are discussed.

China's emergence on the international economic scene over the last three decades has impacted the world in diverse ways, and the scale of these effects has frequently been exceptional. Domestically, however, the changes have been even more dramatic. Starting with decollectivization, many of the socioeconomic structures in China have altered very substantially since Deng Xiaoping formalized and promoted the "reform and opening up" period of China's history with his speech before the Chinese Communist Party plenary in December, 1978. The drive towards a more market-oriented economy has had important social ramifications. Geographic mobility, land tenure and home ownership, labour markets, the health care and education systems and, perhaps most well known of all, the country's demographics have all been dramatically reshaped. All of these are fundamental to the economic structure of the nation and, clearly, comprehending them is important for anyone who wants to begin to understand China today and where it may be going in the future.

In the process of economic development China has faced massive social changes. While in the early process of reform it may have been possible on the economic side to achieve so-called "reform without losers,"

Economic Transitions with Chinese Characteristics: Social Change During Thirty Years of Reform, eds. Arthur Sweetman and Jun Zhang. Montreal and Kingston: McGill-Queen's University Press, Queen's Policy Studies Series.

on the social side the one-child policy is clearly associated with immense loss for many individuals. Starting in the late 1990s, while there have been large economic benefits, development has increasingly generated negative spillovers including a rising income gap, land seizures, the shortage of social insurance, and environmental degradation. All of these issues need to be addressed and they represent a huge challenge not only to China's policy making, but also to social scientists. Divided into three sections, this collection of essays, *Economic Transitions with Chinese Characteristics: Social Change During Thirty Years of Reform*, looks at many of the relevant issues in a primarily economic framework.

Land tenure and internal migration are addressed in the first section since they are crucial underpinnings of many social issues and of what has been China's most important comparative advantage in international trade: its very large low-cost industrious workforce available in the coastal regions. The supply and productivity of that workforce (as seen in the labour market chapter in the second section) is influenced by changes in land tenure and internal migration policies, and the enforcement of these policies. This includes not only the regulation of migration to the increasingly heavily industrialized coastal regions, but also return migration to interior provinces that are currently in need of economic stimulation. Secondly, the volume looks at a range of social issues. These include the interrelated transitions that have occurred in the labour market, the education and health care systems, and the antipoverty efforts that have seen hundreds of millions of people lifted out of extreme distress. Closely related to poverty, China's start at addressing the interregional and interpersonal economic inequality that has been associated with economic growth is discussed, as is the intertwined relationship between the economic reforms and demographic change, in particular, the well-known one-child policy. Finally, the collection is forward-looking and explores ongoing reform, focusing particularly on the ramifications of the announcements of the 17th Chinese Communist Party Congress in 2007 and the role of China in the world going forward. Good governance is a crucial determinant for ongoing growth and success.

This book is complemented by its sister volume, *Economic Transitions with Chinese Characteristics: Thirty Years of Reform and Opening Up*, which looks at the context of the economic reforms, and addresses issues related to economic growth and finance, technology and development, and gives some attention to the environmental issues now arising in China.

Land Tenure, Housing, and Migration

Land tenure is one of the fundamental policies of a society. Guanzhong James Wen (2009) argues, in accord with some recent government action, that China's current system of rural land tenure is in need of reform so that individual ownership rights can be established in a well-defined legal framework that permits resale. He contends that the existing land tenure system, initiated in the early 1980s, injures rural progress and increases rural-urban economic inequality. Initially, the system in rural areas that was started in the 1980s worked very well, increasing productivity and output. However, more recently it has fallen behind relative to the advances seen in the industrial coastal regions. Collective ownership and administrative intervention do not permit rural land to be allocated to its best use, reducing total output. He argues for a more market-oriented approach to land tenure. These reforms, as has often been the case in China, will likely only ratify, codify and extend practices that are already underway in some locations.

Looking at urban land tenure, Weili Ding and Steven Lehrer (2009) analyze its intersection with education policies, using empirical evidence from a survey they conducted. They argue that Shanghai's citizens are sorting themselves into neighbourhoods in accord with socioeconomic status. While, overall, the reforms of the late 1970s and early 1980s have increased the quality of both housing and education, issues of equity are increasingly in the forefront of the government policy agenda. The sorting process is generating inequality in access to high-quality education—so-called neighbourhood effects based on social stratification—are well known in the Western world, but were not previously as obvious in China. Neighbourhood formation and socioeconomic stratification are closely interrelated and extremely important issues that exemplify the interaction of social and economic forces operating in China in the current period.

Zhao Chen, Jie Chen and Xiaofeng Liu (2009) also address urban housing with a focus on housing quality and the challenge China faces in upgrading its housing stock to provide increased quality of life for its residents, especially its poorer ones. They point to a paradox: the reforms to the urban housing system have improved both the quality and quantity of housing available, which is of value to the entire population, and also simultaneously have increased inequality of housing conditions and income. This is an apparent trade-off observable in several areas of the changing Chinese socioeconomic structure as discussed in several of the chapters in Arthur Sweetman and Jun Zhang (2009a, 2009b). A current question is whether this trade-off between increasing standards of living, and increasing inequality of outcomes, is a permanent or a transitory phenomenon. More fundamentally, it is necessary to understand in the Chinese context whether the growing inequality is a requirement of growth, if it can be managed by government policies and programs, and whether its roots are primarily economic or political. Of course, there are also substantial issues about the magnitude of the inequality associated with the reforms. Chen, Chen and Liu address the role of government, considering the pros and cons of market reforms and alternative government policies. Arguing that the class of individuals who benefited under the previous housing allocation regime is the same one that disproportionately benefits under the current more market-oriented regime, they contend that further reform is needed, but that it is constrained by a type of path dependence as a result of political and social power being monetized in the housing market. They suggest that this implies that successful future housing policy to assist low-income households should operate more on the supply of, rather than the price of, dwellings.

Naoki Murakami (2009) takes a different tack, looking at internal migration and the return of individuals to the poor interior regions of China from the wealthier and industrialized coastal ones between which regions there has been a substantial increase in inequality since 2000. The central government has undertaken several major initiatives to reduce this gap. In this context, Murakami focuses on migrant entrepreneurs to Zhongyuan (or Henan province). The individuals involved are important sources of regional economic stimulation who transfer knowledge by defusing new ideas and entrepreneurial ability to underdeveloped regions. Initial outward migration of such individuals, he argues, should not be seen as a loss of human capital to the origin province. Rather, it is beneficial to economic growth in the economically disadvantaged region since some of these individuals return ready for entrepreneurial success after they have accumulated significant human capital in other locations, which is seen as beneficial for the economically disadvantaged region since some of those among the returning group will have entrepreneurial success. One caveat is that, in an example of the difficulties of transferring technology across alternative contexts, returnees have a tendency to employ more capital-intensive investments than is required in the relatively low-skilled, and low-cost, interior regions where there is an abundant and underutilized potential workforce.

Social Issues

The workforce is a crucial element of China's reforms, and Gordon Betcherman, Ana Revenga, and Minna Hahn Tong (2009) explore the transition toward a labour "market" that has evolved through a series of small steps that, though sometimes lagging the changing context, have amounted to a radical change over the past 30 years. Labour has moved from the rural and typically interior areas toward the cities, with both urban and rural productivity and wages increasing. Beneficially, the reallocation of workers from one sector to another has been well timed so that those exiting one sector have been absorbed into the other without massive disruption.

Despite the very large changes, however, China cannot be said to have a fully flexible labour market yet. There are substantial differences across areas, and elements of the former "managed" employment system still operate, though the current model is quite efficient. However, the increased average level of output has come at a cost. It is associated with the introduction of unemployment, job insecurity and a marked increase in wage/annual earnings inequality. China is now facing the dual challenges of redesigning its social security net, and also of upgrading the productivity / skills of its workforce, to address the new reality of its population. Success in both areas is essential as China seeks to move up the development ladder.

Although China has made great economic strides, there remain serious poverty issues that are particularly prevalent in rural areas. Yuan Zhang (2009) discusses these issues and points out the growing inequality between urban and rural areas. He argues for active government intervention, particularly pointing to the need not only for cash and resource transfers to impoverished rural areas, but for a large-scale strategy to assist these areas in development and growth. Improvements in educational accessibility in rural areas are clearly an important part of long-term development. More immediately, he contends that the residence registration system makes life difficult for the rural poor, and reduces allocative efficiency within the labour force. He suggests that the government continue its reform of this system in order to make it more beneficial to rural residents.

Health care is one of the key social programs in any country, and government policy in this area is particularly relevant for the well-being of the poorer segments of society. John Cai (2009) describes the evolution of the Chinese health care system since the late 1970s, looking especially at its interactions with the economic reforms. He also describes its current problems and future challenges. Prior to the economic reforms, China's health care system funding model was employment-based, and there was effectively perfect employment security. As the labour market has evolved, the health care system, and especially its sources of funding, have not changed as quickly. Access and funding are the crucial issues, and the restructuring of China's health care system in response to its new instructional context remains an ongoing challenge. A fundamental issue is that of a funding model that provides appropriate risk sharing in the *de facto* provision of health insurance. The groups for which risk was formerly pooled have broken down, and it is not clear that there are stable new ones to replace them. It may be that the optimal approach is to fund health care, at least to some base level, from the national government's general revenues.

China's so-called one-child-per-couple rule was among the first major policy changes—and it remains as one of the most interventionist—following Deng Xiaoping's speech in 1978. There was great fear at the time that population growth would prevent economic development and cause significant food, especially grain, shortages since the rate of growth in agricultural production was expected to increase at a slower rate than the demand for food from a growing population. In many ways, therefore, the demographic and economic reforms are intimately intertwined. Moreover, the one-child policy has had, and will continue to have for a substantial period into the future, a very significant impact on China's demographic structure. Zheng Wu, Christoph M. Schimmele, and Shuzhuo Li (2009) provide an overview of the evolution of the policy itself, its relationship to the economic reform, and its impact on China's demographic structure. They argue that while there was likely (although there is some debate on this issue) some early economic benefits from the policy, the demographic dividend is now almost completely spent. Moreover, there have been enormous social and human costs of the policy, and the follow-on of having had a low youth-dependency rate in the past is that in the not-too-distant future there will be a substantial rise in the old-age dependency rate.

Looking Forward

In October 2007 the 17th Chinese Communist Party Congress had a remarkable development agenda placed before it. Having experienced extremely high growth in the past three decades, the nation aimed to continue with high rates of economic growth in order to become a more prosperous, harmonious and technologically advanced state. Overall, while the plan that was laid out is extremely ambitious, given the economic advances of the last 30 years it is not implausible. Shujie Yao, Stephen Morgan and Kailei Wei (2009) analyze the plans developed at the 2007 Congress and discuss the implementation of these proposals going forward. They argue that the most significant challenge facing China is the quality of its leadership, and especially the issue of corruption among administrators from Beijing to local villages. In accord with the ideas discussed above, they also point to the need for growth to be put on a sustainable path to prevent environmental degradation and excessive resource depletion, as well as the need to alleviate the increasing economic inequality of Chinese society. As argued regarding the reform period to the present day in the first section of the affiliated volume, *Economic Transitions with Chinese Characteristics: Thirty Years of Reform and Opening Up*, Yao, Morgan and Wei see political and economic reform moving together in the future with success on each side depending on the other.

It is not yet clear what impact the financial crisis of 2008 will have on China's economic and social aspirations. But it is almost certain that the rate of growth will slow somewhat in the short run, though it will likely remain high by international standards. However, it is quite possible that economic growth will be somewhat lower in the longer-term than it has been in the last decade, since a sustained high rate imposes appreciable adjustment and/or transactions costs, and sustainability is also increasingly important. But China may well gain international prestige and authority as a result of the crisis, and this may change its relationship with many nations. Moreover, given its recent history of adaptation, China may be better positioned to learn from the current crisis and use it as an opportunity to learn and avoid future pitfalls to its long-term benefit. For example, it may be motivated to reform its financial system and reduce corruption as a result of the crisis, and this would likely be of substantial value. Overall, the crisis has appreciable short-term costs, but what is not yet clear is how large the cost will be in the long-term and whether there will be any silver lining. Whatever happens, the ramifications of the last 30 years of "reform and opening" have been quite dramatic and, looking forward, they will continue to be felt in subsequent generations.

References

Betcherman, G., A. Revenga, and M.H. Tong. 2009. "The Transition from a Managed Employment System Toward a Modern Labour Market." Pp. 93–114 in *Economic Transitions with Chinese Characteristics: Social Change During Thirty Years of Reform*, edited by A. Sweetman and J. Zhang.

Cai, J. 2009. "Turning Away from Dependence on the Economic System: Looking Forward and Back on the Reform of China's Health Care System." Pp. 135–148 in *Economic Transitions with Chinese Characteristics: Social Change During Thirty Years of Reform*, edited by A. Sweetman and J. Zhang.

Chen, Z., J. Chen, and X. Liu. 2009. "Finding Housing in China: The Market-Oriented Reform of China's Urban Housing System." Pp. 55–72 in *Economic Transitions with Chinese Characteristics: Social Change During Thirty Years of Reform*, edited by A. Sweetman and J. Zhang.

Ding, W., and S.F. Lehrer. 2009. "Housing and Education Reform in Urban China: No Longer Separate and Increasingly Unequal." Pp. 35–54 in *Economic Transitions with Chinese Characteristics: Social Change During Thirty Years of Reform*, edited by A. Sweetman and J. Zhang.

Murakami, N. 2009. "The Zhongyuan Economy and Returning Migrant Entrepreneurs." Pp. 73–90 in *Economic Transitions with Chinese Characteristics: Social Change During Thirty Years of Reform*, edited by A. Sweetman and J. Zhang.

Sweetman, A., and J. Zhang. 2009a. *Economic Transitions with Chinese Characteristics: Thirty Years of Reform and Opening Up*. Montreal and Kingston: Queen's Policy Studies Series, McGill-Queen's University Press.

——— 2009b. *Economic Transitions with Chinese Characteristics: Social Change During Thirty Years of Reform*. Montreal and Kingston: Queen's Policy Studies Series, McGill-Queen's University Press.

Wen, G.J. 2009. "The Incompatibility of China's Rural Land System with an Increasingly Urbanized and Marketized Economy." Pp. 11–34 in *Economic Transitions with Chinese Characteristics: Social Change During Thirty Years of Reform*, edited by A. Sweetman and J. Zhang.

Wu, Z., C.M. Schimmele, and S. Li. 2009. "Demographic Change and Economic Reform." Pp. 149–168 in *Economic Transitions with Chinese Characteristics: Social Change During Thirty Years of Reform*, edited by A. Sweetman and J. Zhang.

Yao, S., S. Morgan, and K. Wei. 2009. "Ongoing Reform: The New Economic Policies Promoted by the 17th CCP Congress in 2007." Pp. 171–196 in *Economic Transitions with Chinese Characteristics: Social Change During Thirty Years of Reform*, edited by A. Sweetman and J. Zhang.

Zhang, Y. 2009. "The Thirty-Year Anti-Poverty Battle of a Large Agricultural Country." Pp. 115–133 in *Economic Transitions with Chinese Characteristics: Social Change During Thirty Years of Reform*, edited by A. Sweetman and J. Zhang.

Part I

Land Tenure, Housing, and Migration

1

The Incompatibility of China's Rural Land System with an Increasingly Urbanized and Marketized Economy

GUANZHONG JAMES WEN

Although China's current land system has made an outstanding contribution to agricultural production, by its nature it is based on compromises that are incompatible with a market economy. As China moves toward reliance on market mechanisms to allocate its resources, the flaws in the current land system are becoming increasingly apparent. Its institutional barriers regarding land allocation are not only hurting China's rural areas, but also deepening rural-urban income disparities and causing rural infrastructures and ecology to deteriorate. This chapter concludes that it is now time for China to further reform its current land tenure system.

Introduction: China's Land Tenure System

One of the most fundamental institutions of any society is its land system. The impacts of this system are by no means limited to the farming sector. As one of the three most important factors of production (the other two being labour and capital), land is indispensible for all the sectors. For this reason, land has to be allocated in a unified land market before it can realize its maximum value. Therefore, land ownership and property rights need to be well defined before they can be traded. This is especially true when a society is undergoing rapid urbanization and industrialization. Distortion of land allocation, either because of segregated rental markets or—worse—administrative intervention, will negatively affect every facet of a society. It usually takes a long time, however, before the impacts of such distortions become fully apparent.

Economic Transitions with Chinese Characteristics: Social Change During Thirty Years of Reform, eds. Arthur Sweetman and Jun Zhang. Montreal and Kingston: McGill-Queen's University Press, Queen's Policy Studies Series.

China's land tenure system is still very incompatible with a typical market economy. When the Household Responsibility System (HRS) gradually replaced the commune system in the early 1980s, the only acceptable rule for distributing land among farmers was the principle of egalitarianism. Instead of privatizing land ownership and letting the market allocate land, governments allocated land according to households' shares in the village population. Under this arrangement, land was still owned collectively by administrative villages (the former production brigades under the commune system) or villagers groups (the former production teams or natural villages); farmers obtained exclusive use rights to land for 15 years, which was later extended to 30 years.

China's constitution stipulates that farmers in a village own the village farmland collectively, but they cannot buy or sell it at land markets, as farmers in a typical market economy can.

The late 1970s and the early 1980s was a period when China was just emerging from rigid government policies of egalitarianism, self-sufficiency, and isolationism. To privatize the rights to land use alone already represented a significant break from the collective farming system. No wonder the new system greatly stimulated productivity and total output (Lin 1992; Wen 1995), giving China badly needed time to prepare itself for a more open and competitive world. As China moves toward a market-oriented economy and decides to fully integrate its economy into the world community, however, the limitations of the current non-market-oriented land tenure system become increasingly apparent.

Impacts of the Land System

As a vast country with great local diversity, China always poses a serious challenge for anyone trying to get "the big picture" of it. This is especially true for the HRS and its land tenure system. The long-term impacts of this system on farmers' income, migration, land-specific investment, rural infrastructures, rural ecology, urbanization, and industrialization in a globalizing world have not often been clear for several reasons. First, long-term impacts of the land system, by definition, need time to reveal themselves. Second, the land tenure system has many variations across China's regions. Using regional data has sometimes produced conflicting results, while national data of high quality have always been hard to obtain. Most importantly, despite the many variations of the land system, cases of complete private land ownership are missing from the data. Therefore, there is no way to tell what might have happened had a complete privatization of land ownership been in place. No region has been allowed to experiment with such a system for the past 30 years. Hence, there has been no way to compare the performance of the HRS with that of a private farming system in a systematic way. Third, most published studies have focused exclusively on the impacts of the land system on China's agricultural productivity and output. The obvious success of this system by these two measures made it look unnecessary to assess impacts of the land tenure system on other sectors.

Since China plans to build an all-round affluent society by 2020, farmers must find a way to share in the prosperity that the market-oriented economic reforms and resultant rapid urbanization, industrialization, and globalization have been bringing to urban and coastal areas. One can no longer ignore the possibility that the nation may eventually polarize into two different and disconnected worlds if farmers' relative income continues to lag. Not only has this possibility been long pointed out by some scholars (Li and Qiu 2004; Yue et al. 2007), it has also been finally recognized in recent official documents. Among them the most citable ones are the No. 1 Documents of the Central Committee of CCP issued since 2004.[1] This alarming situation is confirmed by a UN document entitled "The China Human Development Report 2005."[2] Obviously if this trend is not reversed soon, China's goal to build a harmonious and prosperous society with equity will sound very hollow.

Developments under the HRS

Here are some facts about the real situation Chinese farmers have faced during the past decade under the HRS.

1. While China enjoyed a sufficient and more diversified food supply, and most farmers were doing better in absolute terms compared with the commune days, farmers were also facing heavy burdens of taxes and fees until recently, when the Central Government, alarmed by the rural situation, decided to intervene.
2. Corruption and abuse of power in village and township cadres have been widespread (Li 2002; Chen and Chun 2003).
3. An increasing number of farmers (40 to 60 million) have been displaced without proper compensation as a result of rapid industrialization and urbanization (Qu et al. 2004).
4. A large amount of arable land has been left idle either by farmers who migrated to urban sector or by developers who bought land at a very low price but did not have enough capital to develop it. At the same time millions of farmers could not expand the scale of their operation (He 2007; Li 2008).
5. Land disputes and contests in rural areas sharply increased and often escalated into violent confrontations (Chen 2006; Yu 2005).
6. Farmers had little, often decreasing access to rural formal financial services (Zhang and Chui 2001).
7. Although rapid urbanization and large amount of migrant workers have theoretically made more land available to those remaining in rural areas, periodic land adjustments and reallocations have resulted in worsening land fragmentation, increased volatility of rental markets, and frequent elimination of more successful and efficient farmers (Liao et al. 2003).

8. China's farming sector is being increasingly relegated to those who are weak, aged, or handicapped, and many farm families are headed by women, since most males have left for urban sectors. These farmers often need government subsidies and financial help for survival. In many rural areas infrastructures are neglected.[3]
9. Farmers feel poorly prepared, often helpless, in an increasingly open and globalizing environment after China's WTO accession in 2001.

These problems can be predicted by economic theory. They boil down to one central question: can a modern farming sector emerge under a land tenure system that gives farmers land use rights for a period of time that is often not well defined and protected, and that denies them land ownership and land transfer rights? In other words, can China's agriculture retain its viability, or will it have to increasingly rely on government subsidies and outside interventions in the absence of a truly functioning land market?

All developed economies had to adopt private land ownership protected by a legal system before they succeeded in modernizing agriculture. Is their historical experience relevant to China? Or can China be an exception? Are basic economic principles about property rights and market allocation not valid in China? Or is the current land system at most a temporary institutional arrangement that needs further reform? If it needs reform, in which direction the current land tenure system should go?

Organization of this Chapter

The following section summarizes the main merits and demerits of the current land system. It is followed by a discussion of farm scale, rental markets, and sustainable growth. It then discusses the relationships among rural financial services, increasing displaced landless farmers, and worsening rural ecology. The final section concludes the paper.

Advantages and Disadvantages of the Current Land Tenure System

Advantages

After more than two decades of experimenting with the commune system, Chinese farmers found themselves unable to feed themselves and the rest of the nation. The rampant free-rider problem under the commune system deprived farmers of incentives to work hard. It was under this miserable situation that in the late 1970s and the early 1980s farmers began to desert the commune system and replace it gradually with the HRS. Under the new system, land is distributed to each household according to its share in village population.[4]

The current land tenure system claims to have many advantages. Some of them are real, but others are not well grounded. One real advantage is improved production. By distributing collectively owned land to households according to their respective shares in village population, village farmers gain exclusive rights to use of the land and exclusive residual claims over what they produce. China has thus eliminated the once rampant free-rider problem in production and greatly increased agricultural productivity and total output (Lin 1992; Wen 1993). Since the 1980s, the food supply has been greatly improved both in urban and rural areas.

HRS also claims to be a system that prevents farmers from becoming landless. For the following reasons, the alleged merit is only a myth. First, rapid urbanization has been taking away an increasing amount of farmland from farmers. As a result, a growing number of farmers have become landless. Second, the allegedly benevolent government is often in a monopsonic position in purchasing farmland and in a monopoly position in selling land. It often colludes with developers by allowing them to pay minimal compensations to farmers, but sharply raise housing prices.[5] The resentful farmers often confront the local government or developers, demanding for more compensations. The number of disputes over land has sharply risen (Yu 2005).

Another alleged advantage of the current land system is its effect on urbanization. Some believe that China's recent rapid urbanization owes a great deal to the current land system. Collective ownership makes land much cheaper and much more accessible to government and developers; however, this does not mean that urban development is really inexpensive. This argument neglects the severe negative effect on farmers' income and social justice on one side, and the fact that skyrocketing urban housing prices have become increasingly unbearable for an average urban family. It is true that the government and developers can get farmland at relatively low prices. The result, however, is like that of any other monopoly—sharply raising housing prices. The growing number of rural land disputes and displaced landless farmers reveals that many of the advantages that the current land system allegedly has are no more than a myth.

Disadvantages

The current land tenure system has the following serious disadvantages.

1. Under the HRS system, the scale of a farm's operation is determined mainly by the household's share in the village population. Under a typical market economy, where land can be owned privately and traded, the scale of land operation of a farm would be determined by the prevailing prices of inputs and outputs. Farmers whose production is more efficient at the prevailing prices would be able to expand their operation scale by legally acquiring or renting in land from the land market. Those whose production is not efficient at the prevailing market prices could choose to rent out or sell their land.

But under the current land system, those who have a higher share in village population but cannot use land efficiently or intensely may still have more land than those who have small family size but can use land more efficiently and intensely.

2. Because rural land cannot be traded, farmers collectively suffer great financial losses, especially when land value appreciates rapidly in areas undergoing rapid urbanization. In addition, many village and township cadres, tempted by bribery, collude with developers and local government officials to sell village land below the market value (He 2007). This not only opens a door to corruption but also leads to increases in land disputes and confrontations in rural areas. According to Yu (2005), land disputes in rural areas have risen sharply in recent years. Qu et al. (2004) point out that the total number of landless farmers amounts to 40–60 million.[6] Thus, it is only a myth that the current land tenure system does not generate landless farmers. Actually, farmers' situation could be even worse than under a private land system for two reasons. First, under a private land system, farmers' land ownership is protected by the legal system. A developer has to negotiate with individual farmers directly; hence farmers are more likely to get prices that reflect the real market value of their land, or they can simply refuse to sell. Second, under a private land system, the village and township cadres have no rights to intervene in a land deal as long as it is legal. In contrast, under the current land system, only village cadres, and increasingly only the township cadres, negotiate land sales. Farmers are kept in the dark throughout the whole negotiation process. Bribery and corruption then lead to contests and confrontations between cadres and developers on one side and farmers on the other side.

   The recent tragedy in Dongzhou, a village in Shanwei of eastern Guangdong where a land dispute resulted in deaths, is only one of many such incidents that have escalated into violent confrontation and loss of life (Cody 2005). As long as the current land tenure system remains unchanged, more unrest and confrontations will happen as urbanization expand from coastal regions to vast inland. The goal of building a generally well-to-do and harmonious society is very much in doubt.

3. Under the current land tenure system, China has been facing the so-called three agrarian issues (*san nong Wenti*) since the mid-1990s: deteriorating rural areas, stagnated agricultural production, and worsening farmers income relative to the rest of the country. According to No.1 document of 2004 issued by the Central Committee of the CCP, farmers' income in general has been growing slowly, and the income of full-time grain-growing farmers in particular has stagnated, sometimes even declining absolutely in the years before 2004.

4. Providing rural households with access to financial services is very important for modernizing China's agriculture (Rozelle, Huang, and Otsuka 2006). Market-oriented financial services, however, can hardly

develop under the current land tenure system. Farmers without land ownership cannot use land—the only valuable asset in rural China—as collaterals to obtain loans from banks. Under such circumstances, no commercially sustainable financial services can develop in rural areas. The Agricultural Bank of China (ABC) accumulated a huge number of non-performing loans and decided to withdraw from rural areas. This has left the rural credit co-operatives as the only financial institution left there; they face the same dilemma as long as rural land cannot be used as collaterals.

5. To a great extent, the production structures of China's agriculture is still largely shaped by the past when China was highly isolated and obsessed with grain security out of the deep-rooted fear of famine. Hence, its sown areas are still mostly devoted to grain production despite the fact that China has no comparative advantage in the production of many of the grain crops (except for rice) at prevailing international prices. China's accession to the WTO and the global trend to further liberalize agricultural trade mean that it should restructure its agricultural production according to its comparative advantage. Lack of financial services, however, at this critical moment means that farmers have to use mainly their own savings to finance the restructuring.
6. The current land tenure system also leads to the worsening of land fragmentation. In the late 1970s and early 1980s, under egalitarian pressure, land was divided into several categories according to their quality (measured mainly by fertility), location (proximity to the village), and accessibility to irrigation (proximity to a river, a well, or a ditch), etc., so that all the families could have a mixed plots with similar proportion of different types of land. [7] This egalitarian rule made an average farm scale not only very small but also very fragmented. Since then, population growth and periodic land readjustment and reallocation often made this fragmentation worse. According to Brenner (2003), the Gini coefficient of land distribution has declined from 0.499 in 1988 to 0.378 in 1995. After having adjusted for irrigation accessibility, he found that the Gini coefficient fell from 0.465 in 1988 to 0.365 in 1995.

Farm Scale, Rental Market, and Sustainable Growth

Full-Time Grain Farmers

As the No. 1 document of the Central Committee of the CCP in 2004 points out, full-time grain-growing farmers are faring the worst of all farmers. The reasons can be explained as follows. First, grain crops can only be harvested once or twice a year in most part of China, whereas non-grain crops often grow much faster. For example, a farmer can harvest vegetables 6–10 times a year (or even more if using a greenhouse) because of the short growing period of most vegetables. A grain grower will have much lower income if he or she has about the same amount of land as a vegetable grower. In addition, the price and income elasticities of demand for vegetables are often higher than for grain. This means that grain growers need to have much larger farm size than those who grow vegetables before receiving a similar level of income. But under the current land system farm size is mainly determined by share in the village population, not by market-driven forces.

Under a typical market economy, many small grain growers would first switch to grow non-grain crops, or leave for urban areas, until the remaining grain farmers can expand and reach an average income. Such market forces and signals are lost under the current land tenure system. Unless the Chinese government plans to turn all farmers into part-time farmers—and hence lose efficiency from specialization—it will have to hand out more and more subsidies to the full-time grain-growing farmers. If the government cannot afford to do so, then it is predictable that the income situation of the full-time grain-growing farmers will continue to worsen relative to part-time farmers and urban residents.

Increasing Farmers' Income

Because of the low income and price elasticities of demand for grain, increases in urban residents' income and reduction in grain prices do not easily translate into increased demand for grain or increased farmer income. In recent years, the government has been trying hard to find solutions to this situation. The Central Committee of the CCP issued several No. 1 documents since 2004 that specifically addressed the three agrarian issues. The government has also decided to phase out the agricultural taxes, while at the same time handing out various types of subsidies to farmers. The market prices for grain have rebounded since 2004, but they are still significantly below world prices, and the gap between rural and urban incomes is still widening, though at a slower pace.

In the long-run, the prospect for farmers to improve their income relative to urban and coastal residents through price increases in agricultural products is very dim. First, the rise in market prices for various grain crops is mostly a response to more rapidly rising prices of intermediate inputs. As historical trends show, relative to that of the industrial intermediate inputs, such as chemical fertilizers, oil, electricity, and various parts of farm machines, the market prices for grain and many other agricultural products have been declining over the past hundred years worldwide. The decline in agricultural prices relative to that of industrial intermediate inputs is due to the rapid technical progress in agriculture, especially in high yield varieties and new types of fertilizers. The rebound in grain prices in recent years, internationally as well as domestically, can only be viewed as a response to skyrocketing in prices of oil, chemical fertilizers, and other intermediate industrial inputs to a great extent, and to a lesser extent to the short-term effect of the cumulative effect of consecutive reduction in China's grain production in response to the last five or six years' overproduction of grain since the mid-1990s (Lu 1999). Second, as I pointed out above, the government is not in a financial position to hand out enough subsidies to farmers in the future. Third, the elimination of agricultural taxes only has a one-time effect.

The government is now promoting more technical progress and pushing for more grain production. But these two efforts cannot be conducive to higher grain prices when China is not facing shortage of food relative to its effective demand. Encouraging farmers to produce more grain has often led to stagnated, sometimes even declining, prices, and has hurt farmers' income significantly, as it has during the last few years (Lu 2008).

This explains why farmers have had so much difficulty selling grain at a time when urban income has been rising rapidly and grain prices declining significantly, at least until 2004. Chinese farmers had no choice but to reduce grain production. The Lewis-Rains-Fei model shows that the terms of trade between agricultural goods and industrial goods will change in favour of agriculture after the point when the urban sector absorbs all the rural surplus labour. But this can only happen in a closed economy, and China is now a WTO member. If a temporary shortage of grain develops in China, once its domestic prices rise to the prevailing world level, China will import grain instead of letting the price of grain rise sharply by closing its door to cheaper imports available at the world market. Hence, it is unrealistic to place hope on the rising prices of farming produce relative to industrial inputs as a main way to raise farmers' income in the long-run.

The experience of developed nations shows that in the long run, a more effective way to increase farmers' income is through expanding farm's average scale of production. Even with prices constant, farmers can double their income if they can double the scale of their land operation. If the prices of agricultural goods fall relative to industrial inputs, as is usually true, then farmers need to expand their farm size at an even faster rate. This explains why, in order for farmers to catch up to the average income of a nation the average farm operation scale has to grow.

But to be able to expand the average scale of a farm steadily, a nation either must have a large amount of arable land relative to its farming population, or the non-farming sector must be able to gradually absorb much of the rural population. China does not have a lot of reserved land to explore; but industrialization and urbanization is giving China a rare opportunity to allow its farmers to expand their farm size—if there are good land markets or rental markets to facilitate the transfer of land to other farmers.[8]

Land markets are necessary, even in a static society without urbanization and industrialization, because the demand for and supply of land still change over time across households. Some farmers decrease their demand for land as a result of death, migration, marriage, aging, sickness, or simply poor management skills; while others increase their demand for land for the same reasons. A land market thus is crucially useful to efficiently allocate land among potential suppliers and buyers.

Substitution Effect of HRS for Rental Markets

Under the current land system, farmers do not have the ownership of their land, and have no rights to sell or buy land. The government indeed encourages the emergence and growth of land rental markets by legalizing them in the early 1990s. The question is how well such markets are developing throughout China's rural areas?

Let's look at this issue more closely. In the early 1980s the government first asked all the villages to sign a 15-year contract with farmers. Then in the mid-1990s, when these contracts were expiring, the government asked all the villages to extend contracts for another 30 years. Theoretically, farmers should have uninterrupted use rights for the same pieces of land for 45 years. As population changes across households, and as more farmers migrate to non-farming sectors, there should be an ever-growing amount of land available at rental markets.

Under China's land tenure system, however, many villagers are finding other ways to get access to land. By the very nature of the collective land ownership, they have every right to do so. Under pressure from those whose shares in village population are rising, villages have periodically adjusted and sometimes even reallocated land among farmers to prevent the land distribution from becoming too unequal.

A few words are in order about the difference between land adjustment and land reallocation. Land adjustment refers to the case where village authorities take away some land from households whose population share falls below the village average and give it to households whose share rises above the average. All the other households keep their land unchanged. Land reallocation refers to the case where all the households turn in their land to the village before the land is reallocated to them. Households often receive totally different plots in terms of location, quality, and size.

Land adjustment and reallocation are a much cheaper way for individual households with rising population shares to gain more land. They can get the land for free instead of paying rent; they also acquire higher land security given the volatile situation at the rental markets (see below). Land adjustment and reallocation, however, has a high cost for the community in terms of transaction cost and efficiency loss due to periodically weeding out more efficient farms.[9]

Insecure Rental Markets

Let's look at some very revealing results from a study on China's land tenure system. This study was sponsored by the Ford Foundation and conducted by Liao, Xi, Zhang and a team from the Research Center for Rural Economy, Agricultural Ministry of China (2003). This study is the only one available that describes the national picture of the current land tenure system. Over a course of four years, Liao and his team collected data in six provinces: Hebei, Shaanxi, Anhui, Hunan, Sichuan, and Zhejiang. Except for Zhejiang, these provinces have a relatively large farming population. In each province, Liao et al. selected two counties: Jingxian and Qian'an in Hebei, Dali and Baoji in Shaanxi, Feixi and Suixi in Anhui, Ningxiang and Qiyang in Hunan, Shuangliu and Renshou in Sichuan, and Shaoxing and Rui'an in Zhejiang. Liao et al. then chose three townships from each county, and from each township they chose one administrative village.[10] From each administrative village, they chose three villagers groups, and then chose seven to eight households per villagers group. Altogether, their sample includes 824 households, 90 villagers groups, 36 administrative villages, 36 townships, 12 counties from 6 provinces.

The survey divides the period from the late 1970s to the end of 1990s into two sub-periods and refers to them as the first-round contracting period (from the late 1970s to the mid-1990s) and the second-round contracting period (from the mid-1990s to the present). During the first-round contracting period, 104 units were handling land contracts. During the second-round contracting period, because of merging of some villagers groups, 96 units handling land contracts remained.

Among the 104 units (villages or villagers groups), initially most of them did not specify 15 years as the length of the contract (Table 1).

TABLE 1
Contract Length during the First-Round Contracting Period

	Heibei	*Shaanxi*	*Anhui*	*Hunan*	*Sichuan*	*Zhejiang*	*Total*	*Percent*
Not clear	0	2	2	3	2	1	10	10
Not specified	7	3	10	2	14	0	36	35
10–15 years	3	0	3	0	0	16	22	21
3–6 years	4	13	3	13	2	1	36	35
Total	14	18	18	18	18	18	104	1

Source: Liao et al. (2003, 8).

After the government made it very clear in 1984 that all the villages should have 15-year contracts, 64 of out of 104 units followed the instruction, at least on paper. However, in reality, among the 64 units, 23 units held both land reallocation and adjustment despite the 15-year specification (Table 2). Only nine units, or 14 percent, did not have any type of land changes among farmers during the first-round land contracting period (Table 3).

TABLE 2
Land Adjustment and Reallocation in Villages with the 15-Year Specification (subsample of 64)

	Readjustment		
	Yes	*No*	*Sub*
Reallocation			
Yes	23	14	37
No	18	9	27
Sub	41	23	64

Source: Liao et al. (2003, 9).

TABLE 3
Land Adjustment and Reallocation in Villages with 15-Year Specification (subsample of 64)

	Readjustment	
	Yes	*No*
Reallocation		
Yes	36%	22%
No	28%	14%

Source: Liao et al. (2003, 9).

Out of the 104 units, the other 40 units[11] did not specify the length of contracts even after the government urged them to do so. Using 104 units as a base, only 9 percent of the villages both clearly specified the length of the contract as 15 years and also did not undergo any changes in land distribution after the initial distribution.

The frequency of land adjustment or reallocation was rather high. According to Liao et al. (2003, 24), since the implementation of the HRS, among the 90 villages in the sample, 88 had either land adjustments, or reallocation, or both. They account for 97.8 percent of the total number of the villages in the sample. Table 4 confirms this undesirable situation for the emerging rental markets.

TABLE 4
Frequency of Land Adjustment and Reallocation during the First 15 years

	Number of Villagers Groups	*Number of Changes*	*Average*
Reallocation	46	60	1.3
Adustment	68	435	6.4
Reallocation only	13	19	1.5
Adjustment only	35	233	6.7
Both	33	243	7.4

Source: Liao et al. (2003, 25).

Although since the early 1990s the government has stated that land should not be frequently adjusted or reallocated, most villages have not complied. As recently as the second-round contracting period in the mid-1990s, 66 out of 90 villages, or 73 percent, had already made land changes. Among them, 30 villages, or 45 percent, had already reallocated land during this period (Table 5).[12]

TABLE 5
Frequency of Land Adjustment and Reallocation during the Second-Round Contracting Period

	Number of Villagers Groups	*Number of Changes*	*Average*
Reallocation	36	36	1
Adustment	36	36	1
Reallocation only	30	30	1
Adjustment only	30	30	1
Both	6	12	2

Source: Liao et al. (2003, 25).

The rental markets are highly volatile. Table 6 shows that nationwide, 44 percent of contracts are valid only for one year, 13 percent for two to five years, 4 percent for more than five years, and 35 percent have an unspecified length. The data in Table 7 shows that as many as 60 percent of contracts could be ended any time. In Hunan, this rate is as high as 82 percent. Sichuan and Zhejiang have similar patterns. Relatively speaking, tenants in Shaanxi have the highest security in their use rights to rented land from rental markets.

TABLE 6
The Length of Contracts by Province

Length	*Hebei* (%)	*Shaanxi* (%)	*Anhui* (%)	*Hunan* (%)	*Sichuan* (%)	*Zhejiang* (%)	*Total Sample* (%)
1 year	0.28	0.72	0.04	0.29	0.15	0.57	0.44
2–5 years	0.17	0.14	0.27	0.08	0.12	0.12	0.13
More than 5 years	0	0.09	0	0	0	0.03	0.04
Long-term or permanent	0	0	0	0.01	0	0.04	0.01
Unspecified	0.22	0.05	0.67	0.60	0.72	0.18	0.35
No response	0.33	0	0.02	0.02	0	0.05	0.03

Source: Liao et al. (2003, 61).

The insecurity of the use rights by the tenants is further reflected in the fact that most contracts are verbal. Table 8 shows that nation-wide, about 86 percent of contracts are verbal. This also explains why the land disputes sharply rose in 2004. In that year, the government not only announced the gradual phasing out of agricultural taxes but also handed out various kinds of subsidies to farmers. In response, millions of migrant workers went back to their native villages, either demanding land from the villages, or taking back their land that they had rented out to other villagers. Since most contracts were not in written form, land disputes rose sharply.

TABLE 7
Security of Tenancy by Province

Can a contract be ended at any time?	*Hebei* (%)	*Shaanxi* (%)	*Anhui* (%)	*Hunan* (%)	*Sichuan* (%)	*Zhejiang* (%)	*Total Sample* (%)
No response	0.31	0	0.04	0	0.03	0	0.02
Yes	0.38	0.25	0.80	0.82	0.71	0.69	0.60
No	0.31	0.74	0.17	0.18	0.26	0.31	0.38

Source: Liao et al. (2003, 62).

TABLE 8
Formality of Contracts

	Hebei (%)	*Shaanxi* (%)	*Anhui* (%)	*Hunan* (%)	*Sichuan* (%)	*Zhejiang* (%)	*Total Sample* (%)
Verbal	0.75	0.83	0.80	0.95	0.82	0.89	0.86
Written	0	0.17	0.20	0.05	0.17	0.11	0.13
No response	0.25	0	0	0	0.01	0	0.01

Source: Liao et al. (2003, 63).

As pointed out above, many villages used the opportunity of being asked by the government in the mid-1990s to extend the expiring contracts for another 30 years to reallocate land among farmers. Their practice was supported by many farmers. According to the sample collected by Liao et al. (2003), despite the fact that the government made very clear that for the next 30 years, land should not be adjusted or reallocated, 57 percent of households believe that the government was allowing land adjustment during this period as long as the HRS remained unchanged. Furthermore, around 4 percent of households believe that the government was allowing future land reallocations. This means that more than 60 percent of households in the sample believed that they could have land adjustment or reallocation in the next 30 years as long as they keep the HRS (see Table 9).

Even among the 269 households that thought that government was opposed to any land adjustment or reallocation over the next 30 years, when being asked their own opinion, 174 households of this group believed that land should be adjusted or reallocated as household population shares changed (see Table 10). Therefore, one should expect that land adjustment and reallocation will continue over the next 30 years, as long as the land tenure system is still based on an egalitarianism principle.

TABLE 9
"Do you think that the government allows land adjustment or reallocation?"

	Number of Households	*Percent*
Allow reallocation	31	3.9
Allow adjustment	455	57.3
Not allow both	269	33.8
Do not care	40	5.0
Total	795	100.0

Source: Liao et al. (2003, 163).

TABLE 10
"In your view, should land be adjusted or reallocated in the next 30 years?"

Perception of the government's real intention	*Should*	*Should Not*	*Do Not Care*
Allow reallocation (31households)	27	3	1
Allow adjustment (455 households)	433	20	2
Not allow either (269 households)	174	88	7
Do not care (40 households)	30	10	0
Total (795 households)	664	121	10

Source: Liao et al. (2003, 165).

The question is, given that the Central Government would like to see more secure land use rights and transfer rights, why do most villages still practice land adjustment and reallocation? Obviously, it is cheaper for farmers with growing families to get land this way. Without privatizing land ownership, contracts reached at the rental markets will continue to be ignored, and tenants' rights will continue to be unprotected for two reasons. First, the periodic adjustment and reallocation of land among farmers is backed by the egalitarian principle of the current land system. Those who propose to adjust or reallocate village land according to changed population distribution across households will always have an upper hand legally and ideologically over those who oppose such a practice. Second, for the same reason, there is no way to exclude those farmers who migrate to non-farming sectors from retaining their share of village land. Therefore, the destructive effect on the growth of rental markets caused by the reverse flow of migrant workers back to rural areas will always be present. If the growth of rental markets is something that the Chinese government really wants to seek, land privatization is the only solution.

Infrastructure and Ecology

Stone Edges

Lack of security in property rights can also lead to deteriorating rural infrastructures and ecology (Wen 1995). In China's south and southwest, where most land is hilly or mountainous, farmers are well known for their skills in converting sloping land into terraced fields. Over hundreds—if not thousands—of years, farmers have used stones to build the edges of terraced fields to prevent soil erosion. Therefore, the stone edges have played a great role in keeping the local agriculture sustainable and the local ecology in balanced shape. Typically terraced fields with stone edges look neat and well defined.

In a research trip to Guizhou in the summer of 2005, however, we[13] found that many terraced fields no longer had well-defined edges. Looking more carefully, we found that many terraced fields did not have stone edges. Their mud edges were often eroded by rains and mountain torrents. Later in a meeting with a local township Party secretary, we asked him why some terraced fields had stone edges, and some did not. He told us that farmers' attitude toward stone edges changes under different land systems. During the long period before 1949, landlords hired poor peasants to build the stone edges. This arrangement was mutually beneficial, since landlords had both land and money, and poor peasants had time. During the commune period, farmers were mobilized during winter season to build the edges. However, under the HRS, farmers no longer follow such a practice.

When asked if there were smallholders before 1949 and if they had built stone edges, the Party secretary said yes to both questions. When asked why farmers had not built stone edges after the HRS, he told us that farmers were too busy to take care of this business and that many male labourers had left for urban areas (without realizing what he said was conflicting with his earlier statement when he complained that there were still a high number of idle labourers in rural areas who were redundant in farming sector, but could not find non-farming jobs).

In a follow-up survey conducted by the team from University of Guizhou, International Food Policy Research Institute (IFPRI), and Chinese Academy of Agricultural Sciences, questions were raised specifically to households about the stone edges. The results are summarized in Tables 11 and 12.

As Table 11 shows, out of 19,297 households, only 3,629 households, or 19 percent of total households in the sample, built stone edges under

HRS. Even these households did not do so on their own initiative. Living in villages that are designated as poverty-stricken areas, they received financial support from the government or international organizations, which required them to build stone edges in return as a way to improve the local ecology, in the hope that the improved ecology will raise the productivity of the terraced fields and make local economy sustainable.

TABLE 11
"Have you ever built stone edges since HRS was installed?"

	No	*Yes*	*Total*
Number of households	15,672	3,625	19,297
Percent	81	19	100

Source: Author's compilation based on data collected during a field trip in June 2005 and participated by Xiaopeng Luo from University of Guizhou, Xiaobo Zhang from International Food Policy Research Institute, Li Xing from Chinese Academy of Agricultural Sciences, and myself.

Table 12 shows that farmers gave four clearly specified reasons regarding why they did not built stone edges. Surprisingly, almost 40 percent of farmers chose not to give answers from these choices, while 17 percent attributed to high labour costs, 5 percent attributed to lack of organizers, 22 percent attributed to the high cost of raw materials such as stone, and 18 percent attributed to the low profitability of farming.

TABLE 12
Reasons Not to Build Stone Edges

	Labour Cost Is Too Costly	*No Organizers Initiate Such Projects*	*Raw Materials (Stone) Are Too Costly*	*Farming is Is Not Profitable*	*Other Unspecified Reasons*
Percent	17	5	22	18	38
Number of households	3,247	908	4,295	3,388	7,459

Source: Author's compilation based on data collected during a field trip in June 2005 and participated by Xiaopeng Luo from University of Guizhou, Xiaobo Zhang from International Food Policy Research Institute, Li Xing from Chinese Academy of Agricultural Sciences, and myself.

Property Rights and Long-Term Land-Specific Investment

The answers in Table 12 deserves further analysis. For example, China in general still has a lot of surplus labourers, especially in Guizhou, a poor and remote province in mountainous southwest of China where rural income is among the lowest in China and non-farming jobs are most limited. Economic theory suggests that the shadow price of labour should be close to zero when surplus labour is abundant. Why should labour costs be a prohibitive factor to the construction of stone edges? On our way to villages, we saw several quarries, indicating that stone is abundant in this mountainous region. With modern explosion technology, greatly improved roads, and transportation facilities, the cost of stones should not be too expensive. With regard to the low profitability of farming sector, this argument is valid for more recent years. What about period of the 1980s and the early 1990s, when farmers were doing fine relative to urban residents? If farmers also did not invest in such projects during this period, as the secretary said, then the costs of labour and stone cost should not be relevant.

The construction of stone edges, however, is a long-term land-specific investment, heavily depending on security in land use rights and ownership. If land can be adjusted or reallocated at any time, or its ownership is undefined, individuals will not make such long-term investments in the land. Investment of this type has a very slow rate of return and can be recouped only after a long period of time. Unless farmers are sure that they and their future generations can have secure rights to benefits from such investments, they will not undertake it.

The case of the stone edges serves as a good example of the negative effects of HRS. After nearly 30 years of HRS, the deteriorating of rural infrastructures are widely observed almost everywhere. It is clear that the current land tenure system offers farmers very low incentives to undertake any long-term land specific investment (Wen 1995).

Concluding Remarks

After its initial outstanding performance in raising productivity and output, the current land tenure system is facing increasing problems. Urban and coastal areas are becoming increasingly integrated into the world economy, while the rural population is being left behind. To a great extent they are left behind because of the land tenure system. It is incompatible with marketization, urbanization, and globalization. Under this land tenure system, land is mainly allocated through villages' administrative intervention according to households' shares in village population rather than through rental markets. Because of the collective ownership of rural land, land is not readily accessible relative to factors of production and fails to realize its highest value. Competent farmers feel helpless about expanding their scale of operation as a result of the egalitarian pressure to periodic adjust or reallocate land, or of the volatile rental markets, where most contracts can be ended prematurely at any time.

As China's concerns are shifting from food security to farmers' worsening relative income, the advantages of the current system are becoming less important, while its disadvantages are becoming more pronounced. The numerous disadvantages of this land tenure system are preventing farmers from sharing the urban and coastal prosperity. All the arguments formerly used against private land ownership can now be used to criticize the current land tenure system. In reality, all the so-called "bad" things that supposedly happen only under a private land system are not only happening, but are also happening in a more rampant way.

For examples, farmers have to bear heavy tax burdens, rampant corruption, and power abuse unless the central government directly intervenes; the number of displaced landless farmers is rising; rental markets are often undermined by periodic land adjustment and reallocation; land disputes are unsettling rural areas; rural financial services are deteriorating at a time when such services are important for globalized markets; migrant farmers are keeping their land, despite the fact that other farmers want to expand their scale of operation; competent and more efficient farms are being weeded out; and increasingly China's farming sector is run by those who are old, weak, and handicapped, and by families whose men have gone to work in the cities—all who need government subsidies and financial help. Rural infrastructures and ecology are now often neglected because the current land system offers farmers few incentives to take care of them. Many of these negative effects do not happen under a private land ownership. For examples, under a private land ownership, there would be fewer land disputes; urbanization would automatically take care of displaced farmers because they would be fully compensated; and rural financial services would develop much faster, thus facilitate the restructuring of China's agriculture according to its comparative advantage.

Hence, it is not an exaggeration to say that the current land tenure system has all the problems that a private land tenure system might have without its main advantages—that is, the security of ownership, efficiency in land allocation, and the ability to connect rural population with the urban and coastal areas, and through them, to the rest of the world. Only when farmers are connected with marketization, urbanization, and globalization can they benefit from the urban and coastal prosperity.

When asked why China did not consider adopting the private land ownership—was this refusal based on ideological reasons or on economic rationale?—many people in China would deny that ideology played any role in arriving at such a collective land system (Chen 2006). If so, then why should China not be more open-minded and take a closer look at the disadvantages of the current land system and the advantages of a private land system, especially when it is clear that the current land system has failed to prevent the full-time grain-growing farmers income from getting worse relative to the rest of the population?

The time is right to take another look at the current land tenure system. China has already spent 30 years to experiment with this rural institution, longer than the amount of time China had actually spent with the commune system. The Chinese government once used political power to vehemently defend the system, only to find that the system was failing to feed its growing population. The Chinese government should avoid making another blunder by ignoring basic modern principle on property rights and the rich experience from all the developed nations and from its own long history of land private ownership which once enabled China to create one of the greatest civilizations in the world.

Notes

I want to thank Zhang Jun and an anonymous reviewer for their helpful comments. In particular, deep gratitude should go to Liao Hongle, Xi Yinsheng , and Zhang Zhaoxin for constructive discussion of their remarkable research, on which this paper heavily draws on. I also want to thank Luo Xiaopeng, Zhang Xiaobo, Xing Li for inviting me to join them to conduct a field trip to Guizhou province in 2005 and later for allowing me to use part of the data collected during that trip. Thanks also go to Du Rensheng, Yao Jianfu, Jiang Zhongyi, Li Shi, Chen Zhiwu, Dang Guoying, Zhou Qiren, and Cai Jiming for insightful discussions on China's land tenure system and farmers' income situation. All the remaining errors and mistakes of the paper are exclusively mine.

1. The Central Committee issues many numbered documents each year to address various issues that it thinks important to the nation. It usually saves No.1 document to address the most important or urgent issue for that year. For example, since 1982, when agriculture was viewed as a possible liability to China's modernization plan, No. 1 documents were devoted to agricultural issues for four consecutive years. When the HRS turned out to be a great success after the mid-1980s, the No. 1 documents turned attention away from agriculture. At the beginning of 2004, after 18 years' interruption, alarmed by the situation in rural China, the Central Committee of the CCP decided to resume this tradition and issue No. 1 document to address the three agrarian issues. Since then it has issued four agriculture-oriented No. 1 documents consecutively. It is expected that in 2009 No. 1 document will again be devoted to agrarian issues.
2. Calum MacLeod, "Report illustrates huge gap between China's rich, poor" *USA TODAY*, Dec. 16, 2005. According to MacLeod, Khalid Malik, United Nations resident coordinator in China, said: "China's urban-rural income gap is among the highest in the world," and "The public health access in the Chinese countryside has fallen dramatically."
3. It has been reported by many studies, however, it is now recognized by the Central Committee of the CCP, as is reflected in its most recent decision to devote more resources to build new socialist countryside, including improving the very fragile rural infrastructures (*People's Daily* overseas edition, Dec. 21, 2005).
4. There are several variations. Village land can be distributed according to each household's share in village population, or in village labour pool, or a combination of these two types of shares (Wen 1995). For brevity, in what follows, I will use population share only whenever the land distributing rule is referred.
5. According to China's Constitution, a village can only sell its land to the state, usually at a price significantly lower than the market prevailing prices.

6. As more farmland is being taken over by the government for urban and other non-farming uses, such as building highways or railways, an increasing number of farmers are losing their land and become landless. Compensation is often far below the market value of the land taken away by the government. Two measures are used to calculate land compensation. Both are arbitrary because there is no real land market in China; therefore, there is no true land price formed in a competitive land market. One method is based on the present value of the average product produced from a said piece of land over the past 3–5 years. A different measure is used when there are properties involved. In this case, the value of the properties will be estimated to decide how much the owner of the properties should be compensated. In most countries, the government can take over land owned by citizens only exclusively for public interest; otherwise it should be left to developers to negotiate with land owners. In China, however, the public interest is often broadly and arbitrarily interpreted. The main reason why the government has been taking so much land directly from farmers lies in the fact that farmers can only collectively own farmland, but have no right to sell it collectively, let alone individually, for non-farming use according to China's Constitution. Therefore, a piece of farmland that has changed its zoning for non-farming use must first be taken over by the government at very low price (in the form of so-called compensation discussed above) before the government sells the land to developers. The government typically splits the huge profit from the land appreciation with their favoured developers. This type of corruption is widespread and causes increasing resentment among farmers.
7. Where this is impossible, a household is compensated by a larger plot of poor quality.
8. Given that China has 1.8 billion mu of land, and a rural population of more than 700 million (farmers and their dependents), everyone in rural areas should have 2.5 mu land on average, or for a household of 4, it has 10 mu. Currently more than 100 million rural labourers are working in non-farming sectors. Therefore, theoretically, there should be at least 250 million mu of land, or 11 percent of the total land acreage, available at the rental markets across the country at any point in time. The Chinese government plans to increase the urbanization level by 1 percent every year. At this rate, by 2035 China will reach an urbanization level of 70 percent from the current level of 40 percent. In the last 20 years, China did reach a rate close to this targeted annual rate of 1 percent. The urbanization level was 20 percent in 1980, and by 2004, its urbanization level had reached 40 percent. This means that of the total population of 1.3 billion, 520 million people are now living in urban areas. Suppose that China can reach its goal of urbanization level of 70 percent in 2035, and that China will have a stabilizing population of 1.6 billion by then, as many predict (Sun 1994), the size of urban population will be 1.12 billion, and the rural population will be 480 millions. Assume that the total arable land remains the same, the per capita land will increase to 3.75 mu, or increase by 87.5 percent. Further, as specialization in rural areas develops and income increases, more and more rural population will use modern equipments in production and in consumption. Job opportunities will become increasingly available in rural non-farming sectors such as house construction, mechanics and parts, gas, water and electricity supply,

television and other electronics repairing, shopping centres, education and medical services. Suppose that these rural non-farming sectors can absorb half of the rural population. Then only 240 million rural population will still work in farming sector. The per capita land will be 1800/240 million mu/capita, or 7.5 mu per farming labourer. For a typical household of four, it will have 30 mu. Compared with the average size of 8 mu now, and holding everything else (mainly the prices) constant, a household will increase its income by 375 percent in 30 years, or 12.5 percent per year on average. This is not a bad prospect.

9. Because of the high transaction costs, some villages chose to keep the existing land distribution, but to shift some of the tax and fee burdens from households with less land per capita to those with more before the tax and fees were finally abolished after 2004.
10. Typically, an administrative village is equivalent to a production brigade under the former commune system and has around ten natural villages. A natural village was usually equivalent to a production teams under the commune system, now is called a villagers group (*cunmin xiaozu*).
11. In Liao et al., it is 39 instead of 40.
12. These villages used the opportunity to reallocate the village land according to the changed households' shares in village population instead of extending the existing contracts for another 30 years.
13. Xiaopeng Luo from University of Guizhou, Xiaobo Zhang from International Food Policy Research Institute, Li Xing from Chinese Academy of Agricultural Sciences, and I visited several counties in Guizhou in June, 2005, including Meitan in Zhunyi, and Puding in Anshun among others.

References

Brenner, M. 2003. "The Evolution of Land Distribution in Post-Reform China." Working Paper, Political Economy Research Institute, University of Massachusetts, Amherst, MA.

Chen, G., and T. Chun. 2004. "A Survey on China's Farmers" (*Zhongguo Nongmin Diaocha*). Beijing: People's Literature Press.

Chen, X. 2006. "Conflicts and Problems Facing China's Current Rural Reform and Development." Pp. 33-42 in *China's Agricultural Development: Challenges and Prospects*, edited by X. Dong, S. Song, and X. Zhang. Burlington, VT: Ashgate Publishing Limited.

Chinese Academy of Agricultural Sciences, Guizhou University and IFPRI. 2005. "Rural Poor and Smallholders in Western China under WTO: A Regional and Community Level Analysis." Working paper.

Cody, E. 2005. "Chinese Police Kill Villagers During Two-Day Land Protest." *Washington Post Foreign Service*, Friday, December 9, page: A01. Available at http://convincingargument.blogspot.com/2005/12/chinese-police-kill-villagers.html.

He, D., 2007. "On the Village Governance in light of Rampant Farmland Encroachment". *Zhongguo Jingji Guancha (Observations on China's Economy)*, November. Available at http://rdi.cass.cn/show_News.asp?id=18770.

He, S., and N. Zhao. 2000. "How to Stop Leaving Land Idle." *Legal Daily*, November 11.

Huang, X., et al. 2001. "An Analysis on the Operating Mechanism of China's Rural land Market." *Jianghai Journal* (*Jiang Hai Xuekan*) 2:9–15.

Li, Changping. 2002. *Be Honest with the Premier* (*Wo Xiang Zongli Shuo Shihua*). Beijing: Guangming Daily Press.

Li, Changjin 2008. "Be Alert to the Turning Point of Grain Supply", *China's Reforms* (*Zhongguo Gaige*), No7, 2008. Available at http://www.rural.gov.cn/nyxw/nydt/20050928/118055751.htm.

Li, S., and X. Qiu. 2007. "The Reforms on Income Distribution Should be Furthered as Soon as Possible." *The Southern Weekend (Nanfang Zhoumo)*, Oct. 11, 2007. Available at http://finance.sina.com.cn/economist/jingjixueren/20071011/09414049876.shtml.

Liao, H., Y. Xi, Z. Zhang, et al. 2003. *Rural Household Survey No. 43: A Study on China's Rural Land Contract System.* Beijing: Chinese Financial Economic Press.

Lin, J.Y. 1992. "Rural Reforms and Agricultural Growth in China." *American Economic Review* 82 (March):34–51.

Liu, X. 2005. "A Survey Report on the Current Farmers' Income Situation in Jiangxi Province." *Zhinong* 1, December 12. Available at http://www.zhinong.cn/data/detail.php?id=5048.

Lu, F. 1999. "Be Honest with Grain Overproduction Issue." *Management World*, No. 3, 168–175.

——— 2008. "China does not have Grain Security Problem". *Southern Net*, April 24, 2008. Available at http://view.news.qq.com/a/20080424/000031.htm.

MacLeod, C. 2005. "Report Illustrates Huge Gap between China's Rich, Poor." *USA Today*, December 16. Available at http://www.usatoday.com/news/world/2005-12-16-china-wages_x.htm.

Qu, F., S. Feng, P. Zhu, and Z. Chen. 2004. "Institutional Arrangement, Price System, and Farmland Conversion." *China Economic Quarterly* 4(1):229–248.

Rozelle, S., J. Huang, and K. Otsuka. 2006. "China's Rural Economy and the Path to a Modern Industrial State." Pp. 43-77 in *China's Agricultural Development: Challenges and Prospects*, edited by X. Dong, S. Song, and X. Zhang. Burlington, VT: Ashgate Publishing Limited.

Sun, J., et al. 1994. *The Population of China into the 21th Century*, Vol. 33. Beijing: The Statistical Publishing House of China.

Wen, G. 1993. "Total Factor Productivity Change in China's Farming Sector: 1952–1989." *Economic Development and Cultural Change*, October:1–41.

——— 1995. "The Land Tenure System and the Saving and Investment Mechanism: The Case of Modern China." *Asian Economic Journal*, November:233–59.

Wen, T. 2005. *Rural China's Centenary Reflection* (*San Nong Wenti Yu Shiji Fansi*). Beijing: Sanlian Bookstore Press.

Yu, J. 2005. "A Survey on Farmers' Contests to Protect their Land" (*Nongmin Tudi Weiquan kangzheng de Diaocha*). *China Economic Time* (*Zhongguo Jingji Shibao*), June 28. Available at http://news.km.soufun.com/2005-06-28/449421.htm.

Yue, X., T. Sicular, S. Li, and B. Gustafsson. 2007. "Explaining Income Inequality in China." Pp. 88-117 in *Inequality and Public Policy in China*, edited by B. Gustafsson, L. Shi, and T. Sicular. New York: Cambridge University Press.

Zhang, X., and H. Chui. 2004. "The Key is to Change the Pattern of National Income Distribution." Available at http://www.zhinong.cn/data/detail.php?id=2852.

Zhou, Q. 2004. "Property Rights and Land Requisition System: A Critical Choice for China's Urbanization." *China Economic Quarterly* 4(1):193–210.

2

Housing and Education Reform in Urban China: No Longer Separate and Increasingly Unequal

WEILI DING AND STEVEN F. LEHRER

This chapter discusses how reforms to both housing and education policies have influenced the formation of neighbourhoods in urban China over the last three decades. While reforms in both areas traditionally had impacts in isolation, recent policies are likely to interact and change the process by which individuals sort into neighbourhoods. Using a new survey that we administered to over 4500 families in Shanghai, we document how the structure of neighbourhoods has responded to the combined incentives of recent reforms, leading to rising inequality in access to high quality education in urban China.

Introduction

This chapter discusses how reforms to both housing and education policies have influenced the formation of neighbourhoods in China over the last three decades. Understanding neighbourhood formation is important, as numerous social scientists have suggested that the exogenous and endogenous characteristics of a neighbourhood may have impacts on a variety of individual outcomes. These impacts have been given many names, such as "social capital," "contagion," and "neighbourhood effects." If these neighbourhood effects are substantial, government policy may exploit them by optimally grouping individuals to achieve desired socioeconomic outcomes. Additionally, several economists have constructed formal models (e.g., Benabou 1996; Kremer 1993) that illustrate how optimal organization of individuals within neighbourhoods and jobs of different skill levels respectively can lead to higher levels of macroeconomic growth.

Economic Transitions with Chinese Characteristics: Social Change During Thirty Years of Reform, eds. Arthur Sweetman and Jun Zhang. Montreal and Kingston: McGill-Queen's University Press, Queen's Policy Studies Series.

China has undergone remarkable transitions over the last thirty years, and, as the several other chapters in this volume indicate, substantial income inequality has resulted. Yet unlike in many other developing and developed countries, urban housing conditions improved by almost all accounts over this time period (Yu 2006), which may suggest that inequality is not as pervasive in the housing markets as in other sectors. In addition, reforms in basic education have led to an expansion of primary and secondary enrolment and increasing adult literacy levels. Enrolment in senior high schools in 2004 was 2.3 times that of 1988. While much attention has focused on inequalities in housing and on education policies that have created inequality between urban and rural regions, this chapter argues that recent reforms in the housing and education sector may interact in generating segregation across neighbourhoods, which could create inequality in housing and local public goods within urban areas.

This chapter is organized as follows. The first section describes the evolution of housing policy in urban China. It provides a brief overview of a series of reforms that have significantly reduced the role of the state as provider of housing and allowed the re-emergence of a private housing market in China. The next section provides a brief discussion of the basic education system and school admission policies in urban China during this time period. This section documents how government policies established middle schools (Grades 7–12) of different qualities and how competition to attend higher-quality middle schools has changed the system from one that promoted equality in opportunity to one that may result in substantial inequality in access. The final section discusses how these reforms can interact and lead to more sorting of households across neighbourhoods. It presents information on how the structure of neighbourhoods is changing in response to school quality. It draws upon a recent survey that one of the authors constructed and administered to over 4,500 families in a large district in urban China. It also discusses how recent reforms may result in the creation of ghettos in urban China. A concluding section summarizes the findings and discusses the potential implications of recent trends.

Housing Policy

Upon the founding of the People's Republic of China, the new government confiscated the land and buildings belonging to the Kuomintang government and capitalists to lay the foundation for state-owned real estate.[1] But the Communist Party felt that urban housing should not be managed by a centralized housing authority and handed responsibility to local public entities and work units for the distribution, maintenance, and administration of housing. Thus, prior to 1978, the real estate market in China was suppressed, and government policy was the sole factor in the distribution of housing resources. For many people in urban China, housing was distributed by their employers, and residences typically were within or near the work unit. Employees were assigned housing based on their position in the state-owned enterprise. On average, individuals received better housing based on their party affiliation, rank, and tenure.[2] Following retirement, employees and their immediate family members could remain in their last home.

In 1978, the State Council approved and issued a Report from the National Construction Committee on Speeding Up Urban Housing Development, which concluded: "In one sentence, the urban housing problem has reached a stage that has to be resolved." That is, there was substantial underinvestment in housing, and much of the existing stock was considered of poor quality and functionally obsolete. To determine how to reform the housing sector, the government followed an evidence-based approach and embarked on a series of trials.[3] These pilot studies, carried out between 1979 and 1982, allowed occupants in certain geographic areas to purchase their own new housing at either full or subsidized prices, among other reforms. The demand for home purchase was low, due in part to: (i) low rent for housing (considered only a nominal fee to many Chinese workers), (ii) the high cost of homes relative to salaries, and (iii) limited payment options for buyers.[4] Based on these results, the government embarked on a new set of trials in four cities in 1983: they lowered the portion of the purchase price that the homeowner was responsible for (with the remainder the responsibility of the employer and local government) and also allowed the purchase of existing homes. These purchasers, however, became locked in to their housing purchase, unable to re-sell it on the open market. Even in the event that an individual wished to purchase a newer home, the existing home had to be returned to the employer, with only a portion of the original purchase price re-paid to the purchaser. The central government ended the second experiment in 1985, after many complaints from employers and local governments regarding their mandatory subsidies. Yet, even with the subsidies, the price of homes was so much greater than rent that demand remained low.

In 1986, two events occurred that substantially influenced housing reform. The Housing System Reform Leading Group was set up under the aegis of the State Council, and at their first meeting, they decided to raise rent gradually nationwide until it reached market levels. At the same time, a third experiment was being carried out in Yantai city. While simultaneously introducing flexible financing options, the local government designed a system that would weaken the extent to which employers provided housing benefits. Specifically, it built several new houses, and to cover construction costs, it increased rents. To avoid backlash from residents, the government also issued special housing-subsidy coupons that would encourage individuals to purchase housing, but only of a size that they could afford.[5] This plan was very successful and played a major role in the design of the *Implementation Plan for a Gradual Housing System Reform in Cities and Towns* that the State Council issued in February

1998.[6] This plan was implemented nationwide over the next five years, and the Chinese real estate market boomed.

Strictly speaking, the real estate market was not formed until 1992, but it developed rapidly as investment in this sector and construction became more prevalent. Several new laws were passed: some governed how real estate developers could build housing, and some restricted how firms provided housing benefits (to be replaced with cash); most importantly, several urban land reforms allowed firms and individuals to rent land from the government so that the home-owner would, for a period of time, also own the land. By 1999, state and state-owned enterprises withdrew from the direct provision of housing for their employees.[7]

Much of the housing in urban China today has been built since the mid-1980s. Data from the 2000 population census in Shanghai indicates that 36.8 percent of housing was built in the 1980s, and 55.5 percent was built in the 1990s. The situation is similar in other cities, which are being continually renewed. Yet despite this massive amount of construction, there has been substantial demand for housing since 2000, and prices have skyrocketed. In December 2007, the average property price in China's 70 large- and medium-sized cities was up 10.5 percent from the same month of the previous year, while in Beijing, it was up 17.5 percent. Double-digit increases are common, and inequality in access to housing has begun to develop. On the one hand, Huang (2005) documents that many new gated communities have developed, segregated from the surrounding communities, offering larger homes for wealthy individuals. On the other hand, every city is developing pockets of migrant enclaves (Wu 2005); and with urban sprawl, farmland is being converted to housing at a rapid rate.

The provision of housing to low-income individuals had long been a concern for the government. In 1994, the State Council began to consider policies on housing market equality as well as methods to establish adequate housing for people with low incomes. In 1998, the national government started to develop and construct affordable housing. It subsequently produced many housing-related announcements and introduced more comprehensive regulations to implement affordable and low-income housing. In addition, many local governments have also introduced alternative approaches to provide low-income housing. For example, major cities such as Shanghai and Beijing established the *Inexpensive Rental Housing Projects* in 2000 and 2001, respectively. These projects provide access to housing for some low-income individuals, but their extent is limited. For example, Shanghai had approved 17,999 households' applications by the end of 2005, of which 17,200 households had been allocated their residences.[8] Housing for individuals with low incomes is presently the prime reason the government interferes in housing markets, and these interventions are often controversial. Many commentators argue that they have too many objectives to be successful.[9]

Thus, thirty years ago, the government of China offered full housing welfare, but the quality of the housing was poor. Yet by allocating housing through administrative means, the housing level of urban residents were in general fairly equal (though not always fair). To improve housing conditions for all urban residents as urban populations were growing, the Chinese government opened up the housing market to resolve the problems through market mechanisms. Recent years have been characterized by substantial inflation in the housing market, which has made housing in urban areas inaccessible for people with low incomes. Inequality is beginning to result, and this will continue to present challenges for the government as the market continues to expand.

Education Policy

Similar to housing reforms described in the preceding section, since 1978, many reforms have been introduced to decentralize education. This section discusses only reforms to the basic education sector, which covers schooling from Grade 1 through Grade 9.[10] The importance of education in Chinese society cannot be overstated, and it has become even more important with the one-child policy.[11] This section describes how reforms over the past thirty years have changed access to education: the quality of junior, middle, or high school that an urban student attends used to be based primarily on merit but is now increasing based on geographic assignment rules.

Historically, the education sector in China possessed a large number of unique features. First, nearly all of the schools were government funded.[12] Second, the economic reforms in the late 1970s and early 1980s embraced a dual-track schooling system for basic education. That is, key schools (described in greater detailed below) were created to admit the better-performing students and highly qualified teachers in each respective jurisdiction.[13] The goal of the key schools was to produce maximum educational returns in the shortest time.[14] The rationale is that these schools are necessary to effectively train top-level employees for China's developing economy. In certain parts of China, such as Shenzhen, Xiamen, Shanghai, and Changchun, key schools have drawn criticism for being elitist and have been abolished in concept, although not in fact.[15]

Among the local population, people generally know whether a school is a key school or equivalent, or one that focuses on teaching students trade skills.[16] The number of key schools is limited, and these schools have the privilege of recruiting the best students. Admission to key junior middle schools and all senior middle schools has been primarily test based, and schools and teachers are evaluated and ranked to indicate their quality.

Students compete for positions in the higher-quality junior middle schools by taking a municipal-level entrance examination at the completion of elementary school. They also submit a preference list of which school they wish to attend and often face restrictions on the number of quality schools they can list. The examination scores are sent in a sequential manner down the school list, ensuring that the higher-ranked schools have the privilege of recruiting the best students. Schools admit students who score above a cutoff level in their regular classes. Schools additionally admit one or two expansion classes of students who did not score above the cutoff level, but whose families pay a supplemental tuition fee, called a "donation." The size of this donation varies both across and within schools but is often comparable to or much greater than an average household's annual earnings. A 2000 survey conducted by the Wuxi City Statistics Bureau found the average donation was 10,093 yuan.[17]

Education has thus become an important part of family expenditures. In 2000, an affiliated centre of the State Statistics Bureau conducted a survey of 502 urban residents in Beijing, Shanghai, and Guangzhou, which revealed the following:

- Most families (85 percent) paid little attention to the amount of tuition fees and expressed willingness to pay higher fees to have their children attend a better school.
- Only 10 percent of families considered the amount of tuition fees in choosing a school for their children.
- Almost half (45 percent) of all families reported that the money they paid for education was "value for money."
- 43 percent of families reported that education expenditure is an important part of their budget.[18]

The importance of attending a better middle school means that many students move from their homes to live in dormitories when attending school. The funds collected from students living in dormitories help increase investments in the most desirable schools, which widen the quality gap across schools even further.

In earlier work, Ding and Lehrer (2007a) examined data from 11 of the 16 senior middle schools in a county in the Jiangsu province and found that schools of different qualities are significantly different in both the resources available to each student and the level of investment from government and private sources. When we visited these schools, we observed that key schools tend to have more modern facilities. These additional resources, along with higher entry scores, translate into improved education and labour market outcomes at the completion of the senior middle schools.

Although there was a clear ranking of schools, attendance was strictly based on merit, and the above evidence indicates that only a small fraction of families felt constrained by the cost. While admission tests assigned students to schools based on performance, there were exceptions: for example, students showing exceptional ability in a subject area, fine arts, music, or athletics. Social networks (*guanxi*) also played a limited role in determining who gets access to the better senior middle schools. School assignment based on public information (test scores) reflects in part the strong common preference for a fair assignment process, which is monitored by each family whose child is involved. In many urban counties, where people attached extreme importance to education, social networking's effect on the assignment process is minimized.

Moreover, back-door admissions are generally rationalized by indicating that the student had exceptional ability in a particular subject area, fine arts, music or athletics. Yet indicators are available to control for exceptional ability. Ding and Lehrer (2007b) examined a rich dataset of information on school assignment, school quality levels, entrance examinations, and exceptional abilities. Using regression analyses, we verified whether students were truly assigned to type of schools based on the incoming test scores and indicator variables for early admission or talent in subject areas to the rank of the school. We discovered that the regression model could correctly predict 96.67 percent of the matches between students and schools. This test suggests that there is indeed little room for any other factors to potentially influence student assignment in that county.

Under this test-based admissions system, students can attend a school from anywhere within the county, and dormitories are provided at very low cost to accommodate students from neighbouring communities or rural areas. For this reason, there is no need for people to form communities within a county, based on characteristics that henceforth influence school composition. From a policy perspective, test-based admissions and tracking of schools may be desirable if peer group effects exist. If peer group effects are substantial, government policy may exploit them by optimally grouping students in different classrooms to achieve desired socioeconomic outcomes. There has been very limited empirical analysis of this question using data from urban China, however, in part due to data limitations. Ding and Lehrer (2007b) present the strongest evidence that peer group effects indeed exist in urban China and operate in a positive and nonlinear manner, but more evidence is needed to disentangle how a student's performance in school may be influenced by the characteristics and behaviour of her peers.

Although using exam scores to determine school admission tests had several desirable features, this policy also faced a great deal of criticism. Critics of this admissions policy argue that exams present a substantial burden on students who at an early age must write one of the most important exams in their lifetime.[19] In addition, it skews the incentives for a general education for all actors in the education system, possibly resulting in excessive development of test-taking skills and a lack of training on analytical exercises. As a result, reforms in many prefectures in urban China have sought to eliminate this burden on young students: they have changed the basis of admissions from exam scores to locality.[20] That is, students who live within the boundaries of a school district can attend that school. Thus, a student's peers in the classroom may change markedly if the structure of the neighbourhood changes.

While the reform reduced student competition, it has spurred the development of a private school sector (see note 12). In addition, in recent years, there has also been a rise in competition between school administrators in different regions and occasionally within regions. This competition is in part a response to the rise of private schools. Many private schools offer large wage and benefit packages in an effort to recruit the best teachers. School administrators in the top public schools have responded by raiding neighbouring lower-ranked schools and schools in more rural regions for their best-ranked teachers. As the next section explains, this competition for resources may intensify in the coming years.

Finally, it should be noted that the reforms to the basic education sector have been very successful in many dimensions. The relative efficiency of education improved, as measured by diagnostics such as enrolment, completion, and achievement. Resources to the average student increased markedly (greater expenditures per student, annual recurrent public educational expenditures, qualified teachers, facilities, textbooks, and others); and education productivity appears more effective, as both drop-out and grade retention rates fell while educational standards remained stable.[21]

Neighbourhood Formation

Within many developed nations, trends and causes of residential patterns continue to be a major research issue. Many commentators (e.g., Reich 1991) suggest that increased segregation in the form of gated wealthy communities and isolated poor neighbourhoods are a source of increasing income inequality. Substantial literature in the United States uses census data to analyze the underlying dynamics of neighbourhood formation and change. For example, Cutler et al. (2001) examine segregation in American cities from 1890 to 1990. They show that segregation by both race and income across cities has been very persistent and is strongly positively related to city size. In addition to this study, a growing body of research has used longitudinal data to measure movement among neighbourhoods of varying economic and racial composition (e.g., Quillian 1999). These studies have found declines in segregation by race and increases in segregation by income class until the 1990s, when segregation by income declined. In the theoretical models that underlie many of these empirical studies, researchers postulate that parents select a place of residence in part because of neighbourhood composition and its potential impact on their children's human capital accumulation. The characteristics of neighbourhoods in which individuals grow up may be important determinants of their lifetime success or failure (e.g., Brooks-Gunn et al. 1997). In recent years, in part driven by the availability of rich geo-coded socioeconomic surveys, sociologists, demographers, educational researchers and economists have produced a sizeable empirical literature on the effects of neighbourhood. Endogenous sorting of individuals into communities, however, is often posited as source of bias in neighbourhood effects analyses. These biases illustrate the importance of understanding the process by which individuals choose their place of residence.

In China, residential patterns have historically not been a social issue. Yet, the preceding section outlines how in many parts of urban China school admission policies have shifted from merit-based systems to locality-based systems. At the same time, policies that restrict families from moving to different neighbourhoods have been abolished for a subset of the population. Taken together, this has created substantial incentives for families that value education to purchase homes in districts with better schools, potentially leading to segregation based on parental wealth, income, or profession. In addition, in the future, school administrators may respond to this demand by focusing their attention on high-income neighbourhoods, which could exacerbate inequality in education resources.

The notion that local public goods, such as school quality, can lead households to "vote with their feet" has been a key idea in local public finance since Tiebout's (1956) seminal paper. The idea that households sort non-randomly is far from new. While the consequences of segregation have been explored in a large body of research,[22] few papers,[23] attempt to explain the fundamental causes of residential segregation; to date, none have done so with data from China. Since China is currently experiencing this sorting process to reach a new equilibrium,[24] there is a unique opportunity to document history in the making.

This research would be a unique opportunity, since historically China has limited residential moves, and those that occurred were usually not self-initiated, but rather mandated by the government or work units. For instance, research by Chai et al. (2002) indicates that in Shenzhen, mobility increased from less than 1 percent per annum in the early 1980s to more than 10 percent per annum in the later 1990s. Research suggests that mobility in urban areas is non-trivial, with geographers suggesting that in urban China, the mobility rate are currently 7–9 percent per annum, which is nearly identical to that of Western Europe.[25]

In our study of the interaction of housing reforms, education reforms, and neighbourhood composition, we were fortunate to receive the generous co-operation of a local education bureau in Shanghai, which has a population of more than 1 million within its administrative district. This Bureau presides over 46 junior middle schools and their corresponding 42 school districts. In 2005, we designed, administered, and collected a rich survey in 34 of the 47 middle schools. Approximately 4,500 surveys were collected by both students and parents. Additionally, we collected at least five years of detailed data on school inputs from each middle school and obtained extremely rich administrative records on the population of teachers and students in seven of these schools. These data sources provide us with a comprehensive picture of students in school for several years, the teachers and classes they have, the family they have, and the neighbourhoods they live in.

While our research agenda examining how residential segregation develops in response to school admission rules and housing reforms in urban China has only begun, several preliminary findings are worth noting. We compared responses across school districts based on their historical school quality level, as reported by the county education bureau.

First, we asked parents in the surveys to list the most important criteria in deciding where the families should reside. Parents claimed that the single most important dimension was price (43.94 percent), followed by traffic (16 percent). Only 8.52 percent of parents claimed that school quality was the prime determinant of residence choice. Not only was school quality rarely listed as the most important dimension, but the rate at which it was the second most dimension was also fairly minor.

Next, we examined whether there were any dimensions along which parents sort across school districts. We ran simple unconditional tests of differences in means between parental characteristics across districts, based on school quality. We found that in neighbourhoods that contained higher-ranked schools, both parents had significantly higher levels of education, and there was also a significant difference in father's income (all results are from one sided t-tests and are statistically different at the 1 percent level).

We also collected data from a single school to determine if the peer group composition changed during the reform period. This school is highly ranked but was not considered a key school. Figure 1 presents Kernel density estimates of the distribution of test scores from the same entrance examination in three subject areas in 1988 and 2002 for this school. Note that at the prefecture level, there was no significant differences in mean or median performance between these time periods on this exam in any of these subject areas.[26] Yet, as illustrated in Figure 1, in each subject area, the mean entry scores fell over time, and the variance in these test scores dramatically increased. Indeed, as both the housing market and education reforms changed admission, the peer group became substantially more heterogeneous in terms of performance on entry examinations. Taken together, these results suggest that peer group composition in schools and neighbourhood formation along several parental characteristics have evolved quickly in recent years.

In terms of how school administrators have responded to these reforms, it is important to note that 30 percent of teachers transferred schools over this period. While we have not yet formally modelled the process by which transfers occur, simple summary statistics indicate that the top two schools in the district now have faculties in which over 50 percent of their teachers are highly ranked. Conversely, in three of the bottom five

FIGURE 1
Kernel Density Distribution of Incoming Test Scores at One Above-Average Middle School in Urban China, 1998 and 2002

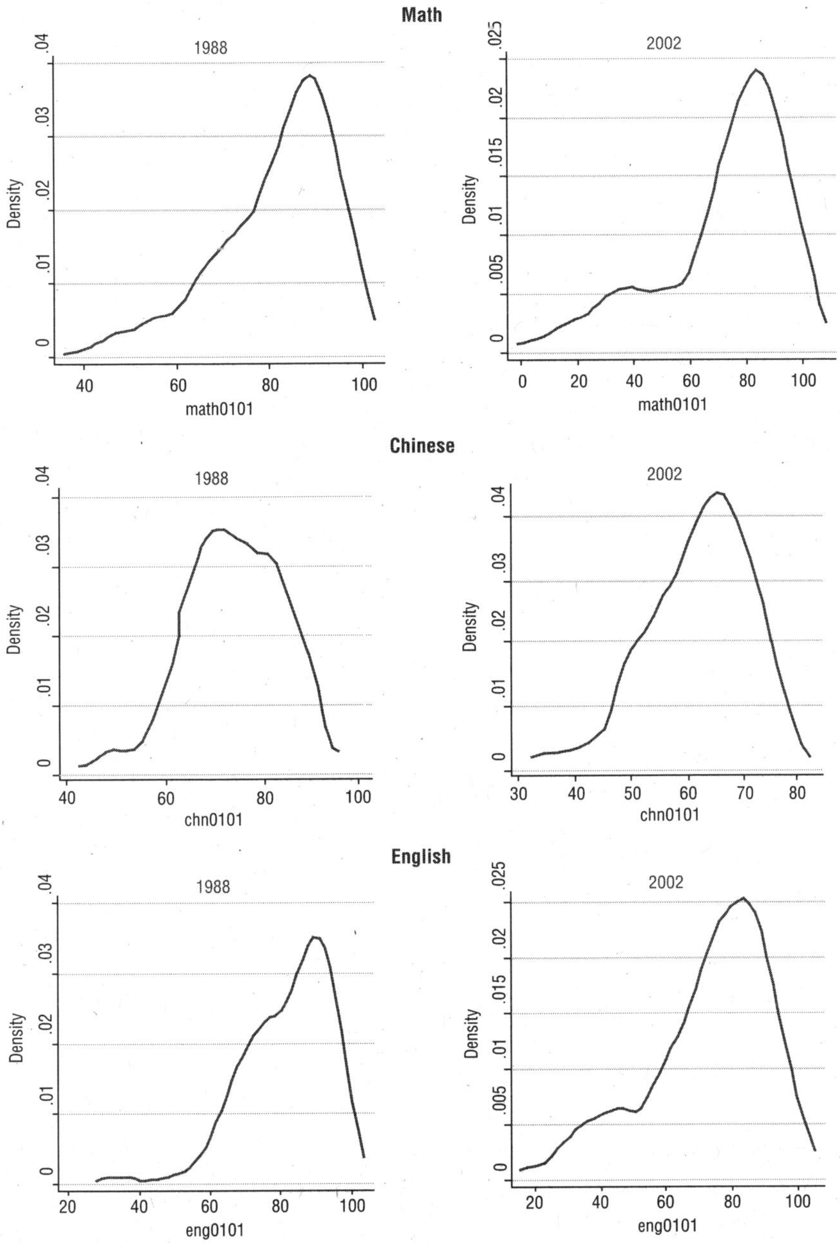

Note: The y-axis presents the percentage of observations at a given percentile test score (which is listed on the x-axis). The area under the density curve sums to 1.

Source: Authors' compilation.

school districts, their faculties do not contain even a single superior teacher. These preliminary results suggest that administrators of highly-ranked schools are actively working on improving their school quality, which is increasing the inequity in access to high quality school inputs.

In contrast, 1998 data collected by the authors from an urban county in the Jiangsu province found that each school within that county had teaching staffs in which 6.09–26.61 percent were ranked as superior teachers. In fact, a provincial key school represented the 6.09 percent (this school had a disproportionately large number of first-class teachers), and the four lowest-ranked schools in that data had 10.0–13.04 percent. This suggests that a lot has changed since the late 1990s due to the rapid expansion of the housing market.

The previous section on housing policy noted that the prime method in which the government currently interferes in housing markets is through housing for individuals with low-incomes. By the end of 2006, 512 of China's 657 cities have had initiated affordable housing strategies, but only 268,000 households, or 2.7 percent of the low-income families nationwide, have benefited from the low-renting housing policy.[27] A challenge that policy-makers must consider in constructing housing for individuals with lower incomes is how homes should be allocated in urban regions.

Policies on construction of affordable urban housing have ignored their impacts on neighbourhood formation. Essentially, these policies have focused on construction of large congregations of high-rise apartments in specific geographic areas selected by the local government. These apartments are affordable to households with low incomes but potentially have significant negative implications for urban planning, education, health and other social policies. As these areas contain a disproportionately large congregation of low-income housing, this could result in the creation of ghettos.

To understand how the current policies are leading to the establishment of ghettos, it is important to understand the historical housing situation for individuals with low incomes. In most cities in China, both the local poor and the floating population together tend to reside in relatively small, older dwellings, generally near the core of the city. These buildings and living facilities are outdated, and the common space and community are sparse as well. The conditions are extremely poor, and governments tend to move inhabitants from the local area to communities located on the periphery of the city, rather that refurbish these dwellings and revitalize old but familiar communities.[28] The older communities were small in size and tended to encompass areas of 6–10 city blocks. Once the government tears down these communities, it often permits construction of new housing in these central areas, which are subsequently sold to wealthy individuals.

Naturally, individuals who have spent much of their life living near the centre of the city are rarely happy with their mandated move to distant communities, despite the improved living conditions of their residence. Pre-reform housing established by working units created communities that did not have much segregation; but today, if affordable housing is concentrated in specific geographic areas within the urban region, ghettos may emerge. Such segregation along income lines could create larger ghettos and lead to social, economic and political tensions. As large sums of funds are being invested to build affordable housing, this also presents an opportunity to reduce the formation of ghettos. The government can reduce the likelihood of the "ghetto" phenomena by strategically spreading affordable housing in socially and economically diverse neighbourhoods (as diverse as the government has influence over), in a way that addresses both the housing affordability problem and the social problem of ghettoization.

Conclusions

Education and housing policies have been undergoing great transformation in China since the initiation of economic reforms and the open-door policy in the late 1970s. These market-oriented reforms have significantly impacted China's development, improving the average quality of housing and nearly all education statistics. While these reforms have led to improvements, however, there are increasing concerns regarding the equity implications of these policies, even though the levels of inequality in housing and education are several orders of magnitude smaller relative to income inequality.

Like many national governments, the Chinese government tends to devise and evaluate economic and social policies in isolation. For housing policies, it has focused on affordability and price stability over the past five years. For education policies, it has focused on affordability and accessibility for rural residents, on basic education, on quality of education (for example, abolishing admission examinations to reduce testing burdens for students), and on increasing college enrolment to meet the demand for urban residents. Economic analysis suggests, however, that any major economic or social policy likely has general equilibrium consequences. That is, housing policies can impact education, and education policies can affect housing markets. We argue that it is important to consider the consequences of the interactions of multiple policies in different areas and demonstrate their impacts on neighbourhood formation.

After all, if the test-based admission policy for schools were abolished in favour of local admission, especially during a period in which residential movements were highly restricted (as was the case prior to the mid-1990s), then it is reasonable to assume that this education policy would have the potential not only to reduce test burden for students but also to increase access to quality education for low-performing students. Other policies, however, have contributed to the rapid development of urban "commercial" housing, which has greatly weakened restrictions on residential mobility, thereby allowing parents to choose schools for their children based their resources. Increasing access to quality education for high-income households may dramatically change the urban landscape, with high-income and high-education families congregating in school districts that have key schools; it may also substantially reduce access to quality education for low-income students, especially high-performing students who could have been admitted to such schools under the test-based admission policy. This chapter presents preliminary evidence that these reforms and their interactions have led to substantial inequality within urban areas, and that the factors that drive inequality in access to education resources are no longer based on merit or tenure.

Similarly, housing affects multiple aspects of a family's life, ranging from neighbourhood safety to local public health and local public education. Thus, these policies cannot be evaluated exclusively on the housing market, the price, and allocation of housing. The Chinese government should take advantage of its unprecedented opportunity in large-scale urban development to influence the formation of "good" neighbourhoods. Neighbourhoods with low crime rates, high sanitation standards, good schools, and increased interaction of social classes will promote tolerance and mutual understanding. To build better neighbourhoods, policy-makers need to study the impact of education and health policies on the formation of neighbourhoods, since these policies do not work in isolation. Understanding and being sensitive to the influence of policies on multiple outcomes (or the mutual impact of policies from different government department) is not easy, but it is critical to the success of policies that tackle China's social challenges.

Future research is needed to document how neighbourhoods and school composition are changing in response to housing and education policies. Ding and Lehrer (2007b) presented evidence that in urban China, peer groups contribute significantly and positively to student performance as measured by test scores. More importantly, we find evidence of substantial heterogeneity, as the same student would respond in a heterogeneous manner to different compositions of their peer groups. Yet these results were obtained with data during an era where students were assigned to schools based on test scores, and the residential choice was severely limited. Thus, it is critical to improve our understanding of how neighbourhood and peer influences affect development trajectories in urban China for outcomes that extend beyond student achievement, particularly as policy-makers engage in future reforms in these areas to continue China's development. This chapter presents an agenda for future research.

Notes

We wish to thank participants at the 2007 Shanghai Forum for helpful comments on a presentation of some of the material presented in the section, *Neighbourhood Formation*. We are grateful to both SSHRC and the Spencer Foundation for research support. The usual caveat applies.

1. Wang and Murie (2000) and Huang and Clark (2002) present a substantial overview of housing policy in urban China.
2. Whyte and Parish (1984) suggest that there was a connection between housing provision and the authoritative position. Longan and Bian (1993) discuss the significance of party membership in obtaining better housing. Other factors related to need, such as family size and number of children, also played a role in housing allocation over this period.
3. It is important to state that over the thirty-year period, a series of urban land reforms played a pivotal role in the development of the housing market. These reforms essentially led the government to lease land so that land use rights could be assigned to urban land users.
4. Cao and Gao (2002) provide details on these early experiments.
5. The Plan suggested that the rent should be automatically withheld from employees' salaries (the housing-subsidy coupon included). "When the coupon value is more than the rent to be paid, the balance should be deposited into funds for individual housing purchase and construction." Other than the balance of the rent, the sources of the housing fund should come from: "(i) government allocated housing funds, (ii) housing funds gathered by the work units, (iii) the maintenance and depreciation expenses that are already calculated into the costs of the enterprises, (iv) a portion of the rent of the newly built houses, (v) proceeds from the sale of the houses." When a family's rent was less than the employer-provided subsidy, the balance of the subsidy would go to a special housing fund administered by a bank. The family would be permitted to apply those funds only for their future home purchase. See Wang and Murie (1996) for more details.
6. The National Plan suggested the following actions: (i) increases in rents to market levels, (ii) sales of public housing to private individuals, (iii) encouragement of private and foreign investments in housing, (iv) reduced construction of new public housing, (v) encouragement and protection of private home ownership, (vi) construction of commercial housing by profit-making developers, and (vii) promotion of self-built housing in cities.
7. In July 1998, The State Council announced a reform entitled *Notice of Further Deepening Urban Housing System Reform and Speeding up of Housing Construction*, which ended public provision of housing.
8. Source: Shanghai Housing and Land Bureau: 17,200 Cheap Rent Houses were allocated in 2005, *East Daily Morning Newspaper*, Jan. 19, 2006.
9. We discuss the implications of many current policies on the composition of communities in the section entitled *Neighbourhood Formation*.
10. In 1985, the Central Committee of the Chinese Communist Party issued the *Decision on the Reform of the Educational Structure*, establishing the principle that local governments should be responsible for mandatory basic education, ensuring that this schooling was "free," and placing education rights

on a firm legal basis in 1986. See Hawkins (2000), Tsang (1996) or Wang (2004) for details. Although the law states that students do not have to pay tuition, there are fees for such items as books, supplies, and uniforms, which can cause difficulty (and have grown becoming increasingly non-trivial) for lower-income families (Kattan and Burnett 2004).

11. The economic importance of education has risen substantially in both rural and urban China, affecting both the levels of income and the types of jobs and associated occupational status a person can attain. Paine and Fang (2005) describe how the rising demand for education has meant that more students are seeking higher education options, which in turn has led to dramatic increases in the number of students enrolled in secondary schools and institutions of higher learning. The literature on the returns to education in urban China is discussed in Maurer-Fazio (2005) and Maurer-Fazio and Dinh (2004). Similarly Zhang et al. (2002) and Li et al. (2005) present recent developments in the literature using data from rural China.
12. Tsang (2000a) estimates only 500 registered non-governmental schools existed in 1994. By 2004, however, China had 78,500 private institutions, enrolling 17 million students.
13. In the basic education reform in the middle 1980s, both key and regular schooling systems were expanded greatly (Lewin et al. 1994), but emphasis was placed on the former (Rosen 1987). Ding and Lehrer (2004) present a description of the teacher ranking system in the key and regular middle schools. The importance of teacher rankings on student achievement is discussed in Ding and Lehrer (2007b).
14. The second mission is to serve as a teaching and learning model for regular schools. Rosen (1985) argues that this mission was never realized.
15. In reality, changes have gone little beyond renaming these schools and/or enforcing local admission. With parents' perception of the quality of these schools unaltered, local admission becomes admission based on means of wealth and social connections, which raises serious fairness concerns.
16. The concept of key schools is similar to that of a magnet or college preparatory school in the United States.
17. Source: *Wuxi Daily* June 13, 2000 available at http://www.hku.hk/chinaed/chinaed_news/chinaednews_no19_2000.html . Note that 10,093 yuan is approximately US$1,225. As a point of comparison, disposable personal income per capita in 1999 in urban areas reached Rmb 5,854 (US$707). Per capita net income for farmers was Rmb 2,210 (US$266.90).
18. Source: *Life Times*, April 15, 2000, available at http://www.hku.hk/chinaed/chinaed_news/chinaednews_no13_2000.html.
19. See Lai (2005) and Ha (2005) for a discussion of these issues in the context of reforms in Beijing.
20. Ding and Lu (2005) present a theoretical analysis of the equity and efficiency implications of these reforms.
21. See *Essential Statistics of Education in China* Volume 1, produced by the Ministry of Education's Department of Development and Planning in 2001, as well as chapters in Hannum and Park (2007), for multiple surveys of many of these accomplishments.
22. More recent contributions to the theoretical literature include Epple, Filimon, and Romer (1984, 1993), Benabou (1993, 1996), Fernandez and Rogerson (1996) and Nechyba (1997).

23. For example, Hoxby (2000) demonstrates that Tiebout sorting has a substantial impact on the competitiveness of the education marketplace, with metropolitan areas that can afford more school choice having more productive public schools.
24. In developed countries, household sorting equilibrium was attained a long time ago. Research on residential mobility in market economies is well developed. Hanushek and Quigley (1978) argue that change in residence is an attempt to achieve consumption equilibrium within the constraint of affordability.
25. In China, an abundance of research and policy discussion focuses on migration patterns from rural to urban areas. The topics of intra- and inter-urban mobility has achieved little attention, despite the current impressive levels of mobility and enormous growth in the rates at which families are moving into new residences.
26. We do not have any information on whether the variance in theses scores changed over time.
27. The Chinese government has stepped up construction of affordable housing for middle- and low-income earners by investing 157.8 billion yuan (US$19 billion) in 2003 and 166.3 billion yuan (US$20 billion) in 2004. In its 2008 budget, 6.8 billion yuan (US$951 million) was allocated to build low-rent houses for urban poor, which is 33 percent more than the previous year. Yet, these efforts have not kept up with demand; and on August 7, 2007, the State Council released *Opinions on Solving the Housing Difficulties of Urban Low-Income Families* calling for more financial support to the construction of low-rent housing and affordable housing. Reports in the popular press indicate that one-tenth of the apartments built in Shenzhen between 2007 and 2010 will be rental for the low-income population. The government hopes these measures can help rein in runaway property prices and reduce public resentment towards its property policies.
28. Temporary dwellers do not have permanency and have to find a new home or room to rent that is affordable. In general, the rental price gradient is steep, which forces them to relocate to the periphery of the city.

References

Benabou, R. 1993. "The Workings of a City: Location, Education, and Production." *Quarterly Journal of Economics* 108(3):619–52.

——— 1996. "Heterogeneity, Stratification, and Growth: Macroeconomic Implications of Community Structure and School Finance." *American Economic Review* 86(3):584–609.

Brooks-Gunn, J., G. Duncan, and L. Aber. 1997. *Neighborhood Poverty: Context and Consequences for Children.* New York: Russell Sage.

Cao, Z., and X.H. Gao. 2002. *The Development and Management of Chinese Real Estate Market.* Beijing: Peking University Press.

Chai, Y., et al. 2002. *The Temporal-Spatial Structure of Chinese Cities (Zhongguo chengshi de shikongjian jiekou).* Beijing: Peking University Press.

Cutler, D., E. L. Glaeser, and J. L/Vigdor,. 1999. "The Rise and Decline of the American Ghetto." *Journal of Political Economy* 107(3):455–506.

Ding, W., and M. Lu. 2005. "Can Educational Equity and Efficiency Both Be Achieved? A General Equilibrium Analysis of Basic Education Finance" (in Chinese). *Social Sciences in China* 6(1):47–57.

Ding, W., and S.F. Lehrer. 2004. "Assessing Teacher's Performance Incentives in China." *World Economic Forum* 156(1):1–24.

——— 2007a. "Improving Teacher Quality in China." Pp. 191–204 in *Education and Reform in China*, edited by E. Hannum and A. Park. London: Routledge Press.

——— 2007b. "Do Peers Affect Student Achievement in China's Secondary Schools?" *Review of Economics and Statistics* 89(2):300–312.

Epple, D., R. Filimon, and T. Romer. 1984. "Equilibrium Among Local Jurisdictions: Towards an Integrated Approach of Voting and Residential Choice." *Journal of Public Economics* 24:281–304.

——— 1993. "Existence of Voting and Housing Equilibrium in a System of Communities with Property Taxes," *Regional Science and Urban Economics* 23:585–610.

Fernandez, R., and R. Rogerson. 1996. "Income Distribution, Communities, and the Quality of Public Education," *Quarterly Journal of Economics* 111(1):135–64.

Ha, W. 2005. "Does School Quality Matter? Evidence from a Randomized School Choice Experiment in Beijing." *mimeo*. Harvard University, Kennedy School of Government.

Hannum, E., and A. Park. 2007. *Education and Reform in China*, New York: Routledge Press.

Hanushek, E.A., and J.M. Quigley. 1978. "An Explicit Model of Intra- Metropolitan Mobility." *Land Economics* 54:411–429.

Hawkins, J.N. 2000. "Centralization, Decentralization, Recentralization: Educational Reform in China." *Journal of Educational Administration* 38(5):442–55.

Hoxby, C.M. 2000. "Does Competition Among Public Schools Benefit Students and Taxpayers?" *American Economic Review* 90(5):1209–38.

Huang, Y. 2005. "From Work-unit Compounds to Gated Communities: Housing Inequality and Residential Segregation in Transitional Beijing." In *Restructuring the Chinese Cities: Changing Society, Economy and Space*, edited by L.J. Ma and F. Wu. New York: Routledge Press.

Huang, Y., and W.A.V. Clark. 2002. "Housing Tenure Choice in Transitional Urban China: A Multilevel Analysis." *Urban Studies*, 39(1):7–32.

Kattan, R.B., and N. Burnett. 2004. *User Fees in Primary Education*. Washington, DC: The World Bank.

Kremer, M. 1993. "The O-Ring Theory of Economic Development." *Quarterly Journal of Economics* 108(3):551–575.

Lai, F. 2005. "The Impact of School Quality on Educational Performance: Evidence from the Middle School Educational Reform in Beijing's Eastern City District." *mimeo*. Berkeley: University of California.

Lewin, K., A. Little, H. Xu, and J. Zheng. 1994. *Educational Innovation in China: Tracing the Impact of the 1985 Reform*. Harlow, UK: Longman.

Li, Q., A. de Brauw, S. Rozelle, and L. Zhang. 2005. "Labor Market Emergence and Returns to Education in Rural China." *Review of Agricultural Economics* 27(3):418–24.

Longan, J. R., and Y. Bian. 1993. "Inequalities in Access to Community Resources in a Chinese City." *Social Forces* 72(2):555–576.

Maurer-Fazio, M. 2007. "The Role of Education in Determining Labor Market Outcomes in Urban China." Pp. 260–275 in *Education and Reform in China*, edited by E. Hannum and A. Park. London: Routledge Press.

Maurer-Fazio, M., and N. Dinh. 2004. "Differential Rewards to and Contributions of Education in Urban China's Segmented Labor Markets." *The Pacific Economic Review* 9(3):173–189.

Nechyba, T.J. 1997. "Existence of Equilibrium and Stratification in Local and Hierarchical Tiebout Economies with Property Taxes and Voting." *Economic Theory* 10:277–304.

Paine, L., and Y. Fang. 2005. "Challenges in Reforming Professional Development." Pp. 173–190 in *Education and Reform in China*, edited by E. Hannum and A. Park. London: Routledge Press.

Quillian, L. 1999. "Migration Patterns and the Growth of High Poverty Neighborhoods, 1970-1990." *American Journal of Sociology* 105(1):1–37.

Reich, R. 1991. "*The Work of Nations: Preparing Ourselves for 21st-Century Capitalism*." New York: Alfred A. Knopf.

Rosen, S. 1985. "Recentralization, Decentralization, and Rationalization, *Modern China 11*(3): 301–346.

——— 1987. "Restoring Key Secondary Schools in Post-Mao China: The Politics of Competition and Educational Quality." Pp. 321–353 in *Policy Implementation in Post-Mao China* , edited by D. M. Lampton. Berkeley, CA: University of California Press.

Tiebout, C.M. 1956. "A Pure Theory of Local Expenditures." *Journal of Political Economy* 64:416–424.

Tsang, M. 1996. "Financial Reform of Basic Education in China," *Economics of Education Review* 15(4):423–444.

——— 2000a. "Education and National Development in China Since 1949: Oscillating Policies and Enduring Dilemmas." *China Review*: 579–618.

——— 2000b. "The Economic Burden of Compulsory Schooling on Families in poor Areas in China." (in Chinese). Pp. 1–20 in *Economic Analysis of Education Policy*, edited by M. Tsang, X. Wei, and J. Xiao. Beijing: Education Science Press.

Wang, Y. 2004. "Governance of Basic Education: Service Provision and Quality Assurance in China." Washington, DC: World Bank.

Wang, Y.P., and A. Murie. 1999. *Housing Policy and Practice in China*, New York: MacMillan Press Ltd.

——— 2000. "Social and Spatial Implications of Housing Reform in China." *International Journal of Urban and Regional Research* 24:2397–2417.

Whyte, M.K. and Parish, W.L. 1984. *Urban Life in Contemporary China*. Chicago, IL: The University of Chicago Press.

Wu, F. 1996. "Changes in the Structure of Public Housing Provision in Urban China." *Urban Studies* 33(9):1601–1627.

——— 2004. "Intra-Urban Residential Relocation in Shanghai: Modes and Stratification." *Environment and Planning* 36:7–25.

Wu, W. 2005. "Migrant Settlement and Spatial Transformation in Urban China: The Case of Shanghai." Forthcoming in *Professional Geographer.*

Xinhua News Agency. 2001 "China Embarks on Basic Education Reform." Available at http://www.china.org.cn/english/2001/Oct/21257.htm or http://www.edu.cn/20011029/3007230.shtml.

Yu, Z. 2006 "Heterogeneity and Dynamics in China's Emerging Urban Housing Market: Two Sides of a Success Story from the Late 1990s." *Habitat International* 30(2): 277–304.

Zhang, L., J. Huang, and S. Rozelle. 2002. "Employment, Emerging Labor Markets, and the Role of Education in Rural China." *China Economic Review* 13(2–3):313–328.

3

Finding Housing in China: The Market-Oriented Reform of China's Urban Housing System

ZHAO CHEN, JIE CHEN, AND XIAOFENG LIU

Recent market-oriented reforms in China's urban housing system are working well and must be continued. Although the reforms have intensified inequality in housing condition and income, since people who benefited under the previous allocation system have been rewarded even more under the new system, market reforms nevertheless are improving the quality and quantity of housing across the country. In addition, new housing policies can compensate those who have been disadvantaged by the housing system reform. However, these reforms should work in the context of a market orientation and avoid distorting the pricing mechanism.

Introduction

"Where can I find tens of thousands of houses?" Even centuries ago, Du Pu, the great poet of Tang Dynasty, was talking about the housing supply problem. Today, after more than twenty years of the housing system reform, the housing situation has greatly improved in China. Yet the problem of improving the living conditions of low-income people and mitigating housing inequality (which Du Pu described as "mak[ing] the people who are freezing under the sky happy") has not been adequately addressed.

In fact, problems with the housing sector have become a major challenge to the socio-economic development of China. The market-oriented reform of the housing system has widened the income gap (Meng 2007). Income-segregated neighbourhoods are developing, and surging housing prices have constrained the aggregation effect in the cities. Taken together, these effects could lead to uneven home ownership, wealth

Economic Transitions with Chinese Characteristics: Social Change During Thirty Years of Reform, eds. Arthur Sweetman and Jun Zhang. Montreal and Kingston: McGill-Queen's University Press, Queen's Policy Studies Series.

inflation boosted by marketization, increases in the income gap, and intensification of the gap between social classes.

Unsatisfied with the status quo, people have tended to believe that government intervention in the housing market will reverse these trends. However, is it really necessary for the government to intervene? What would be the aim of this intervention? How would the policies be carried out? Would the government intervention necessarily involve a degree of "inverse marketization"? In order to answer these questions, we must review the pros and cons of the housing market reform and focus on its impact on different groups of people in the course of the reform. This chapter analyzes the government's efforts to intervene in the housing market and assesses whether it can truly achieve its goals through such interventions.

History and experience in the urban housing reform confirms that market-oriented reform is already taking place in China. However, the people who received the most benefits under the former communist system are still receiving the most benefits today. In other words, the old pervious property right structure endures despite the reform, which only seemed to further intensify China's housing inequality. Therefore, effective intervention must aim at compensating disadvantaged groups whose interests have been ignored under the reforms, in order to minimize its distortion effect on pricing. The following section analyzes the pros and cons of the market-oriented reform of the housing market. Subsequent sections review the current housing policy and suggest a direction and philosophy for future housing policy reform. The final section provides a brief summary.

Pros and Cons of Market-Oriented Reform in the Housing Market

History of Urban Housing Reform in China

Before the economic reforms of the early 1980s, the Chinese government had established a housing system in the style of welfare allocation. This centrally planned system placed a heavy financial burden on the government and distorted the supply-demand mechanism in the housing market, causing sharp discrepancies between supply and demand. At the end of the 1950s, the national per capita living space was 4.5 square metres, which further decreased to 3.6 square metres in 1978 (Chen et al. 2003, 26). According to a survey in 1985, more than 27 percent of city dwellers had to share apartments with other families; 7.4 percent lived in an average space of less than 4 square metres; 37 percent had to share a kitchen with non-family others; and 76 percent didn't have a toilet in their home (Xie 1999). To deal with this problem, the Chinese government began to reform the housing system, as described by Deng Xiaoping in his speeches about housing issues in 1978 and 1980, which focused on selling public houses, modifying the rent, and encouraging people to build and purchase homes.

From 1978 to 1985, housing reforms consisted of selling apartments to workers at subsidized prices. By 1985, about ten million square metres of public housing had been sold to urban employees (Xie 1999). With a better turnover of housing investment funds, the pace of urban housing construction accelerated noticeably. In 1985, 188 million square metres of new apartments were built in urban areas, more than four times that built in 1978. At this early stage in the reforms, the government's goal was to ease the financial burden on its own urban housing budget, rather than to change the fundamental ideology of welfare allocation. However, this goal was not accomplished. From 1978 to 1988, housing subsidies increased at a rate of 28.6 percent annually, while the Gross National Product (GNP) in the same period increased at only 14.5 percent per annum—14.1 percent more slowly than the cost of the subsidies. By 1988, total housing subsidies had risen to 5.84 million yuan (Wang 1991).

From 1986 to 1990, regulators studied the problem and proposed a new reform package that would raise rents to finance subsidies. The first meeting of the national housing reform committee in August 1988 concluded that the object of urban housing reform would be the marketization of houses, and that the welfare allocation system should be changed gradually into a marketized housing system, starting with an increase in the low rents of public apartments. Yet housing construction projects during this period stagnated, due to a slowdown in the sales of public housing and insufficient cash flow. Therefore, the annual construction of new urban housing during this period was just 160–200 million square metres.

In 1991, the Shanghai government implemented a combined reform policy package, which included step-by-step increases in rents and subsidies, the sale of public apartments, the implementation of a housing accumulation fund, the sale of housing bonds, and the setting up of a housing committee. This policy package clarified that the government, the community, and the people all had a share in the responsibilities for urban housing development and the transfer of the housing supply from the government to the market. This policy was copied in many other cities and played a critical role in furthering the national housing reform. In 1991, the State Council issued a *Notice on Actively and Safely Furthering Urban Housing System Reform*, which reaffirmed that new homes would be built according to the new system policy. The reform intensified in June 1994, when the government declared the State Council's *Decision on Furthering Urban Housing System Reform*, which proposed a dual goal for housing system reform: to set up a supply system of economically affordable homes to provide social security to families with low and medium income, and to set up a supply system of marketized homes (i.e., sold at market prices) for high-income families. The Decision gave new direction to the housing reform. By 1997, housing accumulation funds had been set up in all major Chinese cities; rental reform and the sales of public housing had accelerated; and the home ownership ratio was increasing rapidly. During this period, urban housing construction increased by an annual rate of 30 percent. In 1997 alone, 406 million square metres of new housing space was added.

The market for marketized houses was immense; yet out of all the urban homes built in 1997, only 120 million square metres of them were for marketized homes—less than a third of the total. In addition, the proportion of homes actually purchased by the inhabitants themselves was even smaller, because most marketized homes were purchased by employers for welfare allocation. Even in Shanghai, where the housing market was the most developed, only 54 percent of marketized homes were bought by inhabitants (Chen and Hao 2006). Thus, the dual system had become a bottleneck to further reform.

The year 1998 was pivotal in the history of China's housing reform. The Notice of the State Council on Furthering Urban Housing System Reform and Accelerating Housing Construction set up the goal of implementing gradual housing marketization reform. This policy changed the core philosophy of the old housing system. The issuance of this notice symbolized a new era in the real estate industry of China. In retrospect, however, the notice failed to provide clear direction on how to provide housing to lower-income families. This omission was the direct cause of later social dissatisfaction about housing issues.

For quite a long time afterwards, policies centred on controlling the rise of housing prices, since prices rose too fast during the early reform period. On August 13, 2007, the Office of the State Council issued the State Council's Advice on the Settlement of Housing Difficulties of Urban Low-Income Families and gave the urban low-income housing problem top priority in housing policy, reflecting the new attention being paid to this problem by the central government. This Notice was the first to propose explicitly that low-rent homes should be the core of the housing security system and the first to give limited property rights for the purchase of public housing.

Achievements of the Market-Oriented Urban Housing Reform

Starting in 1998, China's housing system entered a new phase of complete marketization. As a key component of the overall step-by-step economic reforms, urban housing reform played an important role in improving urban housing conditions and nurturing the development of property-related industries.

One important effect of China's housing reform was the new prosperity of the real estate industry. In 1990, the annual value added to the national economy from the real estate industry was only 32.53 billion yuan, or 1.8 percent of the Gross Domestic Product (GDP). That decreased to 1.72 percent in 1998. In 2004, however, it rose to 4.5 percent (NBS 1996–

2007).[1] By 2006, national real estate investment reached 2,144.6 billion yuan and comprised 23 percent of gross social investment. Investment in residential homes reached 1,361.2 billion yuan and became a significant part of the economy.

Meanwhile, as shown in Figure 1, national sales of marketized houses rose steadily. In 2006, national sales of residential homes reached 1,728.8 billion yuan, with 554.23 million square metres of new living space. In the ten years following the beginning of the comprehensive housing reform, the housing sector saw unprecedented growth in China. From 1985 to 1997, an accumulated 3.52 billion square metres of homes were built in China's urban areas, an annual average of 293 million square metres. Moreover, in the eight years from 1998 to 2005 alone, accumulated completion of urban housing construction reached 4.54 billion square metres, an annual average of 648 million square metres. This growth momentum has continued in recent years. The rapid development of the real estate industry is also evident in the increase in employment in the real estate industry. National employment in real estate rose from 360,000 in 1985 (0.28 percent of the total employed urban population) to 1.52 million in 2005 (close to 0.45 percent of the total employed urban population).

FIGURE 1
National Residential Sales (1991–2006)

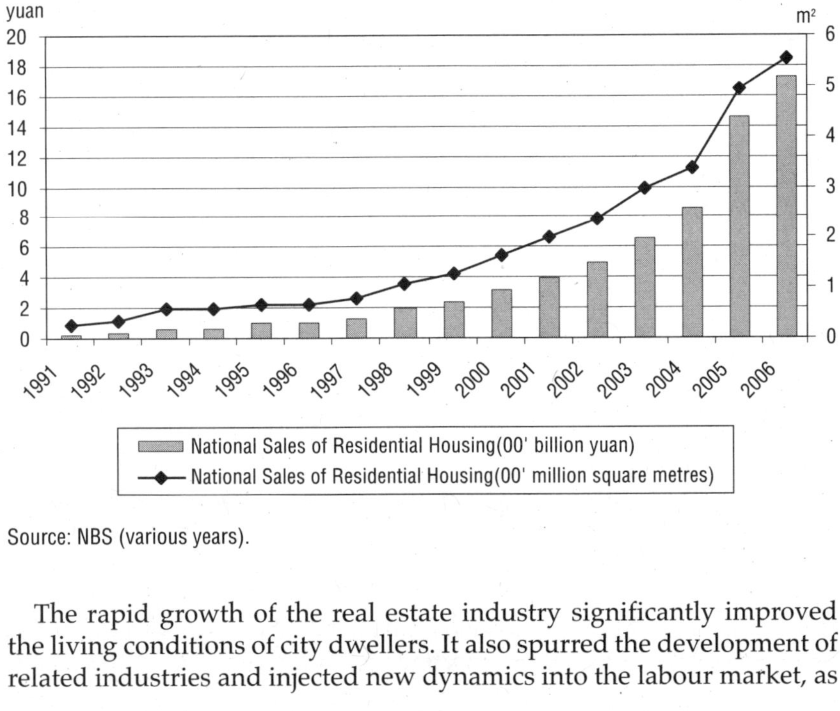

Source: NBS (various years).

The rapid growth of the real estate industry significantly improved the living conditions of city dwellers. It also spurred the development of related industries and injected new dynamics into the labour market, as shown in Figure 2. After the beginning of the housing reform, new construction of urban housing at the national level rose significantly. Average living space per person in urban areas rose from 10.02 square metres in 1985 to 17.78 square metres in 1997, with an annual average growth of 0.65 square metres per person over the 13 years. After 1998, the increase accelerated noticeably. Average living space increased by roughly one square metre every year—from 18.66 square metres per person in 1998 to 25 square metres in 2004.

FIGURE 2
New Urban Housing Construction at National Level and Average Living Space (1985–2005)

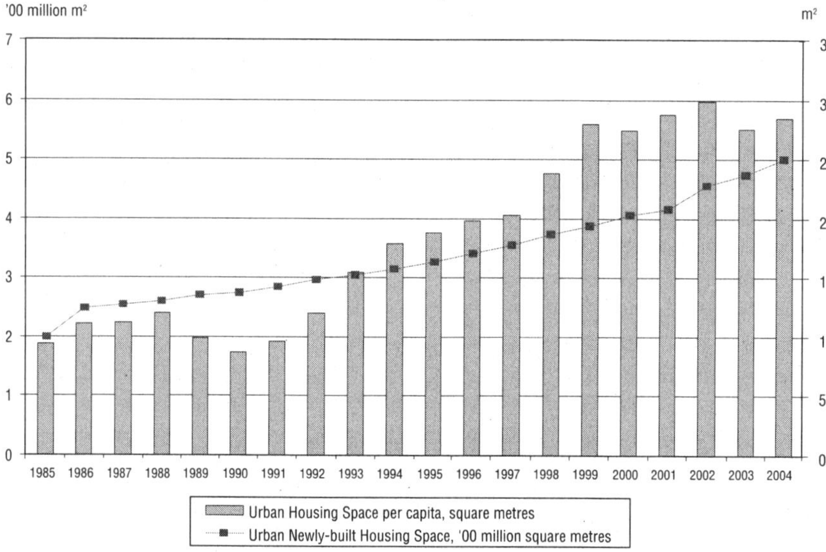

Source: NBS (various years).

In 2004, there were 0.84 independent housing units per family nationally. The total area of independent housing units reached 7.93 billion square metres, or 82.44 percent of all residential homes; by 1995, those figures had risen to 0.85 independent housing units per household, 8.68 billion square metres, and 80.64 percent, respectively (Ye 2005). Meanwhile, infrastructure for residential housing improved significantly. Tap water and gas were supplied to more and more homes each year. These improvements in urban living conditions were the direct result of housing reform and the development of the real estate industry.

As already mentioned, before the reform, the government was almost exclusively responsible for funding the construction and maintenance of urban housing (although businesses also had some responsibility). But this arrangement placed a heavy financial burden on the government.

The market-oriented reform not only relieved much of this burden but also created a major source of income for government finance, especially for regional governments.

The reform also encouraged the emergence of the housing finance sector, particularly due to the surge in the mortgage market. Since 1998, when the personal housing mortgage business became active across the country, the share of housing mortgage loans in personal consumer loans has varied from 75 to 97 percent, which is substantially high. As for the total amount, in 1996 when housing mortgages were still in the experimental stages, outstanding personal mortgage loans accounted for only 42.6 billion yuan. By the end of 2006, this figure had risen to 1,990 billion yuan, a 52-fold increase in just ten years. Personal mortgage loans now account for 8 percent of all loans and 16 percent of mid- and long-term loans.[2] Thus, the real estate industry has intensified the development of the financial market by developing a market for mortgage loans.

Termination of the welfare housing allocation system also gave city dwellers more freedom to choose where they wanted to live and work. Under the previous system, the dominant method (almost the only method) for a worker to obtain housing was through his or her employer, who took the employee's rank and years of work into consideration. If the employee later decided to quit that job, then he or she had to vacate the home. Urban dwellers were thus faced with enormous constraints when they chose or changed their employment. But market-oriented reform ended these constraints. People can now choose where they want to live, and the markets for new apartments and resale houses have increased steadily, along with the rental market. People can now accept employment in different locations and even different cities from where they currently live. Therefore, housing reform has enhanced the flexibility and efficiency of the labour market, facilitating the flow of professionals and workers. Moreover, the development of the rental housing market has enabled a huge pool of labour from rural areas to find a place to live in the cities, thereby providing urban areas with sufficient labour for developing industries.

Effects of Market-Oriented Housing Reform on Social Welfare

Market-oriented housing reforms have improved social welfare, but the effects have not been equal for all social groups. In general, the living conditions of most people have improved, but for some people, conditions deteriorated. An analysis of the effects of the housing reform on personal welfare provides unique criteria for evaluating the reform, while identifying measures for the goals of the government's housing policies.

Improved Living Conditions for Some People. Market-oriented reforms have improved the personal welfare of people with higher incomes. With the abolition of the former quota constraint under the planned allocation system, income has become the only constraint on housing consumption. Thus, more options are available for those with higher income; that is, they can afford larger or better houses and improve their living conditions.

Moreover, people (mainly employers) who owned or controlled a large number of homes under the old system also benefited from the market-oriented housing reform. They were able to acquire property rights to these homes at relatively low prices, then sell or rent them out at higher prices. In other words, the market-oriented reform monetized their right to own more homes and increase their wealth.

Furthermore, government officials in charge of supervising and approving land transfers have had more opportunities to find low-rent homes for themselves. Thanks to poor supervision, these officials benefited as well.

Deteriorating Living Conditions for Others. Without high income, people who had been allocated small homes under the previous system did not fare well in the housing reform process. The increase in housing prices did not bring much endowment income effect, but rather, significant inverse income effect. With the price of housing rising quickly, many people had few real opportunities to improve their housing situation. Even worse, some of them had to move into smaller homes.

Because of marketization, people who migrated to more developed regions also faced poor housing options. Those migrating from rural areas had to pay high city prices for housing without any initial endowment effect, since their rural homes were not tradable with urban residents. For those migrating from small cities, the rise in prices in high-employment areas has been more marked than in their home city; therefore, the endowment income effect from rising prices has not offset the price disadvantages they have faced. There has been only one possible exception: those migrating to a more developed region as a result of endogenous choice would experience an increase in personal income, which would allow them to acquire larger homes. However, the pressure created by rising housing prices in more developed regions has made this option impossible—and is summed up by the new Chinese expression "housing slave."

Table 1 shows the sharp difference in home rental conditions between local urban families and migrant families living in cities. Since migrant families do not have a local *hukou* (residency permit), regardless of whether they are from rural areas or other cities, they are not entitled to low-rent public housing. In addition, they are poorer than local people, which makes them spend a higher percentage of their income on housing for poor housing conditions (Sato 2006).

TABLE 1
Expenditure Structure of Migrant vs. Local Families who Rent Homes, Beijing, 1999

	Migrant Families	*Local Families*
Sample Size	**89**	**355**
Average family size	2.2 members	3.1 members
Average residential area	9.6 m^2	12.4 m^2
Sample Size	**82**	**355**
Annual rent	345 yuan/m^2	12 yuan/m^2
Proportion of income spent on housing	26%	7%
Proportion of income spent on rent	18%	2%
Average overall expenditure	16,804 yuan	23,826 yuan
Ratio of Residential Difficulty	28%	0%

Source: Sato (2006).

The Cost of Market-Oriented Housing Reform

The influence of market-oriented housing reform is not limited to the housing market itself. Costs also affect: (i) the widening income gap, (ii) intensification of residential segregation, and (iii) influence on the aggregation effect of urban area.

The Widening Income Gap. Many of the current problems in the housing market have not been caused by the market itself, nor can they be solved by the market. Increasing housing prices are in some respects the result of a widening income gap. For example, in Shanghai, from 1997 to 2005, middle- and low-income earners lost a great deal of their purchasing power, which left only the high-income earners able to afford bigger homes (Chen and Hao 2006). Thus, the housing market has accelerated the widening of the income gap and the polarization of society.

The housing reforms affected the income gap in China in two ways. First, housing allocation under the former planned system was generally guided by such factors as rights, social status, and personal experience. Inequality of housing was therefore an important source of social inequality under the planned system. For example, surveys of Chinese families in 1988 and 1995 showed that housing allowances were always a significant factor in the widening income gap (Khan et al. 1999). When implementing the reforms, the government simply accepted the status quo of housing resource allocation under the old system. Thus, in the early years of the reform, wealthy people could purchase publicly allocated homes at low prices, before they were put on the market. As housing prices soared, inequality in housing became based entirely on wealth. The controllers of housing rights under the planned economy did not lose those rights in the transition; instead, their rights were turned into monetary income. Since those rights tended to be concentrated in higher income groups, inequality of wealth allocation was inevitable.

Second, because it failed to consider the situation it was inheriting from the former planned housing system, the market-oriented reform allowed the rich to get richer, and the poor to get poorer (in relative terms). While most citizens facing high prices could not improve their living conditions, the wealthy were usually able to buy up many apartment blocks. When the housing prices increased, these owners profited, while the low-income people did not receive much benefit. A recent positive study by Meng (2007) has illustrated this point.

The housing financial market has further intensified this growing income gap. Generally speaking, banks assess the social status and payback ability of borrowers seeking personal housing mortgage. People with higher income have more access to financing and thus to improved housing. As real estate prices have risen, access to financing and financial leverage has allowed the wealthy to magnify their wealth.

Although nowadays rural lands are owned collectively and urban lands are government-owned, conflicts of interests can arise when rural people migrate to cities. The current system favours urban residents, and they benefit most from land revaluation. The enactment of the 2007 Property Law further—and intentionally—reinforced the inequality of property rights between urban and rural areas. Compared with homes in cities, homes in rural areas became less exchangeable. By law, rural land must be sold to others in the same area, which makes the endowment income effect from rises in housing prices less significant for rural people. Furthermore, since the government protects farmers' rights only to carry out agricultural production on their lands, farmers whose land is appropriated for urbanization are compensated only according to the lost agricultural production, rather than according to the market price for the land. Though those farmers effectively become registered urban residents, the benefits and guarantees they receive in cities are limited compared to the loss of their land and its related value increment, mainly because these farmers lack urban work experience. Thus, the market-oriented housing reform in towns and cities has increased wealth inequality between urban and rural areas.[3]

Intensified Residential Segregation. Under the former centralized system, workers' homes were clustered near their place of employment. Therefore, people of different income and social status were often neighbours, with high-level managers and common workers living in the same building or neighbourhood. The market reform in 1998 disrupted this integration. When people gained the right to choose where to live, residential segregation resulted. City dwellers became clustered according to income: higher-income people began to gather in communities with expensive housing, while lower-income people congregated wherever housing prices were low. As the housing reform inevitably and irreversibly dispersed the distribution of housing prices, residential segregation intensified, further accelerating the polarization of the society.

In other countries, governments have begun to tackle social problems related to this kind of residential segregation. It is generally accepted that residential segregation is a severe threat to social stability, because it results in reduced contact between different classes and groups, reduced social agglomeration, and hampered social cohesion. Consequently, the Netherlands is engaged in an experiment of proactively mixing neighbourhoods. Using financial and legal means, the Dutch policy encourages people of different income classes to live together. In contrast, China has not placed much emphasis on this issue, whether in housing or city planning.

Intensified Regional Disparities. From 1998 to 2005, housing prices in China's urban areas increased by 58 percent. However, research shows that in the developed coastal regions and cities, such as Shanghai and Beijing, the increase in housing prices is far above the national average. For example, housing prices in Shanghai increased by 120 percent during those seven years (Chen and Hao 2006). Certainly, differences in economic development between regions account for some of the price difference; but continuously rising prices have increased the local government revenues such that they have been ble to fund more infrastructure projects. Thus, infrastructure in large cities is much more concentrated than in rural area, or even in mid-sized and small cities. In this way, the housing market further magnifies regional disparity in development.

Insufficient Agglomeration in Urban Areas. Although there is a sharp difference between housing prices in large and small cities, lower-income residents in big cities are not motivated to move to smaller ones. Aside from cultural considerations and the cost of moving, endowment income from buying the homes they had been allocated under the old system at a low price allows these city dwellers to stay; or they can also choose to sell the house at a higher market price or just rent it out for a high rent. Because of their unwillingness to move to smaller cities, they bid up housing prices for migrants who are just arriving, which results in an overheated real estate market and extreme housing prices. For the simple reason that some local residents put up with exorbitant rents, big cities cannot attract sufficient labour for their developing industries; and in the process, they exert an aggregation effect. This also results in the relatively low diversity in the sizes of Chinese cities.[4]

Evaluation of the Housing Policy

Given the achievements and drawbacks of the market-oriented housing reform, the goal of new housing policy is clear: to help those who have been disadvantaged by this reform to improve their living conditions. However, there has not been consistency in the proposals and practices regarding what kind of measures to adopt. One generally accepted idea is that this goal could only fulfill a basic housing guarantee—that is, that all people should have a place to live, but that not all of them need to own their own home.

So far, polices involving both direct and indirect support have been proposed to target these goals.

Direct support systems include a system of subsidized rental apartments and public housing that has received much attention in China recently. Logically, improving the living conditions of low-income people by providing subsidized rental and public housing seems reasonable; however, it is hard to correctly identify who should receive these homes. This information asymmetry has turned the system of subsidized rental and public housing into new opportunities for rental income for people who have power and wealth.

China needs to learn lessons from the experience of other countries that have experimented with subsidized rental and public housing policies (Chen 2007a). This experience shows that such policies have two distinct drawbacks. First, public housing systems to some extent reduce market segregation and distort the signalling effect of the market price of housing, thereby limiting choices and causing dissatisfaction. Second, eligibility does not automatically stop for people whose incomes rise above the cut-off. Therefore, in China, this system would be extremely inflexible and would require a long time for adjustment. Moreover, large-scale programs of public housing would widen residential segregation and create urban slums. In contrast, a system of low-rent housing has fewer disadvantages, although it shares the problem of residential segregation.

Indirect support policies should include a housing allowance for low-income people, so that they could choose housing for themselves. Policies at a more macro-level should include tax deductions on home purchases, home financing, and housing price control. However, in practice, the housing tax policy does not provide any real relief to low-income people; instead, it favours people who resell their home five years or more after its purchase. That is to say, current tax deductions do not specifically favour those who have housing difficulties. As for the policies on home financing, neither public housing funds nor commercial housing loan policies help the poor, but instead help those who have higher incomes.

To be considered effective, controls on housing prices must make housing affordable to most people. These policies become most effective when they avoid direct intervention, such as those carried out in the 1990s, and rely on indirect measures, such as interest rate adjustments, housing loans, tax policies, and land provision policies. In addition, effective price control policy should focus on promoting reasonable housing prices. Thus, only if high housing prices appear to be caused by speculation would a price control policy be a reasonable response. Otherwise, such a policy would distort price signals and would become an unnecessary government intervention in the market.

Currently, several demand factors in addition to speculation are causing price increases in the market-oriented housing reform. There are at least three kinds of demand for home ownership in urban areas. First, there is demand from migrant workers. Migrant workers who come from rural areas without a city *hukou* (residence permit) require housing, as do college graduates and migrating elites, who tend to stay in cities. Second, local residents with rising incomes are looking for better housing, which drives prices up through demand. Third, the dismantling and reconstruction of old neighbourhoods leaves more people looking for homes. These three factors explain the surge in prices in big cities in China from the perspective of demand, regardless of speculation.

From a supply perspective, factors such as the rising quality of housing and the increasing costs resulting from land sales all cause price increases. In addition, a lack of investment opportunities for ordinary people means that many workers are investing in the housing market. Similarly, factors such as the expectation that RMB will appreciate has also attracted foreign investment in China's housing market. All these supply factors have resulted in excessively high housing prices.

Therefore, if regulators cannot control speculative behaviours induced by factors outside the housing market and instead rely solely on housing market policies to curb demand, they may end up hampering real domestic demand. Similarly, policies to control housing prices need to be implemented very carefully. If policies rely on administrative measures (such as price limits), they will probably contribute to corruption and flooding of the rental market; moreover, market signals will be distorted.

Future Direction and Approaches for Housing Policies

The analyses above describe appropriate directions and approaches for China's new housing policy. In short, in addition to retaining a market-oriented approach, the government should actively implement policies that would rein in speculation and support socio-economic groups experiencing housing difficulties.

The Need for Market Orientation

The achievements of the market-oriented housing reform in China have been significant. Although the reforms have created some housing difficulties, the market-oriented approach should not be reversed, nor should the government intensify administrative interference of the housing market. If housing prices are being driven by demand and supply, then direct interference will reduce its efficiency. If the government does have to interfere, its measures should be restricted to market-oriented ones, such as housing credits and tax policies that benefit people who purchase smaller or lower-priced homes. Such polices should also be consistent and reliable.

Stronger Rental Markets

Mature housing markets emphasize both rental and sales sectors. However, China's housing market focuses mainly on the sale of new houses; the rental market is not fully regulated and does not have an effective registration and supervision system. Moreover, because rental contracts are not stable or enforceable, both tenant and landlord legal rights are in doubt in rental situations. Under such circumstances, even if social, cultural, and psychological factors were not involved, people would still view renting as a second choice after home ownership.

China needs to focus on developing well-respected alternatives to purchased homes. In developed countries, many high-income people choose to rent their homes. To promote more flexibility and agility in the real estate market, the governments of many countries encourage the development of both private and nonprofit social rental sectors, both of which provide regulated, good-quality rental services to ensure long-term contracts with tenants. Currently, China still needs to develop a regulated rental market and to promote the institutionalization of rental procedures in order to maintain a healthy and sustainable real estate market. A developed rental market could also further encourage the efficient movement of labour. Moreover, by creating building information agencies, property administrative companies, and maintenance services, the real estate market can create new job opportunities and achieve a higher level of professionalization of the real estate industry. Currently, a significant bottleneck in the development of China's rental industry is the *hukou* system. People who rent homes can hold only a collective *hukou*; thus, they face problems when their children go to school, because they are out of their school area.If the *hukou* bottleneck problem is removed, then the rental market in China will develop more quickly.

Speculative Behaviours in the Housing Market

Eliminating speculative behaviours is very desirable in a housing market, but the government must use a market-oriented approach to do so. For example, a policy that prohibits approval of land for villa development is not reasonable. On the one hand, it limits reasonable supply and demand; and on the other, it feeds an expectation of rising prices for villas, which in turn induces more speculative behaviour. Instead, the current policy, which increases transaction costs for selling newly built homes, is obviously more effective, though it harms the liquidity of the property market. Moreover, some policies currently in place in Hong Kong should be applied elsewhere. For example, the government could use the strategic market release of stock of undeveloped publicly-held land to dampen speculation and price volatility.

Public Housing System

Public housing for socioeconomic groups with housing difficulties should be based on the principle that public housing would change the endowment of these people, rather than the market price of real estate. Public housing should also depend on market mechanisms, rather than on administrative forces. Reliance on market mechanisms would ensure the effectiveness of market price mechanism and reduce corrupt rental practices. These policies should be implemented as follows: (i) A fixed proportion of the profit from the sale of land should be mandated to subsidize lower-income people with housing difficulties. Meanwhile, current subsidized rental or public housing policies should be revised so that that people receive subsidies and purchase or rent housing at market prices, rather than being given housing directly. Newly constructed public housing should be available only for rent, not for sale; and purchased public housing should not be available for resale, only for repurchase by the government. Moreover, if owners want to lease out their public housing to others, they would only be allowed to lease it to people with lower income. (ii) The relevant parties should have to treat renters and buyers equally and without discrimination, regardless of *hukou* issues. (iii) Housing tax policy should be modified to emphasize taxes on housing purchase and possession, rather than on any housing transactions (such as rent payments). In addition, property tax should be levied to replace previous taxes to reign in housing vacancy and speculative investment purchases. Moreover, the sale of already-built houses should be promoted. In the end, people with housing difficulties would be able to improve their living conditions.

Conclusions

Every reform exists in a certain historical context, and the market-oriented housing reform in China is no different. History suggests that reform inevitably becomes biased in favour of the interests of people who were benefiting the most under the old system because the reformers have to comply enough with the existing power structure to win the approval of powerful people. Thus, in a market-oriented reform, power becomes monetized: in China's housing reform, this means that as housing price surged, those with the power to acquire more homes had the easiest path to new wealth.

Compliance with the existing power structure increases the possibility that reforms will achieve Pareto improvement. However, since those people who had power in the pre-reform period generally earn higher incomes in the post-reform period, reform ends up widening the income gap as power becomes redefined as money. This point cannot be more obvious than in China's housing reforms. Therefore, even though the reform seems like Pareto improvement in a static sense, in a more dynamic sense, the widening income gap is worsening the situation of lower-income people. Problems such as residential segregation and unbalanced regional development, both of which are increased by the income gap, will pose a big challenge to economic and social development in the future.

Housing policy in China is a result of the government's process of learning by doing. Recent policies to control housing prices are almost entirely ineffective. The Chinese government has begun to realize that to help low-income people, increasing public housing supply is more effective than artificially lowering prices. Clearly, increasing the supply of subsidized rental apartment or public housing without distorting the housing market price mechanisms should become the central task of the Chinese government. The government should rely on more NGOs and NPOs to implement these policies, rather than doing it alone. In addition, in the long run, the central government should equalize the supply of public service (such as high-quality hospitals, schools, etc.) among regions and provide more investment channels for domestic funds. It will thereby decrease housing demand caused by investment and speculation, especially in big cities that already have an adequate supply of public services.

Nevertheless, there are reasons to be optimistic. The government is turning its attention to the problem of compensating vulnerable and disadvantaged groups. However, the real problem lies in the risk that the government may abandon the market-oriented approach in order to accomplish this goal. For instance, new "price-limited housing" (housing with controlled sale prices) is being built to control housing prices. Given that the reform has already accepted the legitimacy of the pre-reform power structure, it is likely that polices such as "price-limited housing" could become the newest channels for people in power to further their own interests.

Notes

Comments from an anonymous reviewer are greatly appreciated.

1. Data source will be the same for the rest of this chapter, if not specified otherwise.
2. All data here about the housing mortgage here come from NBS (various years).
3. When farmers lost their lands in this way (i.e., because of urbanization), they did receive an urban *hukou* and became urban citizens. As a result, their relative poverty become part of the urban income inequality problem , rather than part of the urban–rural inequality problem.

4. If we consider the Gini coefficient of city size, China's value for 2000 is 0.43, much lower than that in other major countries, including Brazil (0.65), UK (0.60), Mexico (0.60), France (0.59), India (0.58), Germany (0.56) and USA (0.54) (Fujita et al. 2004).

References

Chen, B., G. Zhimin, and L. Kaihe. 2003. *Theory and Practices of Urban Housing Reform*. Shanghai: People's Publishing House.

Chen, J. 2007a. "Drawbacks of Economically Affordable Houses and Advantages of Housing Subsidy." *China Real Estate*, February 5.

——— 2007b. "Double Welfare Loss of Limited-Price Houses." *China Real Estate*, April 16.

Chen, J., and Q. Hao. 2006. "Shanghai Residential Property Market: 1993–2005." Paper from Chinese Economists Society.

Fujita, M., J.V. Henderson, Y. Kanemoto, and T. Mori. 2004. "Spatial Distribution of Economic Activities in Japan and China." Pp. 2911–77 in *Handbook of Urban and Regional Economics*, vol. 4, edited by V. Henderson and J.-F. Thisse. Amsterdam: North-Holland.

Hou, X., Y. Hong, and Z. Yaping. 1999. "For the Thousands of Houses: Major Breakthrough in China's Housing System." Guangxi Normal University Press.

Khan, A.R., K. Griffin, and C. Riskin. 1999. "Income Distribution in Urban China during the Period of Economic Reform and Globalization." *American Economic Review* 89(2):296-300.

Meng, X. 2007. "Wealth Accumulation and Distribution in Urban China." *Economic Development and Cultural Change* 55(4):761–791.

National Bureau of Statistics (NBS). 1996–2007. *China Statistical Yearbook*. Beijing: China Statistical Press.

Sato, H. 2006. "Housing Inequality and Housing Poverty in Urban China in the late 1990s." *China Economic Review* 17:37–50.

Wang, Y. 1991. "The Calculation of China's Housing Welfare and Its Implication." Gaige (Reform), No. 3:106–112.

Xie, Z. 1999. "Breakthrough: Major Actions in China's Housing Reform." Social Sciences Academic Press (China).

Ye, H. 2005. "Personal Housing Loan: Risk and Control." Pp. 89–98 in *Report on the Development of Real Estate Industry in China, No. 2*, edited by N. Fengshui. Beijing: Social Sciences Academic Press.

4

The Zhongyuan Economy and Returning Migrant Entrepreneurs

Naoki Murakami

Zhongyuan (or Henan province) is in the limelight after a long period in the country's shadows. The development of this area is expected to reduce China's regional income disparity. This chapter provides a brief overview of regional discrepancies, then discusses the role of returning migrant entrepreneurs in the development of rural Zhongyuan. Our analysis suggests that: (i) the promotion of out-migration to urban centres is not inconsistent with the promotion of return migration, (ii) human capital accumulated in urban areas allows returnees to succeed in their own businesses, but (iii) returnees tend to adopt capital-intensive technology, which is of less comparative advantage in a rural area.

Introduction

Zhongyuan, a region in the Central plains of China, is in the limelight after a long period in the country's shadows. The slogan "The rise of Zhongyuan" (*Zhongyuan Jueqi*) often appears in the Chinese mass media. Zhongyuan is the region lying in the middle reaches of the Yellow River; but in its narrow sense, and the sense in which it is used in this chapter, Zhongyuan is synonymous with the present-day Henan province (Hereafter we shall use "Zhongyuan" and "Henan" interchangeably). In short, Zhongyuan is the region where the Yellow River Civilization emerged 7,000 years ago. Furthermore, from the Spring and Autumn Period (770 BCE–476 BCE) to the age of the Song Dynasty (960 CE–1279 CE), this region was economically the most developed part of China and was perhaps one of the most prosperous areas in the world at that time (Wu 2006).

Why is Zhongyuan receiving public attention now? The main reason is that development of this area is expected to contribute to a reduction

Economic Transitions with Chinese Characteristics: Social Change During Thirty Years of Reform, eds. Arthur Sweetman and Jun Zhang. Montreal and Kingston: McGill-Queen's University Press, Queen's Policy Studies Series.

of China's regional income disparity. Since the inception of the reform and the introduction of the opening-up policy in 1978, Chinese economy as a whole has been experiencing remarkable economic development. At the same time, however, the economic disparity between the eastern coastal region and other regions, especially the Central region, has increased significantly. Reduction of this disparity is one of the most urgent problems China is currently facing. The development of Zhongyuan is regarded as key to developing the entire Central region and reducing the economic disparity. Chinese policy-makers believe that "the rise of Zhongyuan" will usher in the rise of the whole Central region.

Needless to say, various approaches or models have already been considered and implemented for the development of Zhongyuan, including the promotion of out-migration to urban areas (Key Research Institute of Humanities and Social Sciences of Universities and Research Center of Central China Economic Development, NanChang University 2007) and attracting factories in from more developed areas (Geng 2006; Liu and Wang 2006). This chapter takes an alternate approach—examining the role of returning migrant entrepreneurs in the industrialization of rural areas. It discusses the current situation in Henan and the potential for regional development through the entrepreneurial activities of returnees. To do this, it uses results from informal and formal surveys conducted in Henan province in 2007.

Although the amount of literature about out-migration and return migration in both internal (rural–urban) and international contexts is large, research focusing on the impact of migration on the area of its origin (in this case, rural areas in internal migration) is relatively new and scarce. Furthermore, almost all the research on the impact of migrant entrepreneurs is concerned with their investments in their native area (i.e., financial capital flow); studies focusing on human capital flow that returnees directly bring to their native areas are much fewer in number (Zhao 2002). As a result, this human capital flow from return migrant entrepreneurs needs to be examined.

The return migration phenomenon in China is gradually drawing attention from researchers. Recently, some academics have analyzed the role of return migrant entrepreneurs in the development of their native area (Murphy 2002; Lin 2002; Bai and Song 2002; Hu et al. 2006 etc.). Much of this literature, however, is based on sociology and population study, rather than economics, while other relevant papers are mostly policy oriented. However, Ma (2001, 2002) and Zhao (2002), among others, may be considered important exceptions, since their studies analyze the human capital flow by return migrant entrepreneurs in terms of economic models. The present study has been inspired by their work.

Some other research provides important data surrounding the economic issues of return migration. In particular, Hare (1999) should be mentioned as a relevant piece of literature analyzing return migration in Zhongyuan. This study used data obtained in the fall of 1995 on the sample of 309 households in Xiayi county of Henan province to investigate the determinants of individual return migration decision. Yet this study barely examines at all any economic impacts from this return migration. In addition, the report by the People's Government of Xinyang City and the Xinyang City Committee of the Chinese Communist Party (2005) is also valuable as a document concerning the return migrant entrepreneurship in Zhongyuan; but again, it does not contain a formal economic analysis.

This chapter aims to provide a foundational analysis of the role of return migrant entrepreneurs for the regional economic development of Zhongyuan from an economics perspective. Because the wave of enterprises established by returnees has been a relatively new occurrence, at least in Zhongyuan, it has not yet been possible to comprehensively assess their contribution to the Zhongyuan economy on the whole. Instead, by conducting informal and formal surveys in Zhongyuan, we examined the relationship between a return migrant's urban work experiences and the performance and characteristics of the enterprises he / she established upon return. Endowed with a large labour force, but poor in capital, rural areas have a comparative advantage to urban areas for labour-intensive industries (Otsuka et al. 1998). In other words, a labour-intensive technology is appropriate for and effective in a rural area. Hence, from the viewpoint of economics, it is important to examine whether return migrant entrepreneurs bring the adequate labour-intensive technology to their native area.

The organization of this chapter is as follows. The first section offers a brief overview of the regional discrepancies in China and then discusses regional development in Zhongyuan (Henan) and its contribution to the development of the Central region as a whole. The following section describes the phenomenon of return migrant entrepreneurs in Henan and describes the cases of two Henan cities, Xinyang and Zhoukou. It also conducts a simple regression analysis by using original data obtained in Zhoukou. The final section presents our conclusions.

Regional Development in Zhongyuan

Regional Differences in China

Table 1 details the current situation in the four large regions of China: Eastern, Central, Western, and Northeastern. Based on these indicators, we can briefly summarize the features of regional differences in China as follows:

i. Economic development in the Eastern region is by far the strongest among the four regions (see total GDP, per capita GDP, etc.), especially regarding economic relations with foreign countries (see the total value of imports and exports, as well as the total investment by foreign enterprises).

TABLE 1
Some Economic and Social Indicators by Regions (2006)[a]

	Units	Eastern Region	Central Region	Zhongyuan (Henan Province)	Western Region	Northeastern Region
Population at year end	10,000 persons	46,906.00	35,251.13	9,820.00	36,157.18	10,817.00
	as % of national total	36.32	27.30	7.60	28.00	8.38
Proportion of urban population	%	54.12	38.00	32.47	35.72	55.53
GDP	100 million yuan	128,593.05	43,217.98	12,495.97	39,527.14	19,715.17
	as % of national total	55.66	18.70	5.41	17.11	8.53
Share of primary industry	%	7.27	15.30	16.40	16.18	12.11
Share of secondary industry	%	51.95	48.50	53.81	45.23	50.77
Share of tertiary industry	%	40.79	36.20	29.78	38.58	37.12
Per capita GDP	yuan	27,567.27	12,268.58	13,313.00	10,959.49	18,276.79
Per capita area of cultivated land	mu/person	1.27	1.63	1.59	2.98	7.94
Total investment in fixed sssets	100 million yuan	54,637.11	20,896.58	5,904.70	21,996.94	10,519.98
	as % of national total	50.57	19.34	5.46	20.36	9.74
Local government revenue	100 million yuan	10,844.39	2,950.10	679.17	3,059.36	1,449.72
	as % of national total	59.25	16.12	3.71	16.71	7.92
Local government expenditure	100 million yuan	13,591.01	6,103.85	1,440.09	7,626.84	3,109.63
	as % of national total	44.66	20.06	4.73	25.06	10.22
Total value of imports and exports	100 million US$	15,795.92	539.76	97.95	576.67	691.61
	as % of national total	89.73	3.07	0.56	3.28	3.93
Total investment by foreign funded enterprises	100 million US$	13,409.00	1,252.00	233.00	1,024.00	1,390.00
	as % of national total	78.53	7.33	1.36	6.00	8.14
Average annual wage (manufacturing)	yuan	19,310.61	15,094.20	14,982.00	16,808.41	17,105.05
Per capita disposable income of urban households	yuan	14,967.38	9,902.28	9,810.26	9,728.45	9,830.07
Per capita net income of rural households	yuan	5,188.23	3,283.16	3,261.03	2,588.37	3,744.88

Notes: [a]As the sum of some indicators by region is different from the national total, while calculating the percentage of Eastern, Central, Western and Northeastern regions to all country, the denominator is the sum of 31 provinces, autonomous regions and municipalities.

Eastern region: Beijing, Tianjin, Hebei, Shanghai, Jiangsu, Zhejiang, Fujian, Shandong, Guangdong and Hainan.
Central region: Shanxi, Anhui, Jiangxi, Henan, Hubei and Hunan.
Western region: Inner Mongolia, Guangxi, Chongqing, Sichuan, Guizhou, Yunnan, Tibet, Shaanxi, Gansu, Qinghai, Ningxia and Xinjiang.
Northeastern region: Liaoning, Jilin and Heilongjiang.

Source: National Bureau of Statistics of China (2007); Henan Statistics Bureau et al. (2007).

ii. Though the population is almost the same, the Central region lags behind the Western region in some economic aspects (see the total investment in fixed assets, local government revenue and expenditure, the average annual wage, etc.).
iii. The importance of agriculture and rural areas in the Central region is relatively high compared to the other three regions (see the proportion of urban population and the share of primary industry).
iv. The agricultural economy in the Central region is not necessarily at an advantage compared with other regions (see the per capita area of cultivated land and net income of rural households).

Economic Growth in Zhongyuan

Henan province belongs to the Central region, and the largest part of the province is located south of the Yellow River. Though the area of Henan makes up only 1.7 percent of the country's geography, its population is 98.2 million, which accounts for 7.6 percent of the China's total population (see Table 1). This population size is the largest among the 31 provinces in China (excluding Hong Kong, Macao, and Taiwan). The total GDP of the province ranks fifth in the country, but, owing to its large population, its per capita GDP ranks 16th.

Despite stagnation at the end of the 1980s, both Henan's total and per capita GDP keep growing by double digits. Especially remarkable is the recent real growth rate of 14.4 percent in 2006 (Henan Statistics Bureau et al. 2007). Dominated by industry, the growth rate of its secondary industry sector is prominent, whereas the growth of its primary industry sector is relatively sluggish, and its tertiary industry sector continues with stable growth. Because of different growth pattern by industries, the composition of the total GDP from industries has changed significantly. The share of primary industry, which used to account for 41.7 percent of the total in 1978–1984, recently fell to only 16.4 percent in 2006. The proportion of secondary industry, however, increased from 38.8 percent to 53.8 percent during the same period, with the share of the tertiary industry declining slightly.

Zhongyuan is currently in China's media spotlight because this area is expected to contribute to the development of the Central region as a whole. The GDP share of Henan in the six provinces of the Central region (Shanxi, Anhui, Jiangxi, Hubei, Hunan, and Henan), rose from 25.3 percent in 1996 to 28.9 percent in 2006. The contribution rate of Henan to the nominal GDP growth in the Central region also increased—from 21.5 percent in 1997 to 31.9 percent in 2006. Both figures from 2006 were the highest among the Central region's six provinces (Murakami 2008).

Development of Zhongyuan and the Industrialization of Rural Areas

The agricultural sector still occupies an important position in the Zhongyuan economy. Table 1 indicates that Henan's share of primary industry is 16.4 percent, much higher than the average for the Central region as a whole. Also, the 2006 structure of employment by primary, secondary, and tertiary industries (not covered in Table 1) is 53.3 percent, 23.6 percent, and 23.0 percent respectively (Henan Statistics Bureau et al. 2007). The corresponding figures for the whole country are 42.6 percent, 25.2 percent and 32.2 percent (National Bureau of Statistics of China 2007). Thus Henan's dependence on agriculture is so significant that industrialization of its rural area as well as the modernization of agriculture hold the key to the development of the province.

Agriculture is the first sector that has achieved success as a result of economic reforms. A major reform was the establishment of individual household farming systems. Prices of agricultural products were also raised, which must have stimulated production and, coupled with the productivity gain, resulted in higher incomes for farmers. At the same time, enhanced work incentives reduced working time on farms. Thus, savings were accumulated, and the labour supply for non-agricultural purposes increased, which stimulated the development of rural enterprises known as township-village enterprises (TVEs).

TVEs are essentially profit-seeking businesses. They achieve a higher productive and allocative efficiency than other types of enterprises in China, especially the traditional state-owned enterprises (Murakami et al. 1994).[1] The expansion of the TVE sector boosted industrialization in rural areas. As a result, non-agricultural employment in rural areas rapidly increased on the national level. In 1978, almost all residents in rural areas engaged in agricultural activities. But as the TVE sector developed, the proportion of non-agricultural employment rapidly increased, exceeding 40 percent in 2005 (see Figure 1). Although Henan is behind the national rates, the basic trend of increased non-agricultural employment is similar to the national trend. With the total number of employees in rural areas increasing steadily concurrently with national levels increasing, it is not possible to explain the increase in the proportion of non-agricultural employees solely with the outflow of rural agricultural employees to urban areas.

The term TVE is often used to refer to any enterprise in a rural area. Until the beginning of 1990s, most TVEs were collective rural enterprises or township and village-run enterprises. In contrast, private enterprises in the rural areas were engaged mostly in small-scale industrial activities and services. This situation has changed greatly since then. In the middle of the 1990s, the Chinese government began working on ownership reform.[2] The 1999 revision of the constitution

FIGURE 1
Proportion of Persons Employed in Non-agricultural Sector in Rural Area

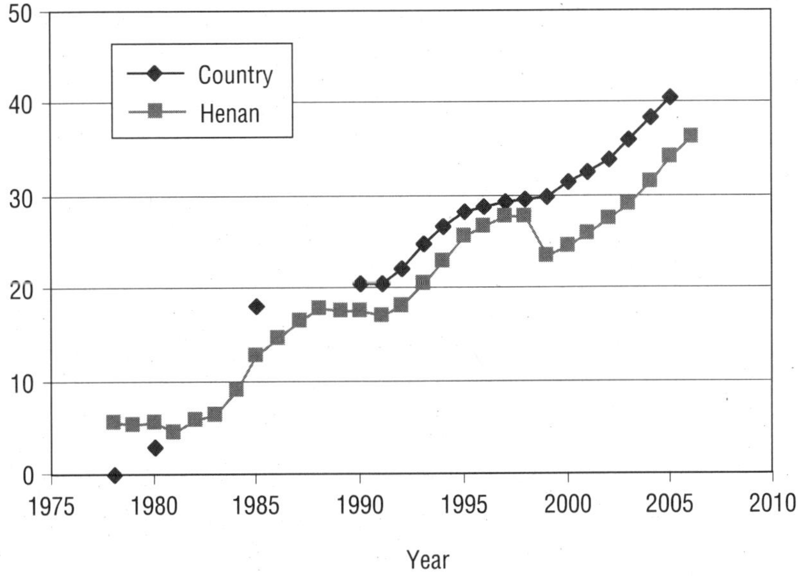

Source: National Bureau of Statistics China (2007); Henan Statistics Bureau et al. (2007).

officially recognized private enterprise. As a result, the private sector, including the individually owned industry (*geti hu*), has expanded rapidly. Table 2 indicates that the recent growth of the private sector (in both rural and urban areas) is prominent in Henan, too. Value added by private sector increased nearly nine times between 2000 and 2006. As a result, Henan's proportion to total also went up from only 9.2 percent to 27.6 percent. On the other hand, although the value added of individually owned industry doubled during the same period, the proportion to total declined from 27.2 percent to 19.0 percent (see last line of Table 2).[3]

In recent Chinese official statistics, all industrial private enterprises are classified into two categories: "enterprise above designated size" and "enterprise below designated size" (the designated size being defined as a 5 million yuan annual revenue from the principal business). Table 2 shows that the growth of the former is more rapid than that of the latter. This finding suggests that while the recent growth of private enterprises is remarkable, the same cannot be fully said about successful establishments of new companies. The problem is, who establishes new enterprises? To put the question differently, who contributes to the rural industrialization? This chapter assesses the real and potential role of return migrant entrepreneurs.[4]

TABLE 2
Value Added of Industrial Enterprises in Henan

	Units	2000	2001	2002	2003	2004	2005	2006
Total	billion yuan	204.51	225.12	250.87	300.91	383.72	489.60	603.12
Private	billion yuan	18.81	22.98	35.01	47.78	80.63	124.12	166.20
	as % of total	9.2	10.20	14.00	15.90	21.00	25.40	27.60
Private	billion yuan	5.95	7.83	11.32	20.66	42.02	73.91	110.01
(above designated size)[a]	as % of total	2.90	3.50	4.50	6.90	10.90	15.10	18.20
Private	billion yuan	12.86	15.14	23.69	27.12	38.61	50.21	56.20
(below designated size)	as % of total	6.30	6.70	9.40	9.00	10.10	10.30	9.30
Indivitually owned industry	billion yuan	55.56	61.09	67.16	81.43	96.08	104.11	114.86
	as % of total	27.2	27.10	26.80	27.10	25.00	21.30	19.00

Note: [a]Designated size implies 5 million yuan annual revenue from principal business.
Source: Henan Statistics Bureau et al. (2007).

Regional Development and the Returning Migrant Entrepreneurs

The Model of Returning Migrant Entrepreneurs

Before the 1978 reforms and opening-up, migration from rural to urban areas was severely restricted in China under the stringent household registration (*hukou*) system. Because of the lack of food and housing in urban areas, rural-to-urban migration was practically impossible. Today, despite the fact that inter-regional migration is still subject to regulation, Chinese economic and political reforms have gradually reduced barriers to migration. As a result, a large portion of the population has moved from rural to urban areas. In general, this migration eases the problem of surplus labour in rural areas. In addition, migrants increase the revenue of their household and native village as a whole by sending back part of their earnings, which means that they contribute to the reduction of the economic disparity between rural and urban areas.

While migrant workers are increasing in numbers in cities, the phenomenon of return migration has started attracting attention. Some workers who have acquired skills and knowledge through labour in the cities are now returning to their rural areas of their origin. More importantly, some have acquired the skill of entrepreneurship à la Schumpeter (Schumpeter 1934; Hébert and Link 2006) during the migration and have established their own enterprises after their return. Thus, return migrant entrepreneurs take home human capital as well as financial capital and contribute their knowledge and expertise to the development of their native rural areas.

Because this wave of new enterprises by returnees is relatively new, at least in Zhongyuan, it is not yet possible to comprehensively assess their contribution to the Zhongyuan economy on the whole. Therefore, the next section will assess the current situation in two different areas in Henan province: the prefecture-level city regions of Xinyang and Zhoukou. Xinyang, in particular, is a more advanced area in terms of the contribution of return migrant entrepreneurs to the local economy. In contrast, in Zhoukou, the wave of returnees has only just started, if it can be said that there is any at all.

Returning Migrant Entrepreneurs in Xinyang

In 2006, the population of Xinyang was 7.9 million. Per capita GDP was 7,444 yuan, third from the bottom among 18 city regions in Henan. The value added share of primary industry in GDP total was 27.9 percent, much higher than the average for Henan. Since the early 1980s, the local government has worked actively on a policy of encouraging surplus workers (mainly in the agricultural sector) to migrate away from Xinyang city. As a result, two million people have out-migrated to urban area in other cities in Henan province and other provinces. These figures are estimated to account for 83 percent of surplus labour in Xinyang's rural areas (The Investigation Group of the Province and Xinyang Social Sciences Association 2006a, 193). The majority of migrants in Xinyang (and Henan as a whole) are temporal or seasonal migrant workers who are not willing to transfer their household registration from the rural to the urban area, since that would mean relinquishing the right to own land. Recently, the local government recognized the beneficial effects of return migration to the economic development and urbanization in the local rural area, and has been working on the policy for promoting return migration. Gushi county is especially well known in this respect.

For example, Gushi, a county within the Xinyang city region, is the most populous county in Henan. The per capita GDP of this county is only 6,141 yuan. Yet Gushi has been designated as one of the "National Major Counties of Assisting the Poor and Development."[5] Although Gushi may still be somewhat lagging behind other counties economically, at present it continues to develop remarkably well. A large portion of the development has occurred thanks to returning migrant entrepreneurs. The estimated number of return migrant entrepreneurs in Gushi reached 49,000 by the end of 2006. This figure corresponds to about 10 percent of the total number of migrants from this county (People's Government of Gushi County 2007).

Indeed, Gushi businesses involved in willow knitting (Liubian Gongyi) and semi-finished medical needles are growing rapidly. Although the willow knitting (Liubian Gongyi) industry was launched in 1960s in Gushi, the founder of the first private enterprise in this industry (in 1988) and the trade association of this industry was a return migrant entrepreneur. Currently the number of enterprises in this industry is as high as 61, the number of employees is close to 40,000, and the annual sales volume is over 300 million yuan (People's Government of Gushi County 2008). Similarly, the scale of the industry that produces semi-finished medical needles in Gushi is also large. In 1996, a return migrant established the first enterprise. Since then, the industry has developed well, with the number of enterprises today exceeding 200, and the annual sales reaching 800 million units, a figure that accounts for 80 percent of the national total for this industry (Li and Zhang 2007). Thanks to the return migrant entrepreneurs' work, both industries have managed to form clusters of national importance in Gushi.

The local government also actively promotes entrepreneurial activities by returnees. For example, the government sends New Year's cards to migrant entrepreneurs living throughout the country, with the aim of reminding them of the benefits of life in their native villages and towns. Furthermore, the local government celebrates the contribution made by return migrant entrepreneurs on various occasions.

Finally, the following two points about Gushi are worth mentioning. First, return migrant entrepreneurs of Gushi invest into infrastructure, such as roads, schools, sanitary facilities, etc.. well as their own business. They invest in these public facilities because Gushi is their birthplace; and more importantly, they invest so that when they return to live in Gushi they can also enjoy (external) benefits from such public goods[6]. Second, policy-makers in Xinyang and Gushi realize that the promotion of out-migration and improvement of migrants' livelihood in the destination city may lead to their return migration in the future. For example, local governments support or directly run the vocational training for potential out- migrants.

Returning Migrant Entrepreneurs in Zhoukou

In 2006, the population of Zhoukou was 10.7 million. The per capita GDP city was 6,313 yuan, the lowest among the 18 cities of Henan. The share of primary industry in GDP total is 33.2 percent, a figure that shows that Zhoukou is an area which substantially depends on the agricultural sector. Even though Zhoukou's economic environment is similar to that of Xinyang, out-migration from Zhoukou has not been as extensive.

Zhoukou Survey

In September 2007, we conducted a sample survey of return migrant entrepreneurs in four counties within the Zhoukou city region: Dancheng, Luyi, Shenqiu, and Xiangcheng. Of these, Shenqiu is designated as one of the "National Major Counties of Assisting the Poor and Development," while Dancheng is one of the "Provincial Major Counties of Assisting the Poor and Development." This survey collected data on personal characteristics of returning migrant entrepreneurs, their migration experience, and the financial performance of the enterprises they set up. The samples are limited to the manufacturing industry, with a maximum number of samples of 69.[7]

Table 3 lists some results of this survey. It shows the distribution of the education level of the returning migrant entrepreneurs. The proportion who have attained high school or above is about 78 percent. According to The Henan Statistical Yearbook for 2007, the corresponding figure for all rural households in Henan is 14.5 percent (2006) and 20.1 percent for

TABLE 3
Sample Results from Zhoukou Survey, 2006

a. Number of Entrepreneurs by Level of Education

Middle School	*High School*	*Junior College*	*College or Above*	*Total Sample Size*
15	32	17	5	69

b. Years in Urban Areas by Profession

	All Professions	*General Worker*	*Engineer*	*Manager*
Average	9.1	2.8	3.7	2.5
Sample Size	64	63	63	64

c. Number of Entrepreneurs with Experience Establishing Own Business

Yes	*No*	*n.a.*	*Total*
14	52	3	69

d. Rated Importance of *Guanxi*

Very Important	*Important*	*Neutral*	*Less important*	*Unimportant*	*n.a.*	*Total*
12	35	16	4	0	2	69

e. Rated Usefulness of *Guanxi*

	For Financing	*For Market Information*	*For Technology*	*For Acquiring Land*	*n.a.*	*Total*
Most useful	25	26	12	6	0	69
Second most useful	19	18	23	9	0	69
Third most useful	17	13	18	17	4	69

Source: Author's survey.

out-migrants from Henan (2006). Thus, the educational level of returning migrant entrepreneurs (in our sample) seems to be relatively high.

The model of returning migrant entrepreneurship emphasizes the importance of human capital, which is accumulated through work experience in the city. As shown in Table 3b, the average length of migration in our survey was 9.1 years. We could say that this figure represents the "quantity" of human capital the migrants accumulate. Then we considered the "quality" of that human capital. To do this, we needed first to consider the length of migration by profession. Table 3b indicates that the average period of migration was 2.8 years for general workers, 3.7 years for engineers, and 2.5 years for managers. Furthermore, the number of return migrant entrepreneurs who experienced working at the managerial level during migration was 51 persons out of the sample of 69. Secondly, we considered whether the returning migrant entrepreneur had already had the experience of establishing his/her own business at the migration destination. Table 3c shows that 14 out of 69 persons had such direct entrepreneurial experience.

Since Ma (2001, 2002) emphasizes the importance of the local social network (*guanxi*) for entrepreneurial activities in rural areas, our survey included questions about *guanxi*. Table 3d shows that 47 persons (68 percent of the total) recognized *guanxi* as very important or important for their establishing their own business. Next we asked these persons in what way they utilized *guanxi*. As listed in Table 3e, *guanxi* have been important for acquiring market information and financing, but of relatively little importance for acquiring technology and land. We also asked respondents what aspect of the local government's policy was most useful for them in the process of establishing a business. The majority of answers related to obtaining land. In general, financial and land markets in rural areas are underdeveloped, such that many businesses need government assistance in procuring what they need to function. The above results suggest that return entrepreneurs in our survey tended to depend on the *guanxi* for overcoming financial constraints while relying on the local government's policy for solving the problem of the site for their firm.

Simple Regression Analysis of the Survey Results

Our survey covered only returning migrant entrepreneurs. Therefore, we could not compare, for example, the personal features of returning migrant entrepreneurs with those of migrants who remain in the destination city, and/or those of non-migrants. Instead, we collected financial data on the enterprises set up by returning migrant entrepreneurs. Using these data, we conducted simple regression analysis, examining the relationship between the features of return entrepreneurs and the characteristics of the enterprises they established.

Firstly, we conducted an estimation based on an equation in which the fixed capital in the establishment period is a dependent variable. There are four independent variables: (i) the formal education level of the return migrant entrepreneur who established the enterprise, measured with a dummy variable that equals 1 if high school or above, and to zero if otherwise; (ii) the "quantity" of human capital that the returnees accumulated during migration, measured by years of migration; (iii) the "quality" of human capital accumulated during migration, measured by the proportion of years of work as an engineer or manager to the total number of years of migration (percent); and (iv) the importance of the local social network (*guanxi*), measured with a dummy variable that equals to 1 if the answer is "very important" or "important," and to zero if otherwise.

One of the purposes of estimating this first model is as follows. So far, we have considered two variables: the years of migration, and the proportion of working years as engineer and/or manager as the index or proxies of the human capital accumulation during migration. Needless to say, however, the earnings and savings of migrants also increase as the migration period lengthens and/or as they rise up the professional ranks. Therefore, these variables may also reflect the amount of financial capital they accumulated during migration. In the case of financial capital, however, these variables must be positively related to the capital scale of the enterprises migrants established after return. To put it another way, if the estimated coefficients of these variables are not significant in our first model, then we can at least say that it is difficult to consider them as the index of financial capital accumulation.

Model (I) of Table 4 presents the estimation result by the ordinary least square (OLS) estimation. The estimated coefficient of the education level (high school or above) is significant (5 percent level), but the estimated coefficients of other three independent variables—especially years of migration and the proportion of working years as engineer and/or manager—are not significant. This estimation result seems to support the idea that we should not consider these variables as the index of financial capital accumulated during migration.

Next, we estimated a model in which the per capita fixed capital is the dependent variable. The higher per capita fixed capital implies that the technology adopted is relatively more capital-intensive (less labour-intensive). The independent variables are the same as in model (I). The estimation result of Table 4 model (II) is somewhat interesting. The estimated coefficients of both the years of migration and the proportion of working years as engineer and/or manager are significant (5 percent level). This implies that more experienced returnees tend to opt for more capital-intensive technology. Since capital-intensive technology generally does not have comparative advantages in rural areas, it seems that their choice is not appropriate. As the technology adopted in a city is likely to be more capital-intensive, the return migrants who get accustomed to such technologies may tend to choose them for their business.

TABLE 4
Estimation Results by OLS[a]

Dependent Variables	*(I)[b] Capital[e]*	*(II)[b] Per Capita Capital[e]*	*(III) Growth of Capital*	*(IV)[c] Growth of Capital*	*(V)[d] Growth of Capital*
Intercept	3.63***	-0.39	29.77*	-11.13	48.98*
	(3.46)	(0.56)	(1.72)	(0.81)	(1.90)
High school or above	0.93**	0.26	1.88	-7.13	15.04*
	(2.31)	(0.99)	(0.30)	(1.38)	(1.72)
Years of migration[e]	0.24	0.43**	-2.37	1.03	-2.63
	(0.78)	(2.15)	(0.49)	(0.31)	(0.33)
Proportion of years as engineer or manager	0.006	0.02**	0.12	0.38***	0.05
	(0.55)	(2.46)	(0.70)	(2.89)	(0.21)
Guanxi	0.27	0.04	-7.02	5.99*	-17.67*
	(0.78)	(0.19)	(1.27)	(1.72)	(1.97)
Per capita capital[e]	-	-	-7.59***	-0.51	-14.09***
			(2.68)	(0.22)	(3.35)
R-squared	0.434	0.466	0.148	0.350	0.440
Number of observations	61	61	60	29	31

Notes: [a]Numbers in parentheses are t-statistics. *Significant at 10%; **significant at 5%; ***significant at 1%.
[b]Three county dummies for Dancheng, Luyi and Shenqiu are included as independent variables.
[c]Samples which have operated for five years or more since the establishment.
[d]Samples which have operated for less than five years since the establishment.
[e]Natural logarithms are taken for the original numbers.
Source: Author's compilation.

In our third model, the dependent variable is the annual growth rate of fixed capital from the time of the enterprise establishment to the present (2006). Here we interpreted this dependent variable as the indicator of the performance of the enterprise established by the returnee. The independent variables are the same as in models (I) and (II), plus per capita fixed capital. Table 4 model (III) indicates the estimation result. As expected, the estimated coefficient of per capita fixed capital is highly significant with the negative sign (1 percent level). Enterprises using more capital-intensive technology seem to show relatively poor performance.

The estimated coefficients of all the other independent variables are not significant. Has human capital no effect on the performance of the enterprise the returnee established? We estimated that the difference in the years of operation clouds the results, so we divided the whole sample into two subsamples: enterprises which have operated for five years or more since the establishment, and those that have operated for less than five years. The two estimation results are contrasted. Table 4 model (IV) presents the result reached using limited samples of five or more years of operation. Here the estimated coefficient of the proportion of working years as engineer and/or manager is highly significant with the positive sign (1 percent level). In the long run, enterprises established by the returnees with a higher "quality" human capital show better performance. The estimated coefficient of the *guanxi* dummy is also significant (10 percent level). This result weakly suggests that the local social network (*guanxi*) is important for long-term success. The estimation coefficient of the per capita fixed capital has lost significance. In the enterprises that survive for a long time, the choice of technology at the time of establishment is not related with later performance.

Finally, we confirmed this estimation result by using the samples with five or less years of operation in Table 4 model (V). In this result, the estimated coefficients of both years of migration and the proportion of working years as engineer and/or manager are not significant. In the short term, migration experience does not have substantial effects on the enterprises' performance. On the other hand, the estimated coefficient of the education level is significant (10 percent level). The estimation coefficient of the *guanxi* dummy is significant with the negative sign. It is not easy to interpret the latter result in a consistent manner. Enterprises that depend excessively on the local social network may have some short-term problems in operation. The estimated coefficient of the per capita fixed capital is highly significant with the negative sign. In the short run, inappropriate technology choice has a negative influence on the performance, and an enterprise with negative performance is likely to go under sooner or later.

Conclusion

Since 2000, to reduce regional economic inequity between the Eastern region and other three large regions, the Chinese government has launched several large-scale regional development projects, such as the "West Development" and "Northeast Promotion." As a result, the development of the Western region and the Northeastern region has received priority, and the Central region seems to have been left out. In recent years, however, the government has become increasingly aware of this situation and has begun to pay attention to the Central region. Zhongyuan, as the core of the Central region, is expected to contribute to the development of the whole Central region. Because rural areas occupy a large portion in Zhongyuan, industrializing these areas is crucial for the development of Zhongyuan.

This chapter discussed the role of returning migrant entrepreneurs in the regional development of Zhongyuan, with a particular focus on its rural part. Although our analysis is simple and preliminary, it suggests some preliminary conclusions. First, the cases of Xinyang and Gushi indicate that the promotion of out-migration to urban areas is not inconsistent with the promotion of returning migration. Second, in the long run, as expected, human capital accumulated during migration to urban areas allows returning migrant entrepreneurs to succeed in their own business. Third, although the problem lessens with time, returnees tend to adopt more capital-intensive technology, which is of less comparative advantage in a rural area. In other words, in order to be successful, returning entrepreneurs must choose technology appropriate for a rural area.

The Chinese government often mentions Chinese tradition and history to strengthen the centripetal force binding the Chinese at home and abroad. As mentioned in opening of this chapter, Zhongyuan, which is the birthplace of the Chinese civilization, has been the driving force behind Chinese culture, science, art, and thought over a long time. As China develops further, the economic and political importance of Zhongyuan is likely to increase.

Notes

I would like to acknowledge support and encouragement I received from Geng Mingzhai, Zhang Junfeng and Zhao Lei (Henan University). This work was financially supported by a grant obtained by the Nihon University Population Research Institute from the "Academic Frontier" Project for Private Universities: matching fund subsidy from MEXT (Ministry of Education, Culture, Sports, Science and Technology), 2006–2010.

1. In machine tool industries, the productive advantage of TVEs can be attributed to the difference in dependence on the purchase of parts (Murakami et al. 1996).
2. See Murakami and Qi (2006) on the situation in Kaifeng, Henan.
3. In China, private enterprises are more efficient than enterprises of other ownership types, such as state-owned and collective-owned enterprises (Murakami and Shen 2006, and cited literatures in it; Murakami 2006).
4. See also Geng (2006).
5. We conducted interviews with government officials and return migrant entrepreneurs in Gushi in May 2007.
6. Our interviews in Xinyang and People's Government of Xinyang City and the Xinyang City Committee of the Chinese Communist Party (2005) etc. revealed many cases in which return migrant entrepreneurs contributed to the construction of the region's infrastructure. Some entrepreneurs invested directly in this activities as a part of their own business. Others made large donations for the same purpose. We think this practice is interesting enough that it merits further investigation.
7. Before conducting this sample survey, we conducted interviews with government officials and returning migrant entrepreneurs.

References

Bai, N., H. Song, et al. 2002. *Huixiang, haishi Jincheng?Zhongguo Nongcun Waichu Laodong Li Huiliu Yanjiu*. Beijing: Zhongguo Caizheng Jingji Chuban She (in Chinese).

Geng, M. 2006. *Qian Fada Pinyuan Nongqu Jingji Fazhan yu Zhidu Zhuanxing: Zhengti Kaocha yu Gean Fenxi*. Henan: Henan Renmin Chuban She (in Chinese).

Hare, D. 1999. "'Push' versus 'Pull' Factors in Migration Outflows and Returns: Determinants of Migration Status and Spell Duration among China's Rural Population." *Journal of Development Studies* 35(3):45–72.

Hébert, R.F., and A.N. Link. 2006. "Historical Perspectives on the Entrepreneur." *Foundations and Trends in Entrepreneurship* 2(4):260–408.

Henan Statistics Bureau and Survey Office of the National Bureau of Statistics in Henan. Various years. *Henan Statistical Yearbook*. Beijing: China Statistics Press.

Hu, M., F. Huang, and W. Xie. 2006. "Waichu Nongmingong Huixiang Chuangye Xianzhuang Fenxi: Yi Jiangxi Sheng Wannian Xian wei Li." *Journal of Jiangxi Agricultural University* 5(1), March:56–59 (in Chinese).

(The) Investigation Group of the Province and Xinyang Social Sciences Association. 2006a,b. "On the Labor Economic Brand in Xinyang and its Improvement." *Henan Social Sciences* 14(5), September:193–196; and (6), November:87–90 (in Chinese).

Key Research Institute of Humanities and Social Sciences of Universities and Research Center of Central China Economic Development, NanChang University. 2007. *Research on Central China Rural Labor Transferring*, Beijing: Economic Science Press (in Chinese).

Li, D., and X. Zhang. 2007. "Zoujin 'Zhongguo Liubian zhi Xiang' Ganshou Shili Gushi," *Sichuan Xinwen Wang* (August 8):1–6 (in Chinese).

Lin, F. 2002. "Dui Anhui Sheng Bai Ming 'Dagong' Nongmin Huixiang Chuangban Qiye de Wenjuan Diaocha ji Fenxi." *Zhongguo Nongcun Jingji* 3:72–76 (in Chinese).

Liu, Y., and Y. Wang. 2006. *Analysis and Forecast on Henan's Economy 2007*. Beijing: Zhongguo Gongshang Chuban She. (in Chinese)

Ma, Z. 2001. "Urban Labour-Force Experience as a Determinant of Rural Occupation Change: Evidence from Recent Urban-Rural Return Migration in China." *Environment and Planning A* 33:237–255.

——— 2002. "Social-Capital Mobilization and Income Returns to Entrepreneurship: The Case of Return Migration in Rural China." *Environment and Planning A* 34:1763–1784.

Murakami, N. 2006. "Ownership and Managerial Targets of Chinese Enterprises." *Journal of Chinese Economic Studies* 3(1) March:1–17 (in Japanese).

——— 2008. "Current State of Zhongyuan Economy: The Performance in 2007 and the Target in 2008." *Chugoku Sangyo Doko Kiho* (April):1–3 (in Japanese).

Murakami, N., D. Liu, and K. Otsuka. 1994. "Technical and Allocative Efficiency among Socialist Enterprises: The Case of the Garment Industry in China." *Journal of Comparative Economics* 19:410–433.

——— 1996. "Market Reform, Division of Labor, and Increasing Advantage of Small-Scale Enterprises: The Case of the Machine Tool Industry in China." *Journal of Comparative Economics* 23:256–277.

Murakami, N., and L. Qi. 2006."Ownership Structural Reform and Its Effect in Collectives Enterprises: A Case of Henan Kaifeng." mimeo, (June):1–21 (in Japanese).

Murakami, N., and Y. Shen (I. Shin). 2006."Efficiency, Productivity of Chinese Firms and its Determinants: A Discussion Based on DEA." *World Economic Papers* 5 (October):1–20 (in Chinese).

Murphy, R. 2002. *How Migrant Labor is Changing Rural China*. Cambridge: Cambridge University Press.

National Bureau of Statistics of China. Various years. *China Statistical Yearbook*. Beijing: China Statistics Press.

Otsuka, K., D. Liu, and N. Murakami. 1998. *Industrial Reform in China: Past Performance and Future Prospects*. Oxford: Clarendon Press Oxford. (Chinese version 2000, Shanghai: *Shanghai Renmin Chuban She*)

People's Government of Gushi County. 2007. *Gushi Xian Laowu Jingji yu "Huigui Gongcheng" Diaoyan Baogao*. (in Chinese).

——— 2008. *Official Homepage*, (May 15th) (in Chinese).

People's Government of Xinyang City and the Xinyang City Committee of the Chinese Communist Party. 2005. *Chuang Shichang de Xinyang Ren*. (in Chinese)

Schumpeter, J.A. 1934. *The Theory of Economic Development: An Inquiry into Profits, Capital, Credit, Interest, and the Business Cycle*. New York: Department of Economics, Harvard University.

Wu, J. 2006. "The Development and Influence of Zhongyuan Exported Economy in Modern Times." *Zhongguo Lishi Dili Luncong*, January:1–12 (in Chinese).

Zhao, Y. 2002. "Causes and Consequences of Return Migration: Recent Evidence from China." *Journal of Comparative Economics* 30(2), June:376–394.

Part II

Social Issues

5

The Transition from a Managed Employment System Toward a Modern Labour Market

GORDON BETCHERMAN, ANA REVENGA, AND
MINNA HAHN TONG[1]

Over the past three decades, China's economic reform has shifted from a "managed employment system" toward a modern labour market. This transformation has occurred through a series of modest steps that, when taken together, have added up to a fundamental transformation in how human resources are allocated, workers protected, and wages determined. The labour market is significantly more efficient now, with positive impacts on productivity and wages. However, these gains have been achieved at the price of increased vulnerability and inequality. Further reforms are needed to strengthen worker rights, facilitate mobility, and improve the skills of the labour force.

Introduction

Over the past three decades, the dramatic transformation of China's labour market has played an integral role in the country's broader economic reform. Various labour market reforms have enabled China to mobilize its massive labour supply effectively, giving it an advantage in low-cost labour which has underpinned its export competitiveness and contributed to double-digit Gross Domestic Product (GDP) growth rates. Meanwhile, large-scale restructuring of the state-owned enterprise (SOE) sector and the movement toward a true labour "market" have changed where and under what conditions workers are employed, with implications for the welfare of individual households as well as the broader economy.

This labour market transformation has been driven by three inter-connected processes: rapid industrialization, the transition from a planned economy to an open market system, and China's integration into the

Economic Transitions with Chinese Characteristics: Social Change During Thirty Years of Reform, eds. Arthur Sweetman and Jun Zhang. Montreal and Kingston: McGill-Queen's University Press, Queen's Policy Studies Series.

global economy.[2] Under central planning, an institutional divide was created between rural and urban areas. Industrialization and economic reforms, combined with a gradual relaxation of restrictions on labour mobility, have weakened this divide considerably and shifted resources out of agriculture and rural areas and into industry and services and urban areas. The shift from a centrally planned economy, under which the government engaged in direct allocation of labour, to an open market system has also been profound, fostering rapid private sector growth. At the same time, China's integration in the global economy has boosted the development of its export sectors and coastal cities.

These three overlapping processes have fundamentally changed China's labour market. The rapidly expanding urban economy has emerged as the main driver of job creation, with migrant labour now accounting for about one-third of total urban employment. The restructuring of the SOE sector, which ended the guarantee of secure, lifetime employment for tens of millions of urban workers, has given rise to the new phenomenon of unemployment. This shedding of labour in the state sector has been accompanied by job creation in the private sector, much of it as informal employment. A side effect of these structural transformations has been a marked increase in income and wage inequality, compared to the situation under central planning when inequalities were systematically compressed.

Although it is remarkable that these transformations have taken place within the space of three decades, it should be recognized that the reforms have been introduced gradually, with synchronization between job destruction and job creation, thanks in large part to the flourishing of the private sector. This experience differs markedly from that of Central and Eastern Europe in the late 1980s and early 1990s, where a "shock therapy" approach was adopted, with painful years of transition including slumps in production, rising prices, and skyrocketing unemployment. In contrast, the hardships associated with transition have been less dramatic in China, where the approach to economic and labour market reforms has been more measured.

Despite these achievements, it should be noted that China's labour market transformation has not been homogenous and remains incomplete along some dimensions. Labour market conditions vary widely across regions and municipalities, with provincial open unemployment rates ranging from below 2 percent to 20 percent. Millions of rural labourers are underemployed or employed in low-productivity activities, while some of China's fastest-growing export industries complain of shortages of both skilled and unskilled labour. At the same time, wage differentials are large and cannot be attributed solely to differences in observable variables. Segmentation persists between rural and urban workers, between the formal and informal sectors, and between the fast-growing coastal regions and the lagging central and western regions. Occupational safety and health, worker voice, and the promotion of labour standards are major concerns. China's ability to address all of these issues will have direct implications for its future economic growth and competitiveness, poverty reduction efforts, and social stability.

This chapter reviews China's labour market transformation over the past three decades, describing the major changes that have taken place in the shift from a managed employment system toward a true labour "market." It traces the reforms along three dimensions: the allocation of human resources, social protection of workers, and wage determination. The chapter then points to the future challenges China faces in carrying out its labour market reforms and further developing its labour market.

The Managed Employment System of the Planned Economy

In order to appreciate the evolution of China's labour market policy over the past 30 years, it is important to characterize the situation as it existed prior to the onset of liberalization. In fact, China did not have a "labour market" *per se* in the period of the planned economy. Labour supply, labour demand, and the matching of the two were not determined in any way by the pricing mechanism that drives markets. Rather, as we will briefly describe in this section, employment was managed through a bureaucratic system, with the allocation of labour and compensation determined administratively.

This review of the transition from the managed employment system toward a labour market considers three interdependent dimensions: how human resources are allocated, how wages are set, and how social protection and related benefits are provided for workers. Table 1 provides a stylized summary of the key features along each of these dimensions, contrasting a managed employment system with a labour market.

China's Employment System Prior to Liberalization

In 1949, the Communists inherited a labour market that has been characterized as "feudal" in the countryside and "colonial" in the urban areas (Knight and Song 2007).[3] In fact, it was not until the mid to late 1950s that the main elements of the managed employment system were in place. In the ensuing two decades, that system, based on administrative allocation and the primacy of the work unit, largely remained intact. The details of the managed employment system had some uniquely Chinese characteristics, but the system was heavily influenced by the model existing in the Soviet Union and much of Central and Eastern Europe over the same period.[4]

While reference can be made to China's "employment system" during the planned economy era, it should be noted that there was some heterogeneity, most notably between the countryside and the cities. The core principles did not differ, especially in terms of labour allocation and

TABLE 1
Stylized Characterization of a Managed Employment System and the Labour Market

	Managed Employment System	*Labour Market*
Allocation of human resources	• Employment needs set by plan • Administrative allocation of workers • Little intra-firm or external mobility • No layoffs (overstaffing) • Very limited flexible employment • Virtually no geographic mobility	• Supply and demand determined by prices • Layoffs possible • Flexible contracting • Mobility in firms, between firms, and geographically
Wage determination	• Administratively determined • Seniority-based • Narrow wage differentials • Limited use of bonuses, other incentives	• Primarily market-determined • Wide differentials heavily reflecting productivity • Performance incentives • Voluntary collective bargaining
Social protection and benefits	• Lifetime employment • Protection tied to work unit • Social insurance and social services (including housing) provided by work unit	• Limited job security • State social insurance plans and programs • Very limited provision of social services by employer

Source: Authors.

compensation, but the bureaucratic divide between rural and urban systems existed in the employment area, as it did in all realms of economic management. There were also some differences depending on the type of enterprise. Lifelong employment and comprehensive social benefits were strongest in the SOEs and large collectively-owned enterprises (COEs). In smaller COEs, there was more temporary employment and less extensive benefits. There were also some shifts, albeit modest, over time. These shifts tended to reflect adjustments in the tensions between solidarity, the need for incentives, and political rewards. For example, Shirk (1981) describes how political factors came into play in the assignment and compensation of workers during the Cultural Revolution.

Allocation of Labour. By the late 1950s, the allocation of labour was fully in the hands of the state. Employment requirements were determined according to the plan, with some overstaffing built in to prevent unemployment. New workers were assigned to enterprises by the local labour bureaus. For the most part, there was little room for choice, either on the part of the employer or the worker. The standard employment form was a full-time position, although a very limited amount of temporary work did exist (Zhu 1995).

Labour economists typically assess labour markets in terms of where they fit on a continuum anchored by flexibility at one end and security at the other. The Chinese situation prior to reform was at the extreme security point of this continuum. As was generally the case in all planned economies, job security was central. Indeed, the connection between the work unit and the worker was stronger in China than in other socialist societies. Expectations were that, once assigned, workers would remain with the work unit throughout their working lives.[5] There was essentially no mobility in the system. Turnover was virtually unknown with a complete job guarantee and benefits that were not portable. Moreover, mobility was uncommon even inside the enterprise, with occupational changes occurring very rarely. As Knight and Song (2007) put it, "the first job was often the last" (18).

The other important feature defining the allocation of labour was the *hukou*, or residency permit. Registration became compulsory in 1958 and, from that time on, access to housing, services, and benefits was essentially limited to the place of residence. This effectively precluded geographic mobility throughout the remainder of the planned economy era and even well into the period of economic liberalization. The *hukou* also reinforced the separation between rural and urban realms, constraining the migration flows that one would expect as the economy developed.

Wage Determination. Wages were set administratively, as well. The compensation system introduced in the first years after 1949 established separate wage scales for administrative, technical, and unskilled workers. While each scale had many grades, the structure was very compressed, with wages differing only very slightly grade to grade. By the mid-1950s, the highest wages within enterprises were only 3–4 times higher than the lowest wages, compared to 40–50 times prior to 1949 (Howe 1973, cited in Knight and Song 2007). Wage levels were overwhelmingly determined by seniority and not by skill or productivity level. Any (modest) occupational premiums that did exist were generally for dangerous work or work under hardship conditions and more often went to unskilled rather than skilled labour.

Through the three decades of the planned economy, wage policy increasingly struggled with the challenge of balancing solidarity with performance incentives. The basics of the system were clearly oriented heavily to the former: seniority is about the most "socially cohesive" determinant of wages there is. However, the need for incentives to encourage effort and productivity was obvious. To this end, the state created various forms of additional compensation, such as bonuses and subsidies, which were meant to be dependent on individual or collective performance. However, these funds were relatively ineffective, in part because the amounts were small. Moreover, the internal dynamics of the enterprises tended to lead to an egalitarian rather than performance-based distribution of these extra funds (Shirk 1981).

Social Protection and Benefits. The relationship between the work unit and the worker went well beyond lifetime employment. Urban enterprises generally provided housing as well as the social protections and benefits that are typically associated with the welfare state, such as health services, pension benefits, various cash benefits, child care and basic education, and recreation. In rural areas, work units offered fewer services and benefits but still provided basic health care and elementary education, along with job security. Although the enterprise provided what became known as the "iron rice bowl" (these benefits and services, coupled with job security), financing was actually through the state, which received all revenues from the enterprises. Since the central government allocated and was responsible for all expenditures, even if they exceeded revenues for a work unit, social risk was, in effect, pooled at the national level (Cai 2003). As noted above, the benefits and services provided by the work unit were not portable, which essentially ruled out changing enterprises as an option for workers.

Incompatibility with Economic Liberalization

The managed employment system, as described here, was in place when the process of market liberalization was initiated by Deng Xiaoping in 1978. As Lindbeck (2006) has written: "It is easy to understand why the economic reforms rendered these social arrangements dysfunctional" (36). Efficiency was the major problem initially. Cai (2003) has pointed out that the employment system created two different types of inefficiencies: the lack of incentives and supervision within the workplace (technical inefficiency) and the misallocation of resources (allocative inefficiency). The former was created by the iron rice bowl and wage compression that, together, offered neither rewards for performance nor penalties for nonperformance. The administrative determination of employment and hiring, wage practices, and the iron rice bowl all contributed to a situation in which labour was not allocated to its most productive uses.

As the economic reforms proceeded after 1978, additional incompatibilities of the managed employment system became apparent. The system could not accommodate the emergence of a private sector which brought new risks and the unwillingness on the part of enterprises to take on traditional work-unit social responsibilities. Moreover, the productivity-enhancing reforms, first in agriculture and then in the state sector, created vast pools of surplus labour, the emergence of unemployment, and mounting social protection demands that became unaffordable under the traditional system. Such developments sparked the changes over the past three decades that have transformed the employment system.

Tracing Labour Market Changes over the Past Three Decades

This section summarizes developments in the three interrelated aspects of the reform of the labour market introduced in the previous section:

the allocation of human resources, determination of wages and working conditions, and social protection of workers.

Allocation of Human Resources

As briefly discussed in the previous section, prior to liberalization, labour was allocated by the state, with workers assigned to jobs as determined by the central plan. Geographic mobility, and even mobility between enterprises, was rare. Over the past 30 years, this centrally managed system has gradually evolved toward a situation where the allocation of labour is based more and more on market-based principles governing supply and demand. Indeed, increased turnover, the convergence of labour productivity across regions, large internal migration flows, and increasing returns to education are all evidence of this evolution. However, substantial labour hoarding in the state sector, very long average job tenures, and significant wage differentials across groups attest to the fact that the transformation from a managed employment system to a labour market remains a work in progress.

There are many aspects to the story of how the matching of workers and jobs has changed over the past three decades. Here, we touch upon three: the end of government assignment of workers, the replacement of lifetime jobs with contract employment, and the geographical mobility of workers.

This transformation in how labour is allocated has not only contributed to fundamental changes in the structure and operation of the labour market but, not surprisingly, has also directly affected labour market outcomes. Unemployment has risen after being virtually unknown in the pre-transition period, while labour force participation has fallen, in part due to limited employment opportunities for less skilled workers (see Table 2). A large informal sector has emerged and has been growing rapidly. At the same time, labour productivity and wages have been rising, as returns to skills have increased. These changes have combined to increase inequality, a trend that we will consider later in this chapter.

TABLE 2
Basic Labour Market Indicators

	2000	*2001*	*2002*	*2003*	*2004*	*2005*	*2006*
Urban employment (millions)	231.5	239.4	247.8	256.4	264.8	273.3	283.1
Labour force participation rate (%)	75.8	74.6	74.0	71.0	71.6	71.0	n.a.
Unemployment rate (official estimates, %)	3.1	3.6	4.0	4.3	4.2	4.2	4.1
Real wage growth (%)	n.a.	n.a.	15.5	12.0	10.5	12.8	12.7

Source: World Bank (2008a).

The End of Government Allocation of Labour. State determination of employment requirements and assignment of labour grew increasingly incompatible with the broader economic reforms that began in 1978. In 1980, allocation became decentralized for much of the collective sector, and labour exchanges were established for the registration of vacancies and many job placements. Momentum continued toward the decentralization of labour allocation through the 1980s: as greater autonomy was given to state and collectively owned enterprises, and as performance-related incentives began to be offered, managers wanted greater authority in many areas, including hiring and firing. Moreover, in the 1990s, when labour surpluses developed in urban areas after SOE restructuring had gained momentum, laid-off workers and the emerging flows of rural migrants became "job seekers" in the sense that this term is commonly used in market economies. These developments added momentum to an opening up of job vacancies and selection according to standard labour market principles in the SOE/COE sector.

Obviously, the growth of the private sector—encompassing both formal and informal enterprises—was also important in determining the end of the allocation of labour by the state. Not only was state control of labour allocation clearly inappropriate, but also the competition from the private sector was a catalyst for further reforms in the state sector. During the ten-year period beginning in 1995, urban employment in the state sector was reduced almost by half, while it grew almost five-fold and four-fold in the formal and informal private sectors, respectively (see Figure 1). This reversal in the state-private mix reflects real job losses in the state sector, new job creation in the private sector, and changes in the ownership of SOEs and COEs. As a result, the labour market over the past 10 to 15 years has changed dramatically from a very stable and low-turnover labour market to one characterized by a lot of churning and job

FIGURE 1
Urban Employment Trends (in millions) by Sector, 1995 and 2004

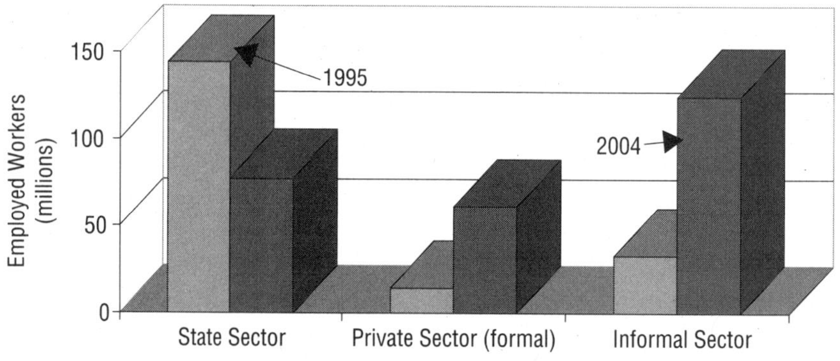

Source: National Bureau of Statistics of China (2005).

creation and destruction rates that are higher than those found in other transition economies (Dong and Xu 2006).

Replacement of Lifetime Jobs with Contract Employment. The lifetime employment relationship, characteristic of the pre-liberalization era, began its transformation in the 1980s with the emergence of the contract system. In 1983, contracts were introduced on an experimental basis, and in 1986, regulations were formally established for the "contract system." All SOEs were required to recruit new workers on a contract basis, and incumbent workers were to be re-selected and contracted on the basis of their performance (Cai 2003). Between 1985 and 1992 alone, the number of contract workers in SOEs increased from 330,000 to over 20 million (Zhu 1995). By 1995, 93 percent of SOE employees were under contract (Meng 2000). The 1994 Labour Code provided a legal framework for fixed- and flexible-time contracts, and various articles stipulated the rules for their legal termination. In 2007, a new Labour Contract Law was passed which is intended to strengthen the legal framework and bring contract law more in line with international practices.

Geographical Mobility. The large-scale movement of workers from the countryside to the cities has been among the most dramatic aspects of China's labour market transformation, given the rigid separation that existed between the two realms. The rural-urban barrier began to erode in the late 1980s and early 1990s, as labour surpluses accumulated in agriculture because of productivity gains and as the township and village enterprises began to exhaust their capacity to absorb these workers. At the same time, reforms spurred economic growth and rising labour demand in the cities, creating the conditions for attracting rural workers. The lure of the cities is demonstrated by the urban-rural income differential, which doubled over the past 25 years (see Figure 2).

FIGURE 2
Urban–Rural Per Capita Income Ratio, 1980–2004

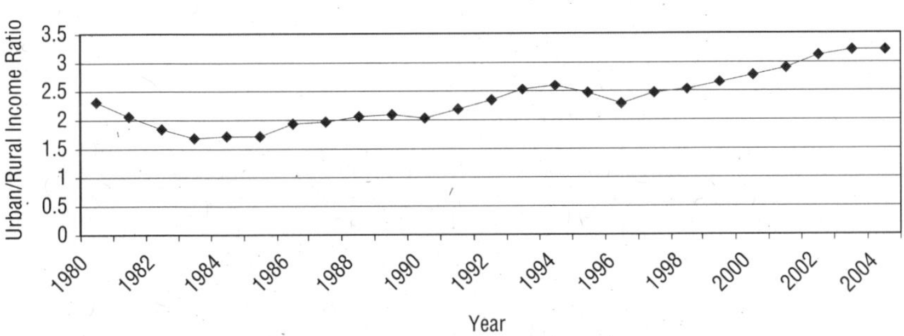

Source: Calculations based on National Bureau of Statistics of China (2005).

The government has also fostered migration by reducing restrictions on labour mobility. Although the *hukou* system has been preserved, its impact has been reduced through a series of reforms that started in the late 1980s when, for the first time, farmers were allowed to work in the city as long as they could secure their own food. Since then, governments at all levels have progressively relaxed the major constraints related to the residency requirements. Now some cities and towns have eliminated the distinction between urban and rural *hukou* and allow migrants to obtain *hukou* and / or access urban services, provided that they have stable incomes and legal housing.

According to the Rural Household Survey of the National Bureau of Statistics, the total number of migrants in 2006 was over 130 million. However, a web of legal obstacles associated with residency rights still needs to be overcome for these migrants to take full advantage of the economic opportunities in the cities. In the largest urban centres that are the major magnets for migrants, residency rules are evolving more slowly, with *hukou* and access to urban services and insurance programs generally granted only to those with high levels of professional and / or economic status.

The benefits of migration have been clear, reducing poverty in rural areas and enabling the dynamic urban centres to meet their rapidly expanding labour demand. At the same time, migration has created a number of social and economic problems. Due to relatively poor education compared to urban residents and discrimination, migrant workers typically fill the lowest-wage and most menial and dangerous jobs in urban labour markets. Unpaid wages and violations of basic employment rights have been chronic issues. Furthermore, migrant workers have typically been excluded from the urban social insurance system; have often faced high local government fees for schooling, health care, and other services; and have faced serious problems finding suitable and affordable housing. In recent years, various guidelines, policies, and programs have been implemented by governments at all levels to facilitate migration and to ease the transition of rural workers to urban centres.[6]

Social Protection of Workers

The shift away from a managed employment system has fundamentally changed the social protection of China's workers. As it aggressively implemented the SOE restructuring program from 1997 onward, the government effectively dismantled the "iron rice bowl" that had provided employees with lifetime job security and social entitlements. Tens of millions of workers were laid off, with most suddenly facing uncertain employment prospects for the first time. Many left the workforce altogether, with the decline in economic activity being particularly severe among older and low-skilled workers who were unable to find new jobs (Giles, Park, and Cai 2006; Betcherman and Blunch 2006). For those who remained in the labour force, most ended up in self-employment or in small businesses in the informal sector, with virtually no job security or benefits.

With responsibility for worker welfare no longer resting with work units, coupled with the new vulnerability of unemployment, China faced the challenge of re-building a social protection system for workers. Previously, social insurance and social assistance programs that provided outside work units had been weak or virtually nonexistent. The government has gradually replaced the old enterprise-based system with a state-administered social protection system that includes pensions, unemployment insurance, and other employment-related social insurance, as well as strengthened worker rights and the development of a dispute resolution system. The evolution of these programs and policies is described briefly below.

Pensions. Over the past two decades, China has experimented continuously with social security reforms in both urban and rural areas. In urban areas, the government has explored different ways of transferring responsibility for pensions from enterprises to municipalities. A new policy framework introduced in 1997 changed the traditional pay-as-you-go defined benefit scheme into a pension system with three pillars: a basic defined benefit plan financed by enterprise contributions, a mandatory defined contribution plan using individual accounts, and a voluntary supplementary pension plan managed by individual employers or private insurance companies. The system applies to enterprises and their employees as well as the self-employed. Contributors are primarily from SOEs, although in many municipalities and provinces, coverage has been extended to workers in private firms, foreign enterprises, personal businesses, and casual workers employed by urban enterprises (World Bank 2005b).

Following the introduction of this new system, the government recognized the persistence of some problems that had plagued the previous pension scheme and undertook a series of initiatives to experiment further with its policies. It launched pilot programs in Liaoning, Heilongjiang, and Jilin provinces which introduced a number of improvements to the pension system. The government then adopted some features of these pilots as national pension policies at the end of 2005, which is expected to improve the financial outlook of the system.

In contrast to urban areas, rural China has had a relatively weak formal social security system. Although a voluntary pension insurance scheme was established in 1992 as the main pension program for rural workers, participation has been very limited. Participation peaked at around 75 million contributors, or 16 percent of the rural population in 1997, then declined to around 54 million participants, or 11 percent of the rural labour force in 2005 (World Bank 2008b). Factors that have created disincentives to participate include high administrative costs, weak financial management, and a continuous fall in interest rates on accumulated pension funds (Lin 2004). In more developed areas, the elderly poor may benefit from commercial pension insurance and rural village collective funds. In addition, a small percentage of township and village enterprises provide pensions for their workers. Overall, however, the social security system in rural areas remains quite weak, heightening the vulnerability of the rural elderly and contributing to segmentation between urban and rural areas.

Unemployment Insurance. China's approach to providing support to unemployed workers has evolved considerably since the introduction of the unemployment insurance (UI) system in 1986. In the initial phase, the system differed considerably from those found in most other countries. It covered only the SOE sector and provided income and other support to redundant workers through their former employers. The second phase of UI program development, which started in 1993, expanded coverage to more categories of SOE workers. However, the role of the UI system remained limited during this period due to the slow pace of SOE reform and low levels of unemployment.

The acceleration of economic reforms in the late 1990s brought renewed attention to the UI program. To handle the large number of laid-off workers, the government required that all SOEs establish Re-employment Service Centres (RSCs) to provide a transition for workers to move into other employment or the UI program. These *xiagang* workers were eligible to receive living support and reemployment assistance from their enterprises for up to three years. As subsequent economic reforms ended the requirement that SOEs take care of their former workers, the UI system was modified accordingly. The introduction of the Regulations on Unemployment Insurance in 1999 marked the beginning of the third and current phase of the UI program, under which the features of China's UI system have become more similar to those found in other countries.

Another important development related to UI was the adoption of the *binggui* policy in 2000. This policy shifted the burden of supporting retrenched workers away from SOEs by merging the RSCs with the UI program. Laid-off workers would no longer maintain a relationship with their former employers through the Centres but would instead be covered directly by the UI program. With these changes, China's UI program has evolved from being a transition measure for mass layoffs to becoming a regular UI program.

The current UI system aims to provide a basic level of income protection to the unemployed as well as help them gain new employment. Coverage has been extended to all enterprises and institutions in urban areas and to rural contract workers employed by urban enterprises. Responsibility for UI contributions is shared between employers and employees. Unlike most other transition and OECD countries, China uses flat benefit levels determined by local authorities rather than earnings-related benefits. Additional benefits include medical subsidies for those receiving UI cash allowances, minor benefits for survivors in the event of a beneficiary's death, and subsidies for vocational training and job matching services.

Other Employment-Related Social Insurance. China has developed a number of other employment-related social insurance programs in recent years. For example, in 1998, the government promoted national reform of the basic medical insurance (BMI) system. This program covers all employers and employees in urban areas and is financed by employer and employee contributions which go into individual accounts and a social pool account. Medical expenses are shared by the individual and the BMI, with outpatient expenses usually being paid from individual accounts, while inpatient expenses are paid mainly from the social pool account. In July 2007, the government announced plans to establish a new urban resident health insurance program to complement the BMI. The new scheme will aim to cover all urban residents not belonging to the BMI, including the children and unemployed. This program will start on a pilot basis and is expected to be rolled out to cities nationwide by 2010.

China has also introduced a work injury insurance system to protect employees against the risks of work-related injuries or occupational disease. The current system, established in 2004, is intended to cover all employees of enterprises and individual businesses. The scheme is funded entirely from employer contributions of about 1 percent of the payroll, although the rates vary by, and within, sectors. Benefits include medical expenses for work-related injuries, injury and disability subsidy allowances, and nursing fees according to the degree of loss of ability to work. If an employee dies due to a work-related accident, the scheme provides a funeral subsidy, lump-sum death allowance, and pension for family members.[7] In recent years, the government's main target group for expanding work injury insurance has been migrant workers, as migrants are concentrated in occupations that expose them to greater risk of work-related injury and illness and account for the vast majority of work-related deaths and occupational diseases.

China also introduced reforms to its maternity insurance system in 1988. The current program is intended to cover urban enterprises and their employees and, in some places, female employees of government agencies, public institutions, and mass organizations. The program provides a "childbirth allowance" for 90 days, and employees can get reimbursements for medical expenses incurred during pregnancy. The program is funded entirely by employer contributions, which should not exceed 1 percent of the total wage bill.

Worker Rights. Under the managed employment system, the interests of the state, employer, and worker were assumed to be aligned. As employment has shifted from the state sector to the private sector, establishing and protecting worker rights has become a major challenge. China has put in place numerous laws and regulations to help clarify the rights and obligations of employees and employers. However, the content of the legislation and its implementation remain concerns. China has ratified only four of the eight fundamental labour conventions adopted by the International Labour Organization (ILO).[8] The conventions that have not been ratified cover freedom of association and collective bargaining and the elimination of forced and compulsory labour.

The adoption of the Labour Law in 1994 provides the overall regulatory framework for the labour market. The law includes fundamental protections such as the right to be employed on a non-discriminatory basis, to take leave and holidays, and to obtain protection for occupational safety and health. The Labour Law also includes the requirement of a labour contract to establish a labour relationship, the introduction of guaranteed minimum wages, arrangements for dispute settlement, and requirements for labour supervision and inspection by the state. The Trade Union Law (last amended in 2001) provides workers with the right to participate in and organize trade unions, but only under the umbrella of the All-China Federation of Trade Unions (ACFTU). Chinese labour legislation does not include the right to strike.[9]

China has recently introduced new legislation that could potentially alter the situation regarding worker rights and the employer-employee relationship. Most significant is the passage of the Labour Contract Law, which became effective at the beginning of 2008. The Labour Contract Law is intended to address some of the gaps in China's legislative framework by strengthening and formalizing the legal protections for workers and by extending the scope of labour legislation to part-time employees and labour dispatching units. It requires detailed written employment contracts, limits the circumstances under which contracts can be revoked, requires severance payments based on years of service, and mandates consultation with trade unions or workers' representatives on matters directly related to employees' interests. It also specifies legal liabilities for breaches of contracts and for use or threats of violence against employees. The Employment Promotion Law, also effective in 2008, strengthens protection against discrimination. It gives workers, for the first time, the right to sue if they believe that they have experienced discrimination. Significantly, it also extends anti-discrimination protection to migrants and to individuals with infectious diseases that are not easily communicable.

The Labour Contract Law, in particular, has been strongly criticized by international corporations operating in China who argue that it will increase labour costs substantially and that it will be difficult to apply. It is important to recognize that some of the more controversial provisions are actually in line with international practice—for example, the reliance on written contracts detailing the terms of employment. However, other aspects of the law are ambiguous and may not be consistent with international practice—for example, severance requirements and the role of trade unions in mass layoffs.

Ultimately, the impact of the law will depend on how it is interpreted and applied in different parts of the country. In any case, existing employment conditions are likely to mitigate any concerns about an excessive shift to worker protection under the Labour Contract Law. The rate of unionization outside the state sector remains relatively low, and a culture of free collective bargaining does not exist. Limited awareness among workers—particularly rural migrants—of their legal rights and entitlements is also likely to weaken the effect of the law's protections on the ground. Even when workers are aware that their rights have been violated by employers, the complicated procedures and short timeframe for arbitration discourage them from utilizing the labour dispute settlement system (Qiao, Lin, and Jiang 2004). Another major challenge is to apply and enforce labour standards in the informal sector, which operates largely outside the reach of government, where workers have a more precarious employment status and are more likely to face poor working conditions.

Wage Determination

Under the old system, wages were based on a grid, with increases based on seniority rather than productivity, and with differentials due to education or occupation severely compressed. Few incentives or rewards were given for skill acquisition or effort. In the early phases of reforms, as greater managerial autonomy was introduced in the SOE sector, wages started to differ between enterprises depending on their profitability, and newly introduced "bonuses" became a significant part of total remuneration (Knight and Song 2007). Since then, with the development of a vibrant private sector, competition over workers and resources has increasingly ensured that wages move to reflect market scarcities and relative productivities. Significant wage differentials have emerged between workers with different levels of skills and experience and across occupations and sectors. A recent study shows that the standard deviation of log urban wages in China increased from 0.45 in 1988 to 0.67 in 2003 (Park et al. 2006). Wage inequality has risen sharply not only between rural and urban areas but also within them.

Much of this increase in wage inequality was necessary to improve market-based economic incentives and reward both risk taking and human capital investments. As wages have moved to reflect productivity and the relative scarcity of skills, returns to education in China have increased sharply, most notably for higher education (see Figure 3).[10] Education is now the single most important determinant of wages. Returns to schooling are high even after controlling for factors such as ownership, sector, and occupation. The World Bank (2008a), for example, estimates the raw return to a year of schooling (not

FIGURE 3
Wage Growth and Returns to Education

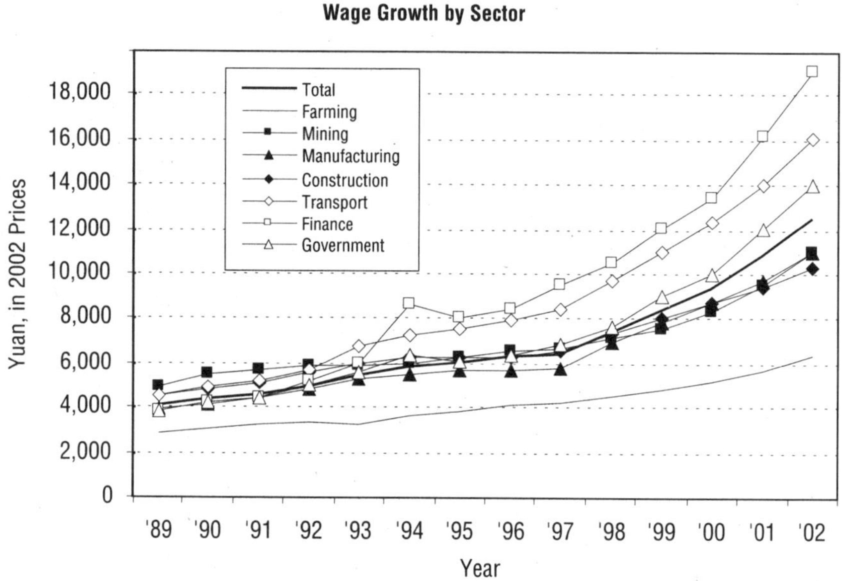

Source: National Bureau of Statistics of China (2005); Park, Song, Zhang, and Zhao (2005).

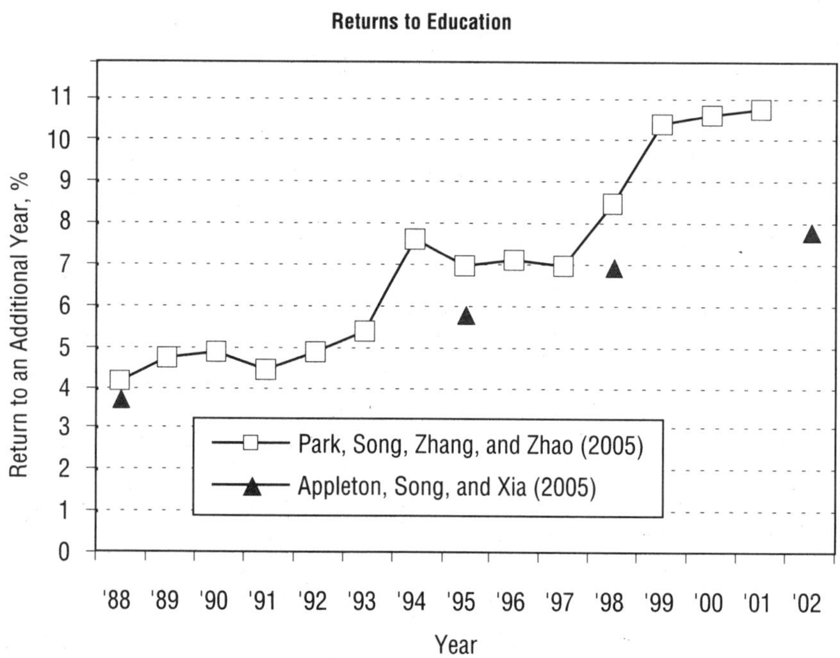

Source: Calculations by the World Bank based on Park, Song, Zhang, and Zhao (2005) and Appleton, Song, and Xia (2005).

controlling for any other factors) at 11.6 percent in 2003. After controlling for other factors, the return to a year of schooling falls to 6.9 percent, which is still high by international standards. Studies suggest that returns to education are higher for women than for men and higher in non-state enterprises than in SOEs. More recent education is also more valuable, presumably reflecting a mismatch between the skills acquired under the old system of education and those demanded by the labour market today.

Besides education, other individual characteristics such as occupation and gender also affect wages. For example, Park et al. (2006) estimate the male wage premium to be about 15 percent. Ownership also seems to matter, with SOEs and foreign-earned firms consistently paying higher wages, controlling for other factors. Significant wage differentials also exist by sector even after controlling for education and other individual characteristics (Park et al. 2006). All these factors are typically important determinants of wages in most market economies.

Indeed, a number of recent studies point to the growing influence of market forces in the determination of wages. For example, the World Bank (2005b) observes a steady convergence in marginal productivity of labour across provinces, although not between agricultural and non-agricultural activities. Cai, Park, and Zhao (2004) interpret increasing returns to education and their convergence to the level seen in other countries as a sign of market forces at work.[11] Park et al. (2005) also find strong evidence of converging returns to education between provinces and between ownership groups during the 1990s. Appleton, Song, and Xia (2005) find that returns to experience have decreased, indicating a move away from seniority-based pay. The relationship between firms' profitability and pay also seems to have strengthened recently (Knight and Li 2005). In sum, wage determination in China today increasingly resembles what is found in more mature market economies.

At the same time, important signs of labour market segmentation persist between rural and urban areas and, within urban areas, between formal and informal employment. Differentials between agriculture and non-agriculture wages are large and growing (recall Figure 3). Part of this disparity reflects the very different underlying endowments of education for rural and urban residents. In 2003, barely 16 percent of rural inhabitants had more than nine years of schooling, compared to more than 75 percent of those residing in urban areas.[12] Part of it also reflects different returns to education in rural and urban wage settings, a sign of segmentation.

Wage disparities are also very pronounced within the urban sector, most notably between formal and informal workers. Wage growth in the urban informal sector has averaged only 2–3 percent per year, compared to the double-digit growth experienced by formal workers. This disparity reflects in part the lower educational achievement of workers in the informal sector, which is heavily populated with rural migrants, as well as the fact that returns to education have been compressed in informal employment. In particular, the education of migrants seems to have been rewarded less than that of urban residents (Knight and Li 2005). Knight, Song, and Jia (1999) find that non-migrant workers in the formal sector are paid higher than their marginal productivity while migrants are paid much below, indicating segmentation.

However, the empirical evidence increasingly suggests that in many growing markets in China, particularly in the coastal areas, wages for informal sector and migrant workers are starting to rise. Du, Cai, and Wang (2006) found a significant improvement in wages of migrants relative to local residents in the formal sector between 2002 and 2005, which they attribute in part to the government's recent migrant-friendly policies. They also find that in the fast-growing coastal areas, returns to education are higher for both local residents and migrant workers, regardless of whether they are employed in the formal or informal sector. Since 2006, firms have been prepared to pay significantly higher wages to migrants they recruit. Since most migrants are employed informally, this trend is a good proxy for rising informal sector wages. All of these factors point toward a gradually more integrated labour market.

Future Challenges

Reforms in the labour market have been implemented with considerable caution since 1978. In fact, employment-related reforms have initially lagged behind changes in other areas (for example, in agriculture, the state sector, residency), with new labour market laws, regulations, and practices finally introduced when the old ones have become completely incompatible with the context in which they were operating. However, looking back on the past 30 years, it is clear that all of these small steps have added up to a fundamental transformation of the managed employment system into a labour market. The inefficiencies of the system that existed in 1978 have largely been eliminated, and today's labour market is contributing to higher productivity and wages while offering choice for workers and employers.

However, these gains have been achieved at a price. Labour market segmentation may be decreasing but remains strong, most notably in three areas: between rural and urban areas; between the state sector and the private sector; and within the private sector, between formal and informal employment. This segmentation has contributed to the growing inequality which has become one of the dominant features of the labour market. The other major, and related, consequence of the employment reforms has been the emergence of vulnerability, with the destruction of the iron rice bowl, the onset of unemployment and informality, and the incompleteness of the modern safety net. China will need to address these issues as it continues along the labour market reform process. The extension of the legal framework through the Labour Contract Law and the Employment Promotion Law may prove to be important first steps.

Looking forward, China now faces a number of emerging challenges in its labour market development. These challenges include coping with a slowdown in labour force growth, meeting the pressures for improvements in worker rights, facilitating mobility, and addressing skill deficiencies.

Coping with the Slowdown in Labour Force Growth

China's demographic transition, accentuated by the one-child policy, is now affecting potential labour supply. The working-age population is projected to peak in 2011, after which it will gradually decline at a rate of 0.1-0.4 percent per year. By 2015, the cohort entering the labour market (ages 15–24) will be 10 percent smaller than in 2005 (World Bank 2008b). These sizeable demographic shifts could possibly reverse what has been a major element of the country's economic success: an abundant and rapidly increasing labour force. However, the tightening of China's labour supply can be mitigated through policies that alter behaviours and incentives to participate in the labour force.

Certainly, one key to increasing the *effective* labour supply will be the continued transfer of workers from rural areas, where there is a slower population aging process, to the cities, where aging is more rapid and where labour demand will be strongest. Measures to equip rural workers with better skills and to improve the flow of information on vacancies and job opportunities could foster greater movement of labour. Demographics and rural-to-urban migration will not be the only determinants of labour supply in China. For example, changes in pension policies to encourage later retirement could expand labour supply substantially by increasing the currently low labour force participation rates among older workers. Policies that aim at providing affordable care for dependents could help boost the labour force participation of women, which fell substantially after economic restructuring.

Enforcing Labour Standards and Worker Rights

The application and enforcement of labour standards remains weak, which is becoming a greater concern for policymakers given pressures from both domestic and international sources. The recent legislation, most notably the Labour Contract Law, seems intended to strengthen the regulatory framework. However, the likely effect is uncertain, due to limited capacity for administration and enforcement and due to weak worker voice.

Strengthening the capacity of labour administration and inspection could help improve compliance in the formal sector. However, it will be of limited benefit for the informal sector, where efforts to strengthen mechanisms that support workers' voices and give employers more incentives to participate are likely to be much more effective. Workers' voices can be supported through a variety of channels, including better access to information on basic rights under the law, access to simplified mechanisms for complaints and dispute resolution, and the integration of migrant and informal workers into labour organizations.

Strengthening Social Insurance Mechanisms and Facilitating Mobility

While the old enterprise-based social protection system has been replaced on paper with mandatory state-run social and health programs, implementation varies widely across provinces and municipalities. Incentives need to be improved for workers and employers to participate. To some extent, this can be achieved through better design that improves portability, equity, and financial sustainability. A critical question is how to extend access to social protection to those outside the formal sector and especially to rural migrants. One possible approach would be to delink coverage from formal employment relationships and to provide a package of universal minimum coverage financed from general revenues. Whatever policy options are considered, they must be assessed in terms of incentive effects for labour force participation and formality.

Addressing Skills Deficiencies

China faces a number of challenges in addressing different types of human capital deficiencies. For the most part, the large pool of unemployed and laid-off workers does not have the skills to be reemployed outside the subsistence-level jobs in the informal sector. Although numerous programs have been created to help these workers upgrade their skills, there is little evidence to suggest that such programs are effective. At the same time, many new graduates are also facing difficulty finding suitable jobs due to a disconnect between the knowledge and skills provided by the education and training system and those demanded by employers.[13] This disconnect points to the need to boost educational attainment and improve the quality and relevance of vocational training and education at the secondary and postsecondary levels. Closing the skills gap will be critical to helping tomorrow's workers find high-productivity employment, which in turn will allow China to maintain its competitive edge as it moves up the development ladder and relies less and less on low labour costs to compete.

Notes

1. The authors are with the World Bank. The analysis and conclusions presented in this chapter are their responsibility and should not be attributed to the World Bank, its member countries, or its Board of Executive Directors.

2. For a more detailed description of China's labor market transformation, see World Bank 2008a.
3. In fact, employment was overwhelmingly rural and agriculture-based. It has been estimated that the urban, non-agricultural labour force was only 3 million in 1949.
4. There is an extensive literature describing the pre-liberalization employment system. See, for example, Knight and Song (2007), Zhu (1995), and Shirk (1981).
5. Indeed, when positions became available because of retirement, children of retiring workers would often have priority for filling the vacancy.
6. For example, the central government has prohibited the imposition of "illegal" fees on non-local workers, and a long-standing law allowing coercive detention and deportation of unregistered migrants has been abolished. A national crackdown on wage arrears was launched in 2003. Training programs and employment services for rural migrants are being widely implemented. The 2006 *State Council Opinion on Rural Migrant Workers* has taken the most far-reaching stance to date, recognizing the significant contributions made by rural migrants to the country's development and underscoring the importance of safeguarding their rights and interests. However, much more remains to be done to implement the measures at the local level.
7. Description from the Social Security White Paper (2004).
8. China has ratified the four conventions relating to equal remuneration, the elimination of discrimination, minimum working age, and the abolition of child labour.
9. However, workers have the legal right to stop working under certain circumstances (e.g., violations of occupational safety and health standards that put them at risk).
10. See Park et al. (2006) and Appleton, Song, and Xia (2005).
11. Cai, Park and Zhao (2004) qualify that not necessarily all of this increase is associated with labour market reform. Other factors, such as skill-biased technical change, could have also played a role.
12. From NBS Rural and Urban Household Surveys, in World Bank (2007a).
13. See, for example, Farrell and Grant (2005).

References

Appleton, S., L. Song, and Q. Xia. 2005. "Has China Crossed the River? The Evolution of Wage Structure in Urban China during Reform and Retrenchment." *Journal of Comparative Economics* 33:644–666.

Betcherman, G. and N-H. Blunch. 2006. *The Limited Job Prospects of Displaced Workers: Evidence from Two Cities in China*, Social Protection Discussion Paper No. 0613. Washington, DC: World Bank.

Cai, F. 2003. "Reform of Labour Policy in China: A Perspective of Political Economy." *China and World Economy* 4:30–37.

Cai, F., A. Park, and Y. Zhao. 2004. "The Chinese Labor Market." Preliminary draft prepared for the second conference on China's Economic Transition: Origins, Mechanisms, and Consequences, Pittsburgh, PA. November 5–7.

Dong, X. and L.C. Xu. 2006. "Labor Restructuring in China's Industrial Sector: Towards a Functioning Urban Labor Market." World Bank. Downloaded from SSRN.

Du, Y., F. Cai, and M. Wang. 2006. "Marketization and / or Informalization: New Trends of China's Employment in Transition" mimeo. Beijing: Institute of Population and Labor Economics, Chinese Academy of Social Sciences.

Farrell, D. and A.J. Grant. 2005. "China's Looming Talent Shortage." Washington, DC: McKinsey Global Institute.

Giles, J., A. Park, and F. Cai. 2006. "How has Economic Restructuring Affected China's Urban Workers?" *The China Quarterly* 185:61–95.

Howe, C. 1973. *Wage Patterns and Wage Policy in Modern China, 1919–1972*. London: Cambridge University Press.

Knight, J. and S. Li. 2005. "Wages, Firm Profitability and Labor Market Segmentation in Urban China." *China Economic Review* 16:205–28.

Knight, J. and L. Song. 2007. *Towards a Labour Market in China*. London: Oxford University Press.

Knight, J., L. Song, and H. Jia. 1999. "Chinese Rural Migrants in Urban Enterprises: Three Perspectives." *Journal of Development Studies* 35:73–100.

Lin, Y. 2004. "The Rural Social Protection System and the Rural Minimum Living Allowance: A Literature Review of Existing Rural Schemes." Washington, DC: World Bank.

Lindbeck, A. 2006. *An Essay on Economic Reforms and Social Change in China*. World Bank Policy Research Working Paper No. 4057. Washington, DC: World Bank.

Meng, X. 2000. *Labour Market Reform in China*. Cambridge: Cambridge University Press.

National Bureau of Statistics of China. 2005. *China Statistical Yearbook 2005*. Beijing: China Statistics Press.

Park, A., X. Song, J. Zhang, and Y. Zhao. 2005. "Economic Returns to Schooling in Urban China, 1988 to 2001." *Journal of Comparative Economics* 33:730–752.

—— 2006. Updated tables and figures (1998–2003) for "The Growth of Wage Inequality in Urban China, 1988 to 1999."

Qiao, J., Y. Lin, and Y. Jiang. 2004. "China Labor Market Policies Review." World Bank Advisory Report, translated by Amy Chang. Washington, DC: World Bank.

Shirk, S. 1981. "Recent Chinese Labour Policies and the Transformation of Industrial Organization in China." *The China Quarterly* 88:575–593.

World Bank. 2005a. *China—Integration of National Product and Factor Markets—Economic Benefits and Policy Recommendations*. World Bank Report No. 31973-CHA. Washington, DC: World Bank.

—— 2005b. *China: Pension Liabilities and Reform Options for Old Age Insurance*. Working Paper Series No. 2005-1. Washington, DC: World Bank.

—— 2008a. *China's Modernizing Labor Market: Trends and Emerging Challenges*. World Bank Report, forthcoming. Washington, DC: World Bank.

—— 2008b. *China's Evolving Poverty Reduction Agenda: An Assessment of Poverty and Inequality in China*. World Bank Report, forthcoming. Washington, DC: World Bank.

Zhu, Y. 1995. "Major Changes Under Way in China's Industrial Relations." *International Labour Review* 134:37–49.

6

The Thirty-Year Anti-Poverty Battle of a Large Agricultural Country

YUAN ZHANG

As a large agricultural country, China has experienced extremely rapid economic growth and poverty reduction in its rural population over the past three decades of reform and opening up. What kind of policies did China adopt to fight rural poverty? How did they work? What caused the dramatic decline in rural poverty? The following chapter provides answers to these questions.

Introduction

As a large developing country, with farmers as the majority of its population, China has attracted the attention of politicians and researchers around the world. Its rapid economic growth during the past three decades has had a tremendous impact on the world economy. Moreover, its impoverished population used to account for one half of the world's poor, and the significant drop in China's rural poverty has made significant contributions to the worldwide battle against poverty. On the other hand, rapid economic growth has sharpened income inequality within China, especially between the rural and urban areas, to such an extent that it has touched, and even been above, the internationally accepted alarm level.[1] These important issues—rapid economic growth, falling rates of rural poverty, and rising income inequality—are intertwined. Therefore, to examine the problem of rural poverty in China, we also need to consider the other related issues.

Without the recent drop in poverty rates in rural China, the number of poverty-stricken people in the world would have risen, not fallen over the past two decades. Given China's large population and the astonishing pace of its economic rise, this chapter will focus on the following key

Economic Transitions with Chinese Characteristics: Social Change During Thirty Years of Reform, eds. Arthur Sweetman and Jun Zhang. Montreal and Kingston: McGill-Queen's University Press, Queen's Policy Studies Series.

questions: as a large developing country that used to base its economy on agriculture, what effects has the implementation of economic policies had on rural poverty in the past thirty years? What lessons has China learned? What have anti-poverty policies actually accomplished? And what other problems does China still need to deal with?

Rural Poverty in China: An International Comparison

The Headcount Ratio

Since the adoption of reform policies and trade liberalization in the late 1970s, the Chinese government has achieved remarkable reductions in poverty. According to official statistics, the number of poor people in China's rural areas dropped from about 250 million in 1978 to about 30 million at the beginning of the twenty-first century.[2] However, this decline has not been uniform. As Table 1 shows, a rapid decline began in the early 1980s, with the Headcount Ratio dropping from 30.7 percent in 1978 to 14.8 percent in 1985. This change was the result of the development of agricultural production under the Household Responsibility System. But in the 1990s, progress slowed; and in 2003, the rural poor population even rebounded slightly upward.

TABLE 1
Rural Poor Population and Poverty Headcount

Year	*Absolute Poverty (10 million)*		*Headcount Ratio (%)*	
	Nationwide	*Key poverty-relief counties*	*Nationwide*	*Key poverty-relief counties*[a]
1978	25.0	-	30.7	-
1985	12.5	-	14.8	-
1990	8.5	-	9.4	-
1991	9.4	-	10.4	-
1992	8.0	-	8.8	-
1993	7.5	-	8.2	-
1994	7.0	-	7.7	-
1995	6.5	-	7.1	-
1996	5.0	-	6.3	-
1997	5.0	2.6	5.4	13.4
1998	4.2	2.2	4.6	11.1
1999	3.4	1.8	3.7	9.2
2000	3.2	1.7	3.4	8.9
2001	2.9	1.8	3.2	9.1
2002	2.8	1.8	3.0	8.8
2003	2.9	1.8	3.1	8.9

Note: [a]Key poverty-relief counties refer to those nominated and mainly funded by the Chinese central government.

Sources: World Bank (2001) and Survey Team in Rural China of National Statistic Bureau (2004).

However, many scholars maintain that the poverty line set by the Chinese government was too low, which greatly underestimated the actual extent of poverty in China. For example, in 1998, the Chinese government set the poverty line at an annual income of 635 RMB—that is, 1.74 RMB per day—which equals only US$ 0.22 (PPP value), far below the international standard of $1 per day (CSLS 2003). Table 2 shows that the World Bank's two estimations indicate that measured against the international standard, the headcount ratio is much higher than that officially announced by the Chinese government. Of course, even though the extremely low official poverty line in China underestimated actual poverty, the World Bank also admitted that regardless of the estimating criteria, the poverty population in rural China has demonstrated a significant decline (World Bank 2001).

TABLE 2
World Bank's Estimation of the Poverty Headcount Ratio in Rural China

Year	*Income Poverty (%)*	*Consumption Poverty (%)*
1990	31.1	42.8
1991	31.7	40.8
1992	30.1	40.9
1993	29.1	40.8
1994	25.9	34.9
1995	21.8	31.0
1996	15.0	24.3
1997	13.5	24.2
1998	11.5	-

Source: Park and Wang (2001).

Rural Poverty in China Compared to Other Countries

Evolving from a semi-colonial and semi-feudal society, China has faced a severe poverty problem. In 1978, the State Bureau of Statistics set the poverty line at 100 RMB per annum, which generated a poverty headcount ratio of 30.7 percent, whereas the World Bank measured an even higher headcount ratio in China, according to the international standard. Table 3 shows the World Bank's estimation of the poverty headcounts in most parts of the world, measured by the standard of US$1 per day.

Table 3 shows that if the poverty line were at $1.08 per day (purchasing power parity value in 1993), then in 1981, China's poverty headcount was at a high of 63.8 percent, topping the list by a margin of 23.4 percent, nearly 10 percent higher than India. However, by 2001, the poverty rate in China had been reduced to 16 percent, about 5 percent lower than the overall poverty rate in all the areas investigated, 18.1 percent lower than that of India, and merely 1.7 percent higher than that of East Asia and the

Pacific Region as a whole. China's drop stood in sharp relief against the rising poverty headcounts of Europe, Central Asia and Sub-Saharan Africa. This global upward trend was especially noticeable in Europe and Central Asia, though the absolute value of the overall headcount was not high.

TABLE 3
International Comparison of Poverty Headcount (%)

	1981	*1984*	*1987*	*1990*	*1993*	*1996*	*1999*	*2001*
East Asia and Pacific Regions	57.5	38.9	28.0	29.6	24.9	16.6	15.7	14.9
China	63.8	41.0	28.5	33.0	28.4	17.4	17.8	16.6
South Asia	51.5	46.8	45.0	41.3	40.1	36.6	32.2	31.3
India	54.4	49.8	46.3	42.1	42.3	42.2	35.3	34.7
Europe and Central Asia	0.7	0.5	0.4	0.5	3.7	4.2	6.3	3.7
Latin-America and the Caribbean	9.7	11.8	10.9	11.3	11.3	10.7	10.5	9.5
Middle East and North Africa	5.1	3.8	3.2	2.3	1.6	2.0	2.6	2.4
Sub-Saharan Africa	41.6	46.3	46.8	44.6	44.0	45.6	45.7	46.9
Total	40.4	32.8	28.4	27.9	26.3	22.8	22.2	21.1

Source: World Bank Website (http://go.worldbank.org/37DLI20JO0).

Table 3 shows the contribution China made to the war against global poverty. Without the decline of China's poor population, the worldwide poverty problem would have severely deteriorated.

Causes of the Rural Poverty in China

Inadequate statistics and survey data relating to China's rural poor has restricted empirical research into the causes of its rural poverty. But economists have still managed to draw significant conclusions. For example, an empirical study based on survey data of farmers in 1995 revealed the following: (i) the characteristics of an urban household play a more important role in determining whether or not a family is poor than the characteristics of a rural household; (ii) talent, gender, occupation, employer, membership in the Communist Party, and ethnicity do not have significant impact on whether or not a rural family is poor; (iii) education past senior high school can lower the probability of being poor; and (iv) land possession per capita exerts important negative effects on poverty (Khan 1998).

Another empirical study based on a large-scale survey of 8,000 families across 19 provinces found that the household poverty level was highly dependent on issues related to location: (i) a family in a minority ethnic group was more likely to be poor; (ii) geographic location was a fundamental determinant of poverty; (iii) education played an important part in poverty relief; and (iv) rural poverty was dependent on household activities, assets, and resources in their control (Gustafsson and Wei 2002).

Other studies have shown that rural poverty occurs not only in remote areas with a shortage of resources, but also in areas with abundant supplies but inadequate infrastructures and limited access to technological services (Gustafsson and Li 1998). Some scholars, however, hold that China's rural population has been intensively distributed in the provinces located in the North China Plain, due to the lack of resources, especially the severe shortage of land and water. They use the simultaneous equations model to examine the effects and impacts of government expenditures on rural production and poverty. Their analysis indicates that agricultural growth, higher agricultural salaries, and increased employment in non-agricultural sectors all play important roles in poverty relief. There is also a negative correlation between the terms of trade and rural poverty—that is, raising the prices of agricultural products could increase farmers' income and reduce rural poverty (Fan et al. 2000). These studies reveal that investment in rural public goods promotes agriculture production, higher prices for agricultural products, and increased employment in non-agricultural sectors, all of which make such investment (or lack thereof) the major determinant of poverty.

These studies all seem to suggest that at the micro level, the physical and human capital possessed by a family and its geographic location have a great impact on the likelihood that the family will be poor. However, there is a common weakness in these studies based on micro level data—they all fail to incorporate macro variables. Thus, these studies don't consider whether the major reason for this concentration of poverty is an urban bias in government policies, owing to its strategy of prioritizing the development of heavy industries (discussed below).

Anti-Poverty Policies in Rural China

In the past three decades, the central and local governments have devoted a great number of funds to fight against poverty, and the anti-poverty policies include tax cuts by the central government, subsidized loans, money transfer, and work-for-food funds from the central and local governments, and so on.

Recent literature and government reports describe the effects of China's anti-poverty policies along these lines: "From 'Period X' to 'Period Y,' the Chinese government successfully implemented a series of anti-poverty policies, reducing the rural poor at a scale of 'XX,' and lowering the poverty rate by 'XX' percent." Obviously, these reports are not precise evaluations, because many factors contribute to the decline of rural poverty, and anti-poverty policies represent only one of these. To evaluate the effects of the anti-poverty policies in rural China, precise empirical analysis is required. However, evaluating the effects of China's poverty relief policies is a daunting task, as researchers lack two kinds of necessary data: panel data on poor populations and their headcount ratio, and data on the distribution and implementation of relief funds. The shortage of the former is due to the fact that the surveillance and statistics system of poor populations has just recently been introduced in China. The reason for the lack of data on relief distribution lies in the failure of the present statistical systems to provide minute data in this respect, though nationwide gross data is available. In addition, obtaining detailed data on the implementation of relief funds is particularly difficult. But existing research still has made great efforts and so far drawn some important conclusions.

For example, a detailed study on the effects of a work-for-food program in rural China showed a connection between this poverty relief program and economic growth and development. With labour-intensive technology as its main feature, this policy was of particular advantage to the labour force in poor rural areas since it improved infrastructure and social services, while increasing the employment rate and income of the poor population (Zhu and Jiang 1994). The 2001 World Bank Report, which cited research by Jalan and Ravallion, also paid much attention to China's rural poverty. Jalan and Ravallion (1998) found that rural residents living in poor counties had a more rapidly increasing rate of household consumption than what was expected.

Similarly, Park analyzed a set of data between 1981 and 1995 related to all counties in China and found that the injection of relief funds increased the per capita income by 2.28 percent each year from 1985 to 1992, and by 0.91 percent from 1992 to 1995. Nevertheless, Jalan and Ravallion pointed out that their estimation might overstate the effect of the poverty relief projects, as they didn't take into account all the public expenditures of poverty relief (World Bank 2001). Moreover, studies using data collected in Sichuan and Shaanxi provinces to investigate the reasons for the decline in the headcount ratio showed that most changes to poverty levels could be explained by economic growth (which is the most important factor in reducing poverty), while anti-poverty policies had little effect (Rozelle et al. 2000).

Another empirical study of various poverty relief initiatives found that among government inputs, anti-poverty policy showed the least effect. The reason lies in the low efficiency of the targeting mechanism of these policies and the inappropriate use of funds (Fan 2003). Moreover, some researchers divided poverty into two groups—transient poverty and chronic poverty—and found many differences in the determinants of these two types of poverty.[3] They concluded that Chinese poverty relief policies focused on fighting chronic poverty rather than transient poverty. Thus, development-oriented poverty reduction policies were helpful to overcome chronic poverty, but ineffective against transient poverty (Jalan and Ravallion 1998).

These studies suggest that researchers generally assume a pessimistic attitude towards the effects of poverty relief policies in rural China.

Therefore, we can conclude that anti-poverty policies adopted by the Chinese government leave much to be desired.

Economic Growth and Poverty Decline

Since nearly all researchers believe that China's poverty relief policy has not contributed much to poverty reduction, why has the poor segment of the Chinese population experienced such a dramatic decline in numbers? We find that existing studies offer a unanimous answer to this question.

Most scholars hold that marketization, trade liberalization, and economic globalization are the major forces driving China's economic growth, which in turn reduced poverty. In the early 1960s, Bhagwati brought forward the "Bhagwati Hypothesis"—that economic growth is the fundamental driving force in reducing poverty. Many empirical studies since then have confirmed this hypothesis (Rozelle et al. 2000; Besley and Burgess 2003; Dollor 2001). Some scholars believe that by promoting economic growth, trade liberalization is particularly helpful in reducing absolute poverty, because it creates new markets for poor populations, urging them to respond to price differences and new market opportunities, and raising government public expenditures (Anderson 2004). Some studies have examined the impacts of China's productivity on rural poverty: they conclude that rapid economic growth in China has been chiefly driven by rapid improvements in productivity, along with a significant decline in the poverty rate (Tian et al. 2003; Fan et al. 2003). But productivity has manifested itself quite differently in the agricultural sector: by controlling for productivities of different sectors, some researchers have found that in the industrial sector, productivity growth was the main driving force behind poverty reduction, while in the agricultural sector, productivity growth had only a minor positive effect (CSLS 2003).

Furthermore, other studies have focused on the impact of public investments in agriculture and rural areas on rural poverty. For example, Tian et al. (2003) studied the impact of agricultural departments on rural poverty and found that the development of agriculture had the greatest impact. Increases in labour productivity in the agricultural sector and the rise of non-agricultural opportunities also influenced poverty levels. The World Bank (2001) has stated that since agricultural income constituted the major part of the income of poor populations, unbalanced development of agriculture directly affects poverty rates. In areas with slow agricultural growth, poverty decreases slowly, whereas in areas where agriculture develops rapidly or catches up with the development of other sectors, poverty drops rapidly (World Bank 2001).

Another study (Fan et al. 2000) investigated the relationship between rural public investments, economic growth and poverty reduction. It found that government expenditures in education played the most important role in poverty reduction and the second most important role in improving productivity. Government expenditures in research and development (R&D) also played an important role in agricultural development and was the third most important factor in poverty reduction; whereas expenditures in telecommunications played the second most important role in poverty reduction and the third in agricultural development (Fan et al. 2000).

A comparative study between China and India showed that funds earmarked for underdeveloped areas could deliver both the maximum value of reducing poverty and the greatest economic returns (Fan 2003). It further concluded that compared with other countries, China had made great achievements in poverty reduction, mainly the result of policies and institutional reforms, fair access to rural social services and assets, and public funds invested in rural areas. Despite the challenges of furthering this reduction in poverty levels, the Chinese government can still make better plans and policies, especially in public investments, so as to reduce poverty and narrow inequality. Other economists agree that economic growth in China has played a vital role in rural poverty reduction (Rozelle et al. 2000; Lu 2001).

Thus, economists hold a rather unanimous perspective on the impacts of China's economic growth on rural poverty relief. We can conclude that stable economic growth in the past thirty years in China, rather than government relief policies, has been the fundamental driving force of the poverty reduction in rural areas.

Development and Rural Poverty in a Large Agricultural Country

The three conclusions at the end of the three previous sections show that China's economic reforms have made great contributions to the worldwide battle against poverty. In addition, these accomplishments have not been directly generated by the anti-poverty policies adopted by the Chinese government; instead, they are the direct outcome of China's continuous rapid economic growth. This then raises questions for economists. How should such a large agricultural country balance development and poverty relief? How should we interpret the contrast between the low efficiency of China's poverty relief policies and the drop in its poverty levels?

Deep insight into these questions can be gained through the study of China's early development strategy, which prioritized heavy industry. Some scholars hold that after the Opium War, China declined from an empire with a splendid civilization to an impoverished, isolated backwater. After the foundation of the People's Republic of China in 1949, China's new leaders were confronted with the challenges of choosing the right development path and establishing a sound administrative system to organize economic construction and ultimately fulfill the goal of building a powerful and prosperous country. Facing severe financial restraints, the new government adopted a series of urban-biased policies aimed at developing capital-intensive heavy industry and expediting the process of industrialization by pumping agricultural profits into industrial sectors, hopefully to prepare for the economic take-off. These decisions reflected both the international, domestic, and economic context of the time and the economic ideology of the political leaders (Lin 1994).

Although the strategy of favouring heavy industry within a planned economy made China's capital accumulation rate climb over 15 percent and establish a relatively complete industrial economic system at a relatively high speed, the implementation of these strategies was difficult and created an unbalanced economic structure and a low-performance micro-economy (Lin 1994). The weakness of these urban-biased policies was their influence on agricultural growth and the corresponding rural poverty. Some economists believe that the fallout from these policies appeared mainly in the slowing down of agricultural growth, along with the distortion of the markets for agricultural products and factors of production (Carter 1997). Other economists hold that urban-biased policies restricted the urban mobility of the rural labour force, eventually leaving farmers as the main victims of poverty in China (Knight and Song 1993). Another problem closely related to rural poverty has been the yawning income gap between urban and rural areas. Income inequality is in fact a yardstick for relative poverty. Expansion of relative poverty is basically unfavourable to the ultimate solution to rural poverty. Many economists confirm that China's urban-biased policies have had very significant impacts on the expansion of income inequality (Brandt and Zhu 1998; Yang 1999; Yang and Zhou 1999; Tian 2001; Zhang 2003; Kanbur and Zhang 2004).

Although urban-biased policies have indeed addressed the issue of capital accumulation confronting China since the revolution, China has paid enormous costs. In the long run, such policies are not beneficial to economic growth, and the prevailing economic theories and practices at the time did not necessarily lead to the overall development and improvement of people's well-being. International comparative studies reveal that countries adopting similar strategies all resulted in poor performance in economic development. Not only did they fail to carry out their original objectives, but they also were confronted with similar problems (Lin 1994; Yang and Cai 2000; Yang and Zhou 1999). Therefore, to realize a sustainable and healthy economic development, China now needs to change its strategy of giving priority to heavy industries. Urban-biased policies may have been necessary for a while because they helped overcome the influences of interest groups and pushed forward reform; but the long-term objectives of the government should now be concerned with developing competitive markets and eventually abolishing urban-biased policies (Yang and Cai 2000).

To reduce China's rural poverty, the central government now needs to invest in agriculture. There is little conflict between agriculture development and poverty relief; and government investment in agricultural R&D,

rural education, and infrastructure in rural areas can greatly influence the development of agricultural production and the reduction of rural poverty. These influences can be direct or indirect, by promoting agricultural growth, reducing the costs of agricultural production, increasing farmers' agriculture income, advancing the processing industry for agricultural products, creating non-agricultural employment opportunities, and boosting the levels of non-agricultural salaries.

The research described in this section suggests that urban-biased policy is a double-edged sword for China. It has contributed to capital accumulation and has established the national economic system, but it has significant drawbacks. China must now choose to address rural poverty, create a harmonious society, and narrow the income inequality gap by integrating the rural and urban economies.

Problems with Poverty Alleviation Policies

According to statistics from The State Council Leading Group Office of Poverty Alleviation and Development, in 2003, despite a slight fall in most provinces, poor populations in such provinces as Heilongjiang, Shanxi, Anhui, and Henan all experienced some degree of poverty rebound, resulting in a net increase of 800 thousand persons, a record annual increase in China's annual reports on rural poverty. This result is intriguing because it occurred during a period when the Chinese government was investing enormous manpower and capital to eradicate poverty.

Because this situation is unexpected, a review of the poverty-relief strategies and policies seems necessary. Therefore, we will discuss the major features of China's poverty alleviation programs and practices, as well as their consequences.

Insufficiency of Poverty Relief Funds

Table 4 show how relief funds were used by key poverty-relief counties, the major beneficiaries from 1998 to 2000. The total volume for the first few years at the beginning of the twenty-first century stabilized roughly at 25 billion RMB, including subsidized loans that exceeded half of the gross. If we remove the principal of compensated use, this figure is even smaller. *The China Rural Poverty Alleviation and Development Program* (2001–2010) put forward two goals: to solve the problem of food and clothing for the 30 million people living in absolute poverty, and to help the 60 million low-income people gradually rise out of poverty. This meant that the 25 billion RMB were used for 90 million rural residents. However, even though all these funds were put to their appropriate use without any "leaks," the average amount of money spent on each person still fell short of 500 RMB, which was obviously inadequate for such significant needs.

TABLE 4
Funds Devoted to Key Poverty-Relief Counties (in RMB 10 million)

Sources of Funds	*1998*	*1999*	*2000*
Loans from the central government's budget	698.2	1,118.3	1,042.5
Refunds after the repayment of subsidized loans	86.6	134.9	160.3
Poverty alleviation funds from the central government's budget	194.6	229.9	276.9
Poverty alleviation funds from local governments' budget	89.6	97.3	89.7
Counterpart funds from local governments	52.9	36.8	40.9
Work-for-food funds from central government	358.7	393.4	385.7
Welfare-to-work funds from local governments	151.4	149.0	121.4
All donations	220.5	82.8	59.7
Donations from The Hope Project	15.3	12.3	7.5
Foreign funds	167.3	188.5	182.9
Other funds	173.8	170.7	69.6
Total	2,193.6	2,601.7	2,429.4

Source: National Bureau of Statistics of China (http://www.stats.gov.cn/tjsj/qtsj/ncjjzb/t20021022_38948.htm).

Table 5 shows the percentage of farmers who benefited directly from the poverty alleviation funds, with the highest rate in the groups receiving less than 100 RMB, 200–500 RMB, and 500–1,000 RMB, respectively—hardly enough to alleviate any kind of poverty.

TABLE 5
Percentage of Farmers Receiving Direct Poverty Alleviation Funds

Amount of Funds (RMB)	0–100	100–200	200–500	500–1,000	1,000–2,000	2,000–5,000	5,000+
Percentage	20.3%	14%	27.5%	17.4%	13.4%	6.5%	0.9%

Source: Survey Team in Rural China of National Statistic Bureau (2004).

Local poverty relief funds have been even worse. The central government determined that work-for-food funds from the central government should be granted to rural participants as part of their wages, and local governments had to arrange matching funds at no less than a ratio of 1:1. However, the majority of provinces were unable to raise the matching funds (Zhu and Jiang 1994). Thus, the work-for-food funds did not get distributed in those regions. In 2002, China's total poverty alleviation funds were 25.08 billion RMB, of which the local governments' funds represented only 0.99 billion RMB (Survey Team in Rural China of National Statistic Bureau 2004). The central government obviously played a dominant role in poverty relief, providing 80 percent of the financial resources. One study by the World Bank (2001) shows that in 1997, in Sichuan province, local subsidized loans, poverty alleviation funds, and work-for-food matching funds accounted for, respectively, 5.2, 6.5 and 0 percent of the funds from the central government; whereas in Yunnan province, the same respective percentages were 2.3, 16.4, and 0. Moreover, Table 4 shows that non-governmental funds accounted for only a small proportion of poverty relief.

These statistics suggest that although governments at all levels were able to raise poverty relief funds, the total amount was still far from adequate to fill the demand–supply gap. And in some cases, those funds could not reach the targeted group.

Poverty Alleviation Funds: A Leaky Basket

The 2000/2001 Report of the World Bank revealed that fiscal constraints faced by underdeveloped counties in China may lead to fund embezzlement. With the adoption of fiscal decentralization and the subsequent drop in tax income, local governments in poor counties feel these fiscal pressures especially strongly. Despite transfers from the higher fiscal department, local governments of some counties still cannot make ends meet for their fiscal expenditures. Under supervision of the Leading Group Office of Poverty Alleviation and Development, poor county governments set different objectives. First, their budget is stringent, which is supposed to, for instance, pay off outstanding wages to employees on the government payroll. Second, revenue-starved county governments feel a strong urge to use poverty funds in ways that quickly enrich local revenues. So they spend a lot of poverty funds promoting rural industries and township and village enterprises (TVEs) instead of directing it to the poor. The central government has recently responded to this problem by limiting the amount of poverty funds spent on rural industries. Yet even though poverty funds are spent on agriculture and basic infrastructure, the poor do not enjoy the direct benefits. The returns of agricultural and infrastructure investments in wealthier townships tend to be higher and more easily taxed than those in the poorest townships and villages (World Bank 2001).

In fact, the problems analyzed by the World Bank occur not only at the county level but also at other levels, from the provincial level to the township level. For example, according to one news report from the website of Fiscal and Economic Issues in China in 2002,[4] the Ministry of Finance once sent a group of finance inspectors to eight provinces to assess the distribution, management, and use of anti-poverty funds. This group discovered various types of misuse and embezzlement. For example, the Poverty Alleviation Office of Gansu province spent 27.5 million RMB of poverty alleviation funds to build a dormitory building for its own staff and to buy a car. The director of the Poverty Alleviation Office of Yun

Lian County in Sichuan province embezzled 1.7 million RMB of the poverty alleviation funds from 1997 to 2000, 64.6 percent of the total poverty funds appropriated by its upper department. The embezzled funds were mainly used to buy fixed assets, pay bonuses, and cover catering bills and business accommodation. In 1999 alone, the Poverty Alleviation Office and Provincial Finance Bureau of Shanxi province used 10.87 million RMB of poverty funds for the maintenance and infrastructure of the poverty alleviation offices and service stations at provincial, county, and township levels. News of this kind reveals fund "leaks" during the transfer from upper-level to lower-level departments.

However, in addition to determining the reasons for the leaks, the central government must also ensure that funds can reach the "real" poor. At the beginning of the 1990s, the Chinese government had already started reforming the traditional practice of sending poverty alleviation funds to impoverished counties rather than to poor households. Now poverty funds are mostly channelled directly either to poor households or to poor villages. Accordingly, instead of flowing to TVEs, the funds are now being widely used on such activities as planting, breeding, and processing.

However, the implementation of this policy has not been as satisfactory as had been expected. The leakiest part of the anti-poverty program is the subsidized loan segment, which constitutes over half of the total poverty alleviation funds. The Agricultural Bank of China issues subsidized loans for the purpose of poverty alleviation; however, since it is a commercial bank, its aim is to maximize its profits. The prerequisite for profits is an assurance of loan and interest repayment. Therefore, securing loan recovery is the bank's primary concern when issuing these loans, a practice that results in three kinds of misallocation of money: (i) loans may go to well-off or comfortably-off regions, which are considered better able to repay than poor regions; (ii) loans may go to well-off or comfortably-off households instead of poor ones, because the poorest households do not have much to mortgage, which reduces the likelihood of repayment; and (iii) loans may not go to households engaging in planting, breeding, and processing activities because of their relatively low technology level, and high vulnerability to environmental factors, such as natural disasters. Thus, by its nature, the Agricultural Bank of China is not very willing to lend to actual poor households in dire need of anti-poverty money. Quite simply, all commercial banks in the world regard loans to poor people as highly risky. Thus, even if Central Finance promised a discount interest rate to the Agricultural Bank, as a commercial bank it would still have a low incentive to lend money to the poor.

Excessive Government Interference

According to regulations under China's current poverty alleviation framework, governments at all levels must co-operate with NGOs. However, governments still hold the pivotal roles. NGOs are engaged only in monetary supply and some other pilot projects. To a large extent, poverty alleviation programs have to be administrated by government instead of the market, because many poverty alleviation programs are economic projects with asymmetric information; yet excessive interference from or participation by the government would lead to low efficiency in the use of funds. For example, it is widely reported that in many areas, local governments invest unwisely in doomed projects. As a result, local residents are getting buried deeper in poverty instead of pulling themselves out. In addition, governments are heavily involved in issuing subsidized loans for poverty alleviation. For example, local governments are responsible for auditing, submitting, and approving loan projects, and banks are excluded from this process. This exclusion produces a serious asymmetry between incentive and liability. The government has the last say on how to use funds, but it is free of the responsibility for collecting repayment on loans. This leads to random decision-making, random censure of the eligibility of borrowers, separation between lenders' and borrowers' objectives, and low efficiency of resource allocation.

Moreover, during the granting process, governments still focus too much on the early stage of issuing funds and overlook the needs of the later stages, such as technology input and marketing services. Such cases are abundant in today's news media. For example, some local governments encouraged farmers to plant pears and oranges, but they neglected to provide them with the necessary technology for growing these fruits, and neglected to provide roads to transport the fruit to markets. As a result, the fruit had to be sold at extremely low prices in local markets or simply thrown away. This example shows that technological assistance is extremely important for the success of poverty alleviation projects. If programs emphasize only the issuing of funds, while neglecting follow-up services, success will be limited, and poverty will not be alleviated. On the other hand, many success stories under the guidance of governments show that these funds can help farmers and poor households escape poverty by planting more economically viable crops. Close examination of these cases reveals that success is closely related to the technological service and managerial support offered by government and to pro-production marketing and sales campaigns.

The contrast between successful and unsuccessful cases shows that poverty alleviation is a comprehensive project. It is not just about supplying the poor with some material comfort or financial aid. It is more important to provide them with a larger set of supports to enable them to escape from poverty, but unfortunately this is often overlooked in the government's poverty alleviation programs, and most of the ill-managed ones are doomed to failure.

The Current and Future State of Affairs

The Current State

Urban-biased policies have created a favourable environment for the development of China's economy, propelling robust Gross Domestic Product (GDP) growth. GDP growth is itself the ultimate impetus for poverty reduction. However, we cannot conclude that the strategy of prioritizing heavy industry is flawless, because even though the economy is growing rapidly, a distortion of economic efficiency is also occurring. In addition, the economic sustainability of this strategy is a big problem, because it cannot bring about uniform social development across the country. In the long term, widening income inequality may be detrimental to economic growth.

Thus, while China congratulates itself on its achievements in the past thirty years, it must also reflect on their negative impacts. China's economy is indeed growing rapidly, which is clearly helping to reduce poverty. However, if farmers cannot equally enjoy the fruits of economic growth—that is, if the pie gets bigger but their piece gets smaller—this will result in a sharp cleavage between urban and rural areas, which will do great harm to the harmony of Chinese society. For example, some experts hold that the role of government in poverty alleviation is not simply to provide financial or material aid, but also to establish sound public policies to create incentives for economic growth. The two goals behind these incentives are: (i) to create a good investment environment for ambitious and talented entrepreneurs, and (ii) to invest in the poor and let them participate in economic activities and share the fruit of economic growth. The second point is of more importance for preventing social disharmony and should be the government's major concern when reviewing poverty alleviation policies.

Considerations for The Future of Poverty Alleviation Programs

Poverty is a multi-dimensional concept, including not only income and consumption poverty, but also malnutrition, poor health, and illiteracy. Therefore, while theorists cling to the traditional money-based methods of measuring poverty, the wider aspects of poverty should not be overlooked. Table 6 indicates the significance of these poverty-related problems in rural China.

The dualistic economic structure shaped by urban-biased policies is also likely to introduce social stratification, which will in turn induce social polarization, weakening the survival skills of the poor and entrapping them deeper in poverty. For example, Amartya Sen (2003) states that poverty is not necessarily a low standard of living, but rather being incapable of maintaining one's livelihood. In this view, social stratification

TABLE 6
China's Urban and Rural Illiteracy Rate and Infant Mortality Rate

	Illiteracy Rate (%)						
	National	*Rural*	*Urban*	*Rural/Urban*	*Female*	*Male*	*Female/Male*
1964	50.2	52.5	29.0	1.81	N/A	N/A	N/A
1981	33.9	35.9	20.3	1.77	N/A	N/A	N/A
1990	21.2	23.4	16.7	1.40	29.7	13.3	2.23
1995	17.9	21.8	12.2	1.78	25.5	10.3	2.47
	Infant Mortality Rate (‰)						
	National	*Rural*	*Urban*	*Rural/Urban*	*Female*	*Male*	*Female/Male*
1964	180.0	N/A	N/A	N/A	N/A	N/A	N/A
1981	26.9	37.0	24.8	1.49	25.9	27.9	0.93
1990	29.5	32.2	19.3	1.67	31.8	27.4	1.16
1995	39.2	44.8	21.1	2.12	45.0	33.7	1.34

Source: Zhang (2003).

will significantly impact future poverty. For example, in many areas, compensation for land confiscation (mainly for industrial or governmental purpose) is extremely low. Land owners can hardly enjoy the added value brought by land development, and farmers and village collectives are often marginalized from the discussion. At the 2002 Yan Fu Annual Economic Seminar in Beijing, Sen (2003) stated the following: "Given this chance to speak about what I hope the direction new research regarding inequality and poverty in China will take, I suggest that researchers should concern themselves more with income inequality and the loss of people's basic survival skills. Sufficient evidences exists to encourage us to conduct deeper research into the trends in inequality and poverty based on what we have and will do to eliminate them, and taking into consideration factors such as mortality, the incidence rate of diseases, and education and related skills" (263–264, my translation).

Malnutrition is also an important fact of poverty. Unfortunately, the severe lack of detailed data concerning residents' health status makes the discussion about malnutrition impossible. It's worth noticing that the rural health care system has not been established yet. Table 6 shows that from the 1980s to the 1990s, the infant mortality rate actually rose—an alarming problem that needs to be studied. Although the development of a new rural co-operative medical system has started, the government still has many social infrastructure responsibilities to fulfill in rural areas.

Another issue deserving attention is the implementation of compulsory education in rural areas. According to statistics, in 2002, there were still 431 counties where the nine-year compulsory education system was still not fully implemented (Survey Team in Rural China of National

Statistic Bureau 2004). Roughly 10 billion RMB is needed to implement compulsory education in these counties. In addition, around 100 million school-age children attend school in China's middle and western rural areas. Although 40 percent of them are from well-off or even affluent families, 60 million children can't afford tuition. The annual tuition fee is 200 RMB for each primary school student and 400 RMB for each middle school student; thus, the total tuition fee gap is approximately 18 billion RMB. Given that the goal of 2007 is to enable all children from poor rural households to enjoy the benefits of the policy of "Free Charge for Incidental Expenses and Textbooks, and Subsidy for Living Costs at School" about 20 billion RMB more in education funding is needed. Judging from this figure, there is still a long way to go before China completely solves this problem.

Moreover, rapid economic growth and incentives brought about by decentralization reform are heavily integrated, and the costs of decentralization are gradually revealing themselves. For example, Table 4 shows that local governments have little incentive to devote funds to poverty alleviation and, in some cases, have embezzled poverty funds for other uses, resulting in the nonfeasance of local governments on poverty reduction.

China's rapid economic growth also benefits from its marketization reforms and urbanization process. However, despite the finding of many researchers that marketization and urbanization help eliminate rural poverty and reduce the income gap between rural and urban areas, these results do not occur automatically. One of our studies revealed that the market participation level of peasants (rural farmers) is relative to income level (Zhang and Liu 2006). The market participation level of poverty-stricken peasants is far below that of the well-off rural population. Therefore, economic development cannot be expected to eliminate poverty on its own. In the process, the government has to play a role, especially by allowing peasants to become more involved in the market, thereby enabling them to share the fruits of economic growth.

China's residence registration system entrenches rather than alleviates rural poverty. Discriminatory policies against rural migrant workers are detrimental to the improvement of the workforce allocation efficiency, which is in itself a setback for China's economy, and also to the elimination of rural poverty and the acceleration of the urbanization process. Thus, for establishing future economic strategies and implementing reforms, the government should prioritize, accelerating the reform of the residence registration system, and gradually phasing out urban-biased policies.

Notes

1. A Gini Index higher than 0.4 is a generally accepted indicator of inequality.
2. The gross population in 1978 was about 8.14 hundred million in China.

3. These include different definitions of chronic poverty and transient poverty. One generally accepted distinction is that chronic poverty refers to people with per capita income or consumption levels persistently between the poverty line during a long period, and transient poverty refers to people with fluctuating income or consumption near the poverty line.
4. Source: http://www.fec.com.cn/scoop/content.php3?id=104.
5. For example, read about a successful program in Hunan Province at http://fpb.xxz.gov.cn/292.html.

References

Anderson K. 2004. "Agricultural Trade Reform and Poverty Reduction in Developing Countries." World Bank Policy Research Working Paper 3396, Washington, DC.

Besley T., and R. Burgess. 2003. "Halving Global Poverty." *Journal of Economic Perspectives* 17(3):3–22.

Brandt, L., and Z. Xiaodong. 1998. "Soft Budget Constraints and Inflation Cycles: A Positive Model of he Macro Dynamics in China during Transition." *Mimeo*, University of Toronto.

Carter, C.A. 1997. "The Urban-Rural Income Gap in China: Implications for Global Food Market." *American Journal of Agriculture Economics* 79:1410–18.

CSLS. 2003. "China's Productivity Performance and Its Impact on Poverty in the Transition Period." Ottawa: Centre for the Study of Living Standards Research Report 2003–07.

Dollar, D. 2001. "Globalization, Inequality and Poverty since 1980." World Bank Working Paper, Washington, DC.

Fan, S. 2003. "Public Investment and Poverty Reduction, What Have We Learnt from India and China?" Paper prepared for the ADBI conference *Infrastructure Investment for Poverty Reduction: What Do We Know?* Tokyo, June 12–13, 2003.

Fan S., L. Zhang, and X. Zhang. 2000. "Growth and Poverty in Rural China: The Role of Public Investments." EPTD Discussion Paper, No. 66, International Food Policy Research Institute, Environment and Production Technology Division.

Gustafsson, B., and S. Li. 1998. "The Structure of Chinese Poverty, 1988." *The Developing Economics* 36:387–406.

Gustafsson, B., and Z. Wei. 2002. "Why Some Peasants are Poor yet the Others Are Not in Rural China?" *World Economic Papers (in Chinese)* 3:1-8.

Huppi, M., and G. Feder. 1990."The Role of Group and Credit Cooperative in Rural Lending." *The World Band Research Observer* 5(2):187–204.

Jalan, J., and M. Ravallion. 1998. "Transient Poverty in Post-Reform Rural China." *Journal of Comparative Economics* 26:338–357.

Kanbur, R., and X. Zhang. 2004. "Fifty Years of Regional Inequality in China: A Journey through Central Planning, Reform, and Openness." United Nations University WIDER Working Paper, No. 2004/50.

Khan, A.R. 1998. "Poverty in China in the Period of Globalization, New Evidence on Trend and Pattern." Development Polices Department of International Labour Office Discussion Paper 22, Geneva.

Knight J., and L. Song. 1993. "The Spatial Contribution to Income Inequality in Rural China." *Cambridge Journal of Economics* 17:195–213.

Lin, J.Y., L. Zhou, and F. Cai. 1994. *China Miracle: Development Strategy and Economic Reform* (in Chinese). Shanghai: People Publishing House of Shanghai and Sanlian Bookstore.

Lu, F. 2001. "China: Probing Into the Second Era of Anti-poverty Strategy." Working Paper (No. C2001004) of China Center for Economic Research, Beijing University.

Park, A., and S. Wang. 2001. "China's Poverty Statistics." *China Economic Review* 12:384–398.

Rozelle, S., L. Zhang, and J. Huang. 2000. "China's War on Poverty." Working Paper No. 60, Center for Economic Research on Economic Development and Policy Reform, Stanford Institute for Economic Policy Research, Stanford University.

Schultz, T.W. 1978. *Distortions of Agricultural Incentives*. Bloomington, IN: Indiana University Press.

Sen, A. 2003. "On the Challenge of the Concept of Inequality and Poverty." *China Economic Quarterly* (in Chinese) 2(2):257–270.

Stern, N. 2003. "Public Policy for Growth and Poverty Reduction." *CESifo Economics Studies* 49, 1/2003:5–25.

Survey Team in Rural China of National Statistic Bureau. 2004. *Poverty Monitoring Report of Rural China-2003* (in Chinese). Statistic Publishing House of China, Beijing.

Tian, Q. 2001. "China's New Urban-Rural Divide and Pitfalls for the Chinese Economy." *Canadian Journal of Development Studies* 22(1):165–190.

Tian, W., X. Wang, and F. Ke. 2003. "The Poverty Alleviation Role of Agriculture in China." Paper prepared for the *Roles of Agriculture International Conference,* 20–22 October, Rome, Italy.

World Bank. 2001. *World Development Report 2000/2001: Attacking Poverty*. New York: Oxford University Press.

Yang, D.T. 1999. "Urban-Biased Policies and Rising Income Inequality in China." *American Economic Review* 89(2). Papers and Proceedings of the One Hundred Eleventh Annual Meeting of the American Economic Association (May 1999): 306–310.

Yang, D.T., and F. Cai. 2000. "The Political Economy of China's Rural-Urban Divide." Working Paper No. 62, Center for Research on Economic Development and Policy Reform. Palo Alto, CA: Stanford University.

Yang, D.T., and H. Zhou. 1999. "Rural-Urban Disparity and Sectoral Labor Allocation in China." *Journal of Development Studies* 35(3):105–133.

Zhang, X.B. 2003. "Inequality of Education and Medical Insurance in China." *China Economic Quarterly* (in Chinese) 2(2):405–416.

Zhang Y., and X.Y. Liu. 2006. "Markitization and Rural Poverty in China: A Micro Perspective." Working paper (No.C 2006011) of the China Center for Economic Studies, Fudan University.

Zhu, L., and Z.Y. Jiang. 1994. *Work for Food and Poverty Relief* (in Chinese). Shanghai: People Publishing House of Shanghai and Sanlian Bookstore.

7

Turning Away from Dependence on the Economic System: Looking Forward and Back on the Reform of China's Health Care System

JOHN CAI

China's health care system has experienced fundamental changes since economic reforms began in 1978. The pre-reform health care system depended heavily on the planned economic system to ensure that it met the needs of the population. The current health care system, however, does not effectively integrate the demands of health care with the demands of the free market economy. This has caused problems and remains a significant challenge for health care reform. Following the interrelation between the health care and economic systems, this chapter summarizes the major themes in China's health care reform, its current problems, and future challenges.

Introduction

The scale of China's reform of its economic system beginning in 1978 has been by far the largest such change in human history. China's economic reform originated in rural areas, spreading from the agriculture sector to the manufacturing sector, service industries, and then other parts of the economy (Zhang 1998). China's health care reform, however, started later than the economic reforms. Because of the economic systems in place before and after the economic reforms, China has not yet been able to develop an independent health care system based on the need for health care. Therefore, in order to better understand the current problems of China's health care system, we need to trace its evolution in the context of China's economic system.

Economic Transitions with Chinese Characteristics: Social Change During Thirty Years of Reform, eds. Arthur Sweetman and Jun Zhang. Montreal and Kingston: McGill-Queen's University Press, Queen's Policy Studies Series.

Although China's health care system was dependent on the economic system both before and after the start of the economic reforms, its position relative to the economic system has shifted fundamentally with these reforms. Under the centralized system, China's national economy and standard of living were depressed. At that time, however, the health care system was a point of pride and was recognized as an example for other developing countries (Ge 2007). In contrast, since the process of decentralization and market orientation of the economy began in 1978, during which time China has achieved extraordinary success in improving its national economy and standard of living, new problems in the health care system have caused universal complaints. These two contrasting situations indicate that simply binding a nation's health care system to its economic system does not necessarily meet people's needs.

By tracing the interaction between the health care system and the economic system, this chapter explores the evolution of China's health care system before and after the economic reform, its current problems, and its need for further reform and development.

Changes in Demand Side: Dissolving and Rebuilding of the Risk-Sharing Mechanism

China's new health care system lacks a risk-sharing mechanism that is relatively independent from its economic system. Before the economic reform, China's health care system had a default risk-sharing function, which operated through three institutional arrangements.

First, the old health care system spread financial risk within an employment unit through employment-based health insurance. In urban areas, the Government Insurance Scheme (GIS) covered government employees and college students, while the Labour Insurance Scheme (LIS) covered full-time employees and their family members. Thus, the health-related financial risks were shared among people within the same employment unit. In rural areas, the Co-operative Medical System (CMS) helped spread the financial risks among the members of a rural commune.

Second, although the risk-sharing mechanism focused on a single employer or a single work unit, the financial risks were redistributed among many work units, industries, and regions due to the highly centralized government financing system, which was able to redistribute insurance funding to some extent.

Third, risk-sharing at that time also included the subsidization of health care providers through direct government funding and regulation of the price of health services, pharmaceuticals, and medical equipment. The government also provided financial subsidies to cover medical infrastructure, equipment, salaries, and public health in rural areas. These subsidies helped reduce the costs of health care and provided free health care to the needy (Ge 2007).

In sum, the former health care system included a risk-sharing mechanism that was highly dependent on the centralized economic planning system. The state-owned economy, the centralized government financial system, the public subsidies to health providers, and strict price regulation formed the foundation of this risk-sharing mechanism. When the economic reform eroded this foundation, the old risk-sharing mechanism lost its anchor.

Changes since 1978

The deterioration of the health care system started with the dissolving of its public financing mechanism. First, in the rural areas, the elimination of the traditional collective economy took away the funding source for the Co-operative Medical System. Afterwards, the Chinese government tried several times to reestablish the rural Co-operative Medical System without resolving the financing issue; thus, these efforts were unsuccessful. In 2003, the government began rebuilding and replacing the Co-operative Medical System. The New Co-operative Medical System was started with government funding in addition to a small contribution from participants (Liu and Rao 2006). Due to its limited funding, however, this new rural risk-sharing mechanism provides only a very limited function.

Moreover, in the urban areas, the public financing mechanism faced other challenges. The Government Insurance Scheme and the Labour Insurance Scheme already had financial sustainability problems before the economic reforms began. Meanwhile, the demand for health services had increased rapidly during this period, resulting in serious problems of low efficiency and waste. Both government and employers had problems providing sufficient funding to match the escalating health care expenditures. After the economic reforms, the central government's share of fiscal revenue dropped substantially, and the government could not maintain its previous support and obligations for welfare systems, including health care (CNSB 2007). The financial independence of businesses freed the government from its unlimited financial responsibility to these firms; however, the old state-owned enterprises have more retirees, which has caused difficulties maintaining the Labour Insurance Scheme. In addition, the old state-owned enterprises also had problems with poor management and had to go through costly industry transformations. Thus, the economic reforms took away the original financial foundation of the traditional risk sharing mechanisms in urban areas (Gu et al. 2006).

The dissolution of the old risk-sharing system is reflected in the changes in the financial structure of China's health care expenditures. Health care expenditure per capita increased 43 times between 1978 and 2005—from 15 yuan to 662 yuan per capita (in nominal terms). Its share in GDP increased from 3.0 percent in 1978 to 4.7 percent in 2005. At the same time, however, out-of-pocket payment of health care expenditures increased 114 times—from 3 to 346 yuan per capita. The personal share of health expenditures in total health expenditures increased from 20 percent in 1978 to 52 percent in 2005. Yet government health expenditures increased only 23 times and dropped from 32 percent to 18 percent of total costs. The social insurance payment of health expenditures increased 27 times, and its share also declined from 48 percent to 30 percent of total costs (see Table 1).

TABLE 1
Growth of China's Health Care Expenditures, 1978–2005

	1978		*2005*		*1978–2005*
Expenditures	*Per Capita Expenditure*	*Percent of Total Costs*	*Per Capita Expenditure*	*Percent of Total Costs*	*Increase in Expenditure*
Total	15 yuan	100%	662 yuan	100%	43 times
Government	5 yuan	32%	119 yuan	18%	23 times
Social	7 yuan	48%	197 yuan	30%	27 times
Personal	3 yuan	20%	346 yuan	52%	114 times
GDP per capita	381 yuan		14,103 yuan		36 times
Health expenditures as % of GDP	3.0%		4.7%		0.6 times

Note: Prices are in nominal terms.

Source: China's Ministry of Health (2007).

The dissolution of the old risk-sharing mechanism reached bottom in 2000 when the government share of total health expenditures dropped to its lowest point since the economic reforms began—15.5 percent. In 2001, the personal share of health expenditures reached a peak of 60 percent. By the end of the 1990s, China had started rebuilding its risk-sharing mechanism: establishing the urban Employment Insurance Scheme (EIS) in 1998, and developing the New Co-operative Medical Scheme (NCMS) in 2003, the Medical Assistance System (MAS) in 2005, and the Urban Resident Insurance Scheme (URIS) in 2007 (Chen 2007b). Thus, since 2000, there has been renewed interest in the funding of risk-sharing mechanisms.

The share of out-of-pocket payment in the current financing structure, however, is still as high as 52 percent, still far above that of a reasonable risk-sharing structure. Therefore, China still has a long way to go, even though the restructuring of its health care financing mechanism has started moving forward. Revitalized risk-sharing mechanisms can provide effective support and protection for China's market-oriented economic system, but they do not have to take the extreme form of exclusively market-oriented mechanisms. If health care financing is to be spread evenly throughout the whole country, then the role of the market will be even more limited. There is great variety in the arrangements of risk sharing in different countries. China needs to explore a specific arrangement that serves its situations and needs.

Changes on the Supply Side: Financial Incentives and Rapid Development

Changes to the financing of health care reflect changes to the provision of health care. Before the economic reforms, the centralized public-owned economic system and the government fiscal system provided the financial basis for the government to subsidize health care institutions. The government health budget provided financial support for labour and construction expenditures of health care institutions. Under this centralized and subsidized system, health care institutions did not need to and were also not allowed to make profits from patients.

The spirit of decentralization and market-oriented economic reform, however, spread gradually from agriculture to manufacture and service industries and, in some ways, to health care. To a considerable extent, the government withdrew financial support from health care institutions, pushing them into the free market system and forcing them to support their own operations. Currently, government funding accounts for only about 10 percent of the total revenues of health care institutions, which thus have to generate the remaining 90 percent from patients. Thus, although about three-quarters of hospitals are still publicly owned, and about 80 percent of health care employees work in the public institutions, these institutions, especially the hospitals, have in fact become self-reliant economic entities in the market, at least from the perspective of financing (CMH 2007).

A Mixed Dual System

Mixed dual arrangements are now standard features of the organizational structure of health care institutions in China. On one hand, most health care institutions still keep the centralized administrative management system carried over from the centralized planning economy, especially for selecting their management teams. On the other hand, institutions have become independent economic entities and generate most of their revenue from the market. This type of dual arrangements has led to peculiar behaviour: institutions have a very strong financial incentive to generate revenue from the market and patients, but they also prefer to spend their revenues on infrastructure construction instead of raising salaries. The unreasonably low pay in the health care sector, lower than government employees on average, provides strong incentives for medical staff to make up their income from patients. In this way, health care institutions have become an extremely powerful revenue-generating machines (Cai et al. 2007).

In addition to dual arrangements, the organization of China's health care institutions has another important feature: physicians, hospitals, pharmaceutical companies, and testing facilities are part of an economic community that shares common financial interests and objectives. Therefore, physicians have a financial interest in admitting more patients into hospitals, keeping them there longer, and using more expensive drugs and tests. In 2005, the 9,643 state-owned hospitals generated 53 percent of their revenues from drugs and tests, which were partly used to compensate their physicians' income (CMH 2007). Therefore, the dual arrangement provides health care institutions and their employees with a financial incentive to generate revenue, while the health care organization structure provides them with powerful revenue-generating tools.

The significant reduction in government funding forced health care institutions to turn to the market, which has in turn expanded their financial resources and led to the rapid growth of health care resources and services. From 1978 to 2006, the total number of health care institutions increased by 82 percent, from 170,000 to 310,000. The total number of hospitals more than doubled, from about 9,000 to 19,000. At the same time, the total number of hospital beds increased 1.3 times, from 110,000 in 1978 to 256,000 in 2006. The total number of health personnel and physicians also increased by 81 percent and 93 percent respectively. Since the total population increased by only 37 percent during this period, health care resources per capita have increased substantially relative to the general population (see Table 2).

TABLE 2
Growth of Health Care Resources in China, 1978–2006

	1978	*2006*	*Rate of Growth 1978–2006*
Number of Health Care Institutions	169,732	308,969	82%
Number of Hospitals	9,293	19,246	107%
Number of Beds in Health Care Institutions (10,000)	204	351	72%
Number of Beds in Hospitals (10,000)	110	256	133%
Number of Health Care Personnel (10,000)	311	562	81%
Number of Doctors (10,000)	103	199	93%
Total Population (10,000)	96,259	131,448	37%

Source: China's Ministry of Health (2007).

Issues of Concern: Affordability and Equity

Lack of affordability (*Kan Bin Gui*) and access (*Kan Bin Nan*) are the two major and related problems under current China's health care system. China's total health expenditures accounted for 4.7 percent of GDP, and the health expenditure per capita was 662 yuan in 2005 (CMH 2007). These aggregate and per capita levels of health expenditures were consistent with China's economic development (WHO 2006). Thus, the affordability / accessibility problem is not at the macro and aggregate level, but rather at the structural level, i.e., in the financing structure of health care. The risks related to illness and medical needs are extremely unevenly distributed among the population, and there is always a small population that needs substantial medical resources and health expenditures at certain times (Berk and Monheit 2001). Therefore, the affordability / accessibility problem is unavoidable without an effective risk-sharing mechanism to spread health care costs between the sick and the healthy.

Several weaknesses in the urban Employment Insurance Scheme (EIS) contribute to the affordability / accessibility problem. Since the EIS covers only employees in formal employment, in 2007, it had about 190 million people enrolled (Han, 2007). Government regulation requires the minimum level of EIS premium to be equivalent to 8 percent of the employee's salary, of which 2 percent is contributed by employees and 6 percent by the employers (CSC 1998). Based on the average employee income in 2000, the average EIS premium for the basic medical insurance coverage is estimated to be about 1,000 yuan per person. Because per capita health expenditures for urban populations in 2005 were 1,123 yuan, the EIS premium covers only about 90 percent of medical costs, and the remaining 10 percent is covered by out-of-pocket payments (CMH 2007).

But family members of EIS employees, contract and informal city labourers, and the urban unemployed are not covered by the EIS. Thus, the EIS is estimated to cover only about one-third of urban residents. In addition, a huge migrant population, about 200 million people, currently live in China's urban areas, and about 120 million of them work in the cities (Hu 2007). This huge migrant population is not covered by any urban health insurance plan, except for a very small number covered by a component of EIS that covers catastrophic illnesses and events. The government planned to extend health insurance to all urban populations through the Urban Resident Insurance Scheme (URIS) starting in 2007 (Hu 2007). In 2008, the URIS has been tested in many cities. Only in a few large cities, such as Shanghai, however, is the insured population extensive, and there are huge variations across different regions (SASS 2007).

Problems in the rural insurance scheme affect affordability and accessibility in the countryside. By 2007, about 80 percent of rural residents were covered by the New Co-operative Medical Scheme (NCMS) (Chen

2007a). The minimum premium is 50 yuan per person, of which 40 yuan is provided by the government (Liu and Rao 2006). The premium level is higher in more developed areas (Wagstaff 2006). But based on the per capita health expenditure in rural areas, this minimum premium level covers only about 15 to 20 percent of medical costs of the rural population. Therefore, although the rural population covered by NCMS is at a very high level, the limited funding prevents any reduction of financial risks and fails to resolve the affordability issue. The government plans to increase its subsidy from the current 40 to 80 yuan per person in 2008; but this is still far below the level needed to reduce the financial risks for the rural population (Chen 2007a).

Without providing sufficient funding for health insurance and increasing the level of risk sharing, expanding coverage by itself cannot effectively resolve the affordability problem. The level of financing of health insurance needs to be raised to match the increase in average income. It is also important to increase efficiency in the use of these premiums. With the current low level of financing, the Medical Saving Account of the urban EIS restricts the effective use of the financial resources and risk sharing (Yip and Hsiao 1997). In addition, significant premium surpluses in many regions suggest that insurance resources are not being used efficiently and effectively (Han 2007).

Urban/Rural Inequities

Furthermore, the equity issue in China's health care system is reflected typically in the differences in per capita health expenditures, medical resources, and people's health status between urban and rural populations. In 2006, about four times more per capita was spent on urban populations than on rural populations in China (1,200 vs. 300), which is greater than the difference in per capita income (13,000 vs. 5,000 yuan) (CMH, 2007). This difference also indicates that affordability is a more serious problem for the rural population than for the urban population. The medical personnel and hospital bed to population ratios in urban areas are double those in rural areas. More important, there are huge differences in the indicators of health status between rural and urban populations. In 2005, the new-born mortality rate (14.7 vs 7.5 per 1,000), the infant mortality rate (21.6 vs. 9.1 per 1,000), the under-five mortality rate (25.7 vs. 10.7 per 1,000), and the maternal mortality rate (53.8 vs. 25.0 per 1,000) in rural areas are all about double those in urban areas (CMH 2007).

Future Directions: Reconstructing a New Health Care System

Dissatisfaction with health care has gradually accumulated into a movement in China which is demanding reform. Analysis of the old system, and proposed designs for a new one have concentrated on the relationship and roles of government and the market (Gu et al. 2006). Main-stream opinion believes that most of the current problems in health care are due to market-oriented reforms and the withdrawal of government funding. It argues that the market-oriented health care reform has been a complete failure, and that the government should take a leading role in a new health care reform initiative (Ge 2007).

This pro-reform, anti-market movement bases its objections on some special features of health care—that is, the nature of "public goods" and the role of "asymmetric information" in a market-oriented system. Yet, an opposing movement argues in favour of the market approach and the monopoly power enjoyed by large public hospitals. It argues that the current problems in health care have not been caused by its market orientation, because there has been no real market competition in health care yet. This movement believes that the government is already playing a dominant role in health care by regulating market entry, labour migration, and insurance reimbursement, all of which favour the monopoly power of large public hospitals and impede market competition. Thus, the market forces in China's health care reform are not said to be too strong, but rather too weak (Zhou 2007–8). This pro-market view is held by many economists and private business people.

In fact, both sides are right to some extent, because China is facing both issues at the same time. On the one hand, given that China now bases its economic system almost entirely on market principles, can it base its health care system on the old government-controlled system? On the other hand, can China's health care system completely ignore the population's need for health care and conduct exclusively market-oriented reforms? The answer to both questions is negative. China should pursue a new health care reform that embraces both the special features of health care and considers how it might operate most efficiently within the current economic system.

In health care, we can neither simply reject market forces and replace all market forces with government regulation, nor can we simply open the door to market forces without adequate preparation and protection. When market forces come into health care, governments face more serious challenges and have more difficulties in managing and regulating health care than under a public system. Therefore, a good system considers what kinds of market forces and government regulations are available. Market forces and government regulations have to be balanced, especially in health care. If the government can understand market forces and match government regulations to the desired outcomes of the health care system, then more powerful market forces might be tolerable and beneficial in health care (Cai 2007).

Current Reform Initiatives

The main direction of China's new national health care reform has become apparent, although its details have not been published so far (Chen

2007b). In the area of financing, three types of health insurance schemes will take the dominant roles: the urban Employment Insurance Scheme (EIS), the Urban Resident Insurance Scheme (URIS), and the New Collective Medical Scheme (NCMS) (Hu 2007). In the area of funding sources, EIS will be financed completely by employer and employee contributions, without any government support. In contrast, the other two insurance schemes will rely on the government as the major funding source; however, the overall funding level for these two schemes is very low. In addition, the Medical Assistance System has not formed an independent insurance scheme. It receives a low level of funding and provides inconsistent medical assistance to low-income people. Yet with the implementation and improvement of these three insurance schemes as well as the medical assistance system, the government's share of total health care expenditures will increase significantly. In addition to providing direct funding, the government must play a dominant role, especially in organizing the funding system, in order to ensure the success of the reforms.

The government is currently playing a weak and limited role in health care financing. It has no effective, developed approach for reimbursing different medical services and products based on their efficiency and quality, except for controlling the total reimbursement amount. In order to improve the reimbursement, China needs to establish an infrastructure for health information technology and develop various payment methodologies and performance measures. It also needs to improve the regulation of insurance funding, increase openness and transparency, increase public monitoring, and improve the effectiveness of its funding.

As for health care provision, the government is pushing for the reconstruction of the basic medical care system by setting up community health clinics and increasing investment substantially (Zamiska 2008). Its goal is to consolidate public health and disease prevention, to treat and manage common and chronic diseases in a timely and consistent manner, to reduce severe illness and medical costs, and to improve people's health. Nevertheless, its success is highly dependent on whether this system can attract patients, play the gatekeeper role in managing people's health and illness, and improve its efficiency in utilizing resources.

While the primary care system is the government's current focus, large public hospitals still play a dominant role in the current system because they have the best personnel and equipment, which attracts the most patients and funding. Although the number of private hospitals has been increasing in recent years, they are unable to compete with large public hospitals on many levels. In addition to the disadvantage of competing for medical personnel, private hospitals also do not receive reimbursement from social health insurance schemes, which gives them a serious competitive disadvantage. Meanwhile, while public hospitals have become more market-oriented institutions with revenue-generating activities, they have managed to stay within the centralized planning management system and therefore lack the management autonomy of private hospitals. Since large public hospitals are currently overcrowded, they have no incentive to improve the quality of service, which causes serious complaints from patients. Public hospitals remain islands in the system, still shielded from reform. A clear direction for further reform of public hospitals is needed. Despite the overcrowded conditions, most people favour keeping these hospitals under government control (Cai et al. 2008).

Resource Use, Expenditure Control, and Quality Control

While most Chinese see affordability as the major problem with the current system, improvements to the financing structure should be able to resolve the affordability issue in time. The effectiveness of resource use, control of health care expenditures, and safety and quality of health care services, however, are going to become more pressing long-term problems.

The effectiveness of resource use is closely related to payment approaches, the price structure, and the economic evaluation of medical technology. The current retrospective fee-for-services payment approach encourages rapid increases in services volume and health expenditures. The current price structure in China's health care is reflected in the under-use of health care personnel and over-use of drugs and tests (DRC 2005). Comparing medical services and products and relating them to their costs and benefits, however, will help focus expenditures on services and products that work. Indiscriminate over-utilization of new technology and interventions contributes to the rapid increase in health expenditures without necessarily improving health (US CBO 2008). The government has to take an active leadership role in technology evaluation, as is the pattern in many other countries.

In addition, all health care systems must control health care expenditures (Feldstein 2007). On the one hand, China needs to reduce out-of-pocket payments and the financial risks caused by high medical costs. On the other hand, it also has to pay attention to the rising pressure on health care expenditures caused by the expanded coverage of health insurance. Since out-of-pocket payments still account for over 50 percent of total health expenditures, the rapid increase in health costs has not become a pressing issue for the government yet. This is going to change, however, with the declining share of out-of-pocket payments under current and proposed reforms (Newhouse et al. 1993). The control of health care costs is also related to the design features of health insurance—what services and products are covered, and what payment level and payment approach are used. The control of health care costs also depends on effective resource use. Providing people with information on cost/benefits and quality of medical services and products will help to improve effectiveness of resource use and reduce waste.

Finally, the safety and quality of health services depend on the availability of information as well as on incentive mechanisms. How to develop incentives for health care providers is a challenging issue faced by every health care system in the world. China's current arrangement unwittingly provides a strong financial incentive for health care providers to use more and expensive medical services and products. This counterproductive consumer protection arrangement hurts patient interests because it also protects medical professionals from blame during medical accidents. Therefore, the reform of incentives for providers is also an important task in China's health care reform.

Conclusion

The important challenge faced by China's health care reform is to free itself from direct dependence on the economic system and become a relatively independent health care system which embraces market-oriented mechanisms as well as the public interest in health care. The emerging trend of international health care reform is one of differentiating two basic components of a health care system: the role of government in financing health care and ensuring equal access, and the role of competition and market forces in providing health services (Chernichovsky 1995 and 2002; Gu et al. 2006, Cai 2006 and 2007). The public and social feature of health care financing helps it achieve social equity and macro-efficiency, while competitive and market-oriented provision helps it improve micro-efficiency and patient satisfaction. China's long-range task is to match this principle to China's specific situation and to establish a new health care system adapted to China's future.

References

Berk, M.L., and A.C. Monheit. 2001. "The Concentration of Health Care Expenditures, Revisited," *Health Affairs*, March / April 2001:9–18.

Cai, J. 2006. "Where is China's Health Care Reform Heading to?" *Jie Fang Daily* (Shanghai, China), November 19:8.

——— 2007. "Market Force: Hero vs. Evil for China's Health Care Reform." *Chinese Social Security* 6:24–25.

Cai, J., S. Hu, C. Huang, and L. Zhang. 2007. "Social Market Cooperative Model: A New Concept for the Reform Of China's Health Care System." *World Economic Papers* 1:1–9.

Cai., J., and the Fudan project team. 2008. *This Separation, Not That Separation: Foreign Experience of Public Hospital Reform, China Health Reform Review*, No. 2, May 9. Beijing: China Health Care Reform Program, National Council of China Economic System Reform.

Chen, X. 2007a. "Further Improving the New Rural Cooperative Medical System." *Economic Daily*, December 6. Available at www.moh.gov.cn.

——— 2007b. "State Council Report on Urban and Rural Health System Reform and Improving Monitory of Food and Drug safety." The 31st Conference of Standard Committee, 10th National People's Congress, December 26.

Chernichovsky, D. 1995. "Health System Reforms in Industrialized Economies: An Emerging Paradigm." *The Milbank Quarterly* 73(3):339–372.

——— 2002. "Pluralism, Choice, and the State in the Emerging Paradigm in Health Systems." *The Milbank Quarterly* 80(1):5–40.

China's National Statistic Bureau (CNSB). 2007. *2007 China Economic Statistic Yearbook*, China Statistics Press.

China's State Council (CSC). 1998. "State Council's Decision on Establishing Basic Medical Insurance System for Urban Employees." State Council Document No. 44.

China's Ministry of Health (CMH). 2007. *2007 China Health Statistic Yearbook*. China's Union Medical University Press.

Feldstein, P. 2007. *Health Policy Issues, An Economic Perspective*, 4th Ed. Chicago, IL: Health Administration Press.

Ge, Y and S. Gong . 2007. *China's Health Care Reform: Problems, Roots and Solutions*. Beijing: China Development Press.

Gu, X., M. Gao, and Y. Yao. 2006. *Diagnosis and Prescription: The Reform of China's Health Care System*. Beijing: Social Science Publishing.

Han, F. 2007. "Speeding Health Information Technology and Improving Health Insurance and Management System." The Second Health and Information Summit, November, Shanghai.

Hu, X. 2007. "Vice Minister of Labor and Social Insurance Hu Xiaoyi's Introduction on the Basic Medical Insurance of Chinese Urban Residents." *China State Council News Press* (Beijing). August 15.

Liu, Y., and K. Rao. 2006. "Providing Health Insurance in Rural China: From Research to Policy." *Journal of Health Politics, Policy and Law* 31(1), February:71–92.

Newhouse and the Insurance Experiment Group. 1993. *Free for All? Lessons from the RAND Health Insurance Experiment*. Cambrige, MA: Harvard University Press.

Shanghai Academy of Social Science (SASS). 2007. *2006 Survey of Shanghai Population's Health and Health Care Services*. Shanghai: Shanghai Academy of Social Science.

US Congressional Budget Office (US CBO). 2008. *Technological Change and the Growth of Health Care Spending*, January.

Wagstaff, A. 2006. "Health Reform in Rural China." Presentation at the Harvard China Review 9th Annual Conference, Harvard University, May.

World Health Organization (WHO). 2006. *World Health Report 2006*.

Yip, W.C., and W.C. Hsiao. 1997. "Medical Savings Accounts: Lessons from China", *Health Affairs*16(6), November/December:244–251.

——— 2008. "Chinese Health System at a Crossroads." *Health Affairs* 27(2), March/April:460–468.

Zamiska, N. 2008. "China Thinks Small in Prescription for Health Care: Primary-Care Clinics to Become First Stop in Revitalizing System." *The Wall Street Journal*, March 11.

Zhang, J. 1998. *History and Analysis of China's Economic Reform*. Taiyuan: Shanxi Economic Press.

Zhou, Q. 2007–8. "Series of Review on Health Care Reform." China Economic Research Center, Beijing University. Available at www.ccer.edu.cn.

8

Demographic Change and Economic Reform

ZHENG WU, CHRISTOPH M. SCHIMMELE, AND SHUZHUO LI

The post-Maoist leadership believed that China's rapid population growth would disrupt its economic development and modernization plans. Hence, China implemented a one-child-per-couple rule in 1979, which was designed to counterbalance foodgrain shortages and increase living standards through strict regulation of birth rates. In this respect, the economic reforms and population policies constitute a dual process of development. The one-child rule has had far-reaching demographic effects, altering China's long-term sex-age structure. The one-child rule paid a demographic dividend that facilitated China's economic success, but this gain came with steep socio-political costs.

Introduction

In 1979, China implemented a strict program of population control, regulating reproductive behaviours and birth rates under a one-child policy. This policy has had far-reaching demographic effects, including an alteration of the age-sex structure of China's population. The fundamental rational for the one-child policy was a neo-Malthusian interpretation of population growth. Chinese economic planners believed that population growth would outpace agricultural production, which created grave concerns about national food security and the prospects for economic development and modernization. The Chinese population almost doubled during the Maoist era (1949–1976), and chronic grain shortages and the economic disaster of the Great Leap Forward intensified the political-economic need to resolve China's population question. After Chairman Mao's death in 1976, the reformist state's answer was the institution of a one-child-per-couple standard, which prevented 300 million births, according to official accounts. This chapter provides an overview of the evolution of the one-child policy, its relationship to the economic reform process, and its major demographic consequences.

Economic Transitions with Chinese Characteristics: Social Change During Thirty Years of Reform, eds. Arthur Sweetman and Jun Zhang. Montreal and Kingston: McGill-Queen's University Press, Queen's Policy Studies Series.

Economic Rationale for Population Control

In China, the basic motivation for stringent population control policies is inseparable from the economic reform process that started in the late 1970s (Liu and Wu 1979). The economic reforms, of course, were implemented to settle the developmental problems that emerged under Chairman Mao's leadership, including the prolonged stagnation of agricultural production, the general lack of modernization, and all-around low economic growth. The commune system generated a more equitable distribution of land, resources, and agricultural produce, an important achievement, but it made deficient strides toward improving per capita income (the average standard of living) or transforming China into a modernized, industrial nation (Goldstein 1996). The Deng Xiaoping administration was certain that China's population question was a fundamental vector of national economic prospects and its modernization goals (White 2006). Hence, the post-Mao regime approached the issue of unchecked population growth (or the threat of overpopulation) as a definite impediment to further social and economic development, and indeed as an imminent condition for another economic disaster similar to the Great Famine of 1959–1961 (Scharping 2003).

This emphasis on the putative economic burden of overpopulation represented a radical departure from Maoist principles, instituting a neo-Malthusian logic into the process of economic reform (Wang and Mason 2008). To be sure, population planning efforts pre-date the reform era, but prior to 1970, the Chinese government did not confront the population question as an *economic* challenge in such unequivocal terms (White 2006). Most earlier population planning policies were, at least in the official justification, implemented as social welfare policies, and focused on issues such as maternal health, child well-being, and the difficulties of educating an increasing number of school-age children (Scharping 2003). While some pundits voiced concern about the effect of a large, increasing population on developmental indicators, the official reasons for Mao-era birth policies side-stepped the exigencies of economic growth per se. Moreover, following Marxist doctrine, Mao at first declared that China's large population base was a great productive asset, and thus discounted Malthusian arguments as groundless, bourgeois economics. In September 1949, Mao remarked that "revolution plus production can solve the problem of feeding the population," which represented an ideological position that birth control advocates would often confront throughout the Maoist era (cited in Tien 1973, 179). Hence, whilst Chinese leaders acknowledged the practical importance of population management during the 1950s, traditional pro-natal attitudes and Communist politics foiled a coherent, sustained campaign of national population control (birth planning) until the Great Leap economic crisis and food disaster made it impossible to side-step the population question (White 2006).

Whether high population growth is an actual barrier to economic development is a matter of disagreement in development debates (Johnson 1999). The literature suggests that although a large population can have negative or repressive effects on economic development, these problems are often surmountable in the long-term via careful institutional adjustments (Johnson and Lee 1987). That said, low population growth appears to be the preferable option, because most underdeveloped countries are ill-positioned to introduce the institutional arrangements needed to counteract the economic and ecological pressures of high population growth. Though controversial, the neo-Malthusian or extremist interpretation of overpopulation dominated the development discourse for several decades. In essence, the neo-Malthusian perspective argues that rapid population growth has a depressive or regressive effect on economic development inasmuch as it decreases the economic surpluses available for capital investments and intensifies demographic pressures on land, food supplies, water, and non-renewable resources. In their classic volume on Indian economic underdevelopment, Ansley Coale and E.M. Hoover (1958) argued for a model of economic development that involves a slow-down of population growth. Coale and Hoover concluded that decreasing fertilities in low-income countries represented a practical formula for raising per capita household income and also redirecting national economic output from personal consumption (human needs) into productive activities. In these neo-Malthusian terms, high population growth slows or retards economic development because personal consumption curtails the economic surpluses available for investing in infrastructure, industrial development, and national welfare initiatives.

The popular success of Paul Ehrlich's (1968) *The Population Bomb*, which predicted that global population growth would result in famines on a cataclysmic scale, epitomized the international pre-occupation with a pessimistic attitude toward overpopulation. Though such apocalyptic demographic predictions proved to be inaccurate, there is little dispute about the pervasive influence of neo-Malthusianism among international development agencies, politicians, and policy-makers. As Seltzer (2002) observes, a demographic rationale was an essential motivation behind the origins of population planning campaigns throughout the Third World. In China, the post-Mao leadership adopted a similar rationale for resolving the Chinese population question, which culminated in the implementation of the infamous one-child policy (Johnson 1999). There is little evidence to refute the idea that Chinese leaders believed that population control and economic development was a dual process. In contrast to Maoist policies, the explicit objective of reform era population control efforts was to facilitate the post-Revolution mandate of increasing per capita income and financing the Four Modernizations (Wang and Mason 2008). The Marriage Law (1980) and the Chinese constitution (1982) transformed the post-Mao administration's political stance toward the population question into a *de jure* institution (Attané 2002). For example, the Chinese constitution specifies that the official motivation for the national population planning policies is ensuring the success of economic reform (Xie 2000).

Perhaps the neo-Malthusian perspective overstated the problem, but it is clear that the post-Mao leadership inherited an economic dilemma that intersected with inadequate policies to limit population growth (Liu and Wu 1979). For most of the Maoist era, China's annual population growth rate remained well above 2 percent (Hussain 2002). The total fertility rate (TFR), or average number of children per woman, was the major impetus behind this alarming rate of population growth. Except for the famine-related declines of 1960–1962, the Chinese TFR averaged over 6 from 1949 to 1971, demonstrating the ineffectiveness of birth planning policies under Mao's leadership (see Figure 1). The Chinese population, as a consequence, almost doubled between the founding of the People's Republic and the eve of economic reforms, increasing from 500 to 900 million (Liu and Wu 1979). The economic debacles of the Great Leap Forward (1958–1960) and Cultural Revolution (1966–1976) compounded the situation, demanding an effective response to China's population question. The Cultural Revolution's fanatical objective of blocking a resurgence of capitalism and purging China of bourgeois ideas almost led to

FIGURE 1
Total Fertility Rate: China, 1950–2000

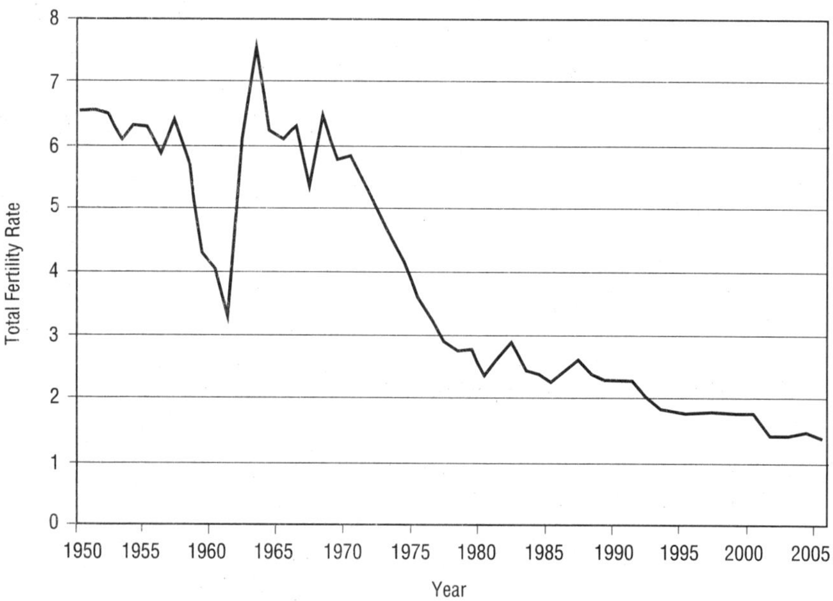

Sources: Sun and Jin (1994); Wang, Wang, He, and Duan (2004); National Population and Family Planning Commission (2006).

an economic collapse (Xie 2000). In this aftermath, most Chinese people desired an increase in their living standards, which prompted a return to economic concerns and abandonment of the class struggle agenda (Wang 1996; White 2006).

Post-Maoist economic planners faced a populace discontent with their living conditions, including housing shortages and overcrowding, inadequate public infrastructure, and deficient educational facilities (White 2006). Their general attention, however, was directed onto China's low per capita gross national product (GNP). The basic objective of the economic reforms was to quadruple GNP between 1980 and 2000 (Xie 2000). As Wang (1996) indicates, economic planners can elevate per capita GNP through increasing the numerator (the total national product) or reducing the denominator, i.e., the population base. Wang observes that a similar numerator / denominator approach was the theoretical foundation of post-Maoist Chinese population control policies. The promise of achieving GNP targets, and thus improving living standards, could not be accomplished without implementing TFR restrictions. Under the scenario of economic reform, Chinese planners anticipated that standards of living could continue to improve provided that the population did not grow by more than 300 million from 1980 to 2000 (Xie 2000). Their demographic objective was thus concrete. For 2000, a ceiling of 1.2 million persons was set, and subsequent Chinese population planning efforts aimed at a TFR of under 1.7 to achieve this target (Wang 1996). The slogan of "One Couple, One Child" promoted this goal, and reflected the strong neo-Malthusian undercurrent in the post-Maoist economic order.

Evolution of Population Planning

As White (2006) details, the seedbed for stringent fertility controls was laid throughout the 1952–1970 period. Albeit somewhat tenuous and opposed for ideological reasons, Maoist era demographic policies were crucial for establishing a political foundation for the controversial one-child-per-couple standard. These earlier policies were not, however, prototypes for the one-child-per-couple standard, which was what White (2006, 7) describes as the "logical and radical outcome" of a long-term national birth planning (*jihua shengyu*) effort. Though pro-natalism, an attitude grounded in Marxist politics and traditional values, muddied this effort, there were almost continuous discussions about the relationship between population planning and economic development (socialist industrialization) throughout the Maoist era. Adherence to Marxist doctrine prevented neo-Malthusianism from gaining a stable foothold before 1970, but Chinese Communist Party (CCP) officials, including Mao, could not ignore the population question. Hence, starting in 1952, the CCP began a reversal of its pro-natalist position.

During the 1952–1970 period, there were several key phases of the population control effort, including a campaign of birth control, the emergence of birth planning, the Great Leap interruption, and then a resurgence and gradual deepening of birth planning after the Great Leap disaster (see Scharping 2003; Tien 1973; White 2006). As noted, the PRC began upon a pro-natalist note, viewing population as an asset, not a burden, for China's prospects. In September 1949, Mao (Zedong 1975, 452) emphasized this view point, remarking that "it is a very good thing that China has a big population. Even if China's population multiplies many times, she is capable of finding a solution; the solution is production." This pro-natal idea would be echoed in later official pronouncements about population numbers, but, as Tien (1973) notes, these later statements appeared to be an ideological denouncement of neo-Malthusianism, rather than a practical stance against birth control per se. Though retaining a strong anti-Malthusian position, Mao would lose some confidence in his original pronouncements, observing that while a large population base is a good thing, it also presents serious contractions that cannot be corrected through a production-based solution alone (see MacFarquhar, Cheek, and Wu, 1989).

The earliest discussions of the population question after 1949 concerned the effects of China's imbalanced geographic distribution of population (Tien 1973). The bulk of the Chinese population (525 million) were peasants concentrated in traditional agricultural regions, which resulted in both high and low person-to-land ratios across China. For the moment, population size remained an indirect issue for the CCP; the population question was interpreted as a need to stabilize urban growth and deploy industrial and agricultural labor in a rational manner. That is, the population question was peripheral to the question about how to achieve the socialist transformation (White 2006). The concerns over the unbalanced distribution of labour, however, could not evade the problem of population size itself. Tien (1973) argues that only a limited, short-term solution could be achieved in population redistribution (planned migration) and land reclamation, which underscored the need for a population management initiative that went further than these efforts. The first direct references to population size were restrained, according to Tien, perhaps reflecting the anti-Malthusian attitude prevalent among CCP political elites; but the growing attention on population numbers initiated a national political debate that would engender a series of campaigns intended to slow population growth.

As White (2006) observes, the reversal of public commitment to a pronatalist stance occurred for several reasons, including a growing emphasis on comprehensive economic planning and subsequent uneasiness over agrarian development and potential shortages of food supplies. The first phase of slowing population growth focused on promoting birth control, stopping short of direct management of population growth. The economic planners, as White outlines, confronted two demographic-related problems that could derail the socialist transformation. The first problem was unemployment. Two million people were unemployed in 1952. The shortage of agriculture work prompted large-scale migration to urban areas, but these migrants could not be absorbed into the nascent industrial sector. Second, food shortages were common in the cities because of agricultural underdevelopment, which posed a serious threat to industrialization since secure (and inexpensive) supplies of foodgrains are needed to sustain the urban workforce. Facing these circumstances, the CCP started to shift its political position on population.

In 1953, the State Council directed the Ministry of Health to assist the masses in birth control (Tien 1973). The economic imperatives of birth control were buttressed because of pressure from elite women within the CCP, who pushed for greater access to contraception and abortion as a matter of individual rights (White 2006). Shao Li-tzu, a leading advocate of birth control, acknowledged Mao's original stance that a large population is a "good thing," but, stressing the health and welfare of mothers and children, insisted that limits on population size should be set (Tien 1973). Hence, even though the practical motivation for birth control was economic, the public justification remained a so-called health issue. In 1954, the Ministry of Health presented its first plan for controlling birth rates, just as a liberalization of contraceptive regulations was unfolding (White 2006). Birth control, however, remained a controversial issue, and advocates of population control still confronted socio-cultural resistance and serious reservations about its putative benefits (Tien 1973). There persisted, moreover, some optimism that China could indeed accommodate further population growth.

An adequate level of political support for birth control (and the rationale behind it) appears to have coalesced around late 1956 (Tien 1973). In February 1957, Chairman Mao provided a decisive endorsement of birth control in a speech to the State Supreme Council that outlined the numerous challenges of high population growth. Around this time, birth control emerged as an essential mechanism of population control, whereas before it was treated as an appropriate, but not a *requisite,* answer to China's population question. Mao insisted that China "need[ed] planned births" for similar reasons as China needed economic planning to coordinate labour and rationalize national production (cited in MacFarquhar et al. 1989). In this respect, Mao formulated birth control as an essential component of the general planning process. This marked the transition from an emphasis on birth control to a program of birth planning for developmental purposes, the second phase of population control during the Maoist era. In addition to its focus on actual birth control (promoting contraception), the concept of planned childbirth (preventing excess or unwanted pregnancies) was introduced at this time (White 2006). According to White, this was the catalyst for the "collectivization" of reproduction or the rationalization of child-bearing through sustained State intervention.

This initial birth planning effort would be interrupted in 1958 because of the dogmatic politics propelling the Great Leap Forward, which silenced questions about China's potential for rapid socialist development, and also the economic rationale for birth planning (White 2006). However, the economic fallout of the Great Leap disaster would concretize the practical need for integrating a national birth control plan with the State's economic objectives. In addition, political support for population control, as White observes, was galvanized through Mao's later commitment to birth control and his conceptualization of "births according to plan" as a *collective* need. This insulated the concept of birth planning from getting labeled as neo-Malthusian, a characterization that had denigrated earlier anti-natal policies. These politics aside, the revival of birth planning in 1962 was a response to poor agricultural production, and the Great Leap famine in particular. Whereas previous birth control efforts focused on a few cities, the revived program included all urban areas and began to extend its reach into rural areas, where most of the population resided.

The Great Leap Forward was Mao's inopportune attempt to achieve a rapid transition to socialist industrialization. The economic goals and production targets of the Great Leap were ill-planned and often unrealistic, and once for all revealed that agricultural production (grain output) was too underdeveloped to support large-scale industrial development (Peng 1987). Though natural disasters also had a significant effect, Great Leap policies, such as the reduction in grain-sown areas and the ill-timed diversion of agricultural labour into industrial production, caused grain supplies to plummet, resulting in 20–30 million famine-related deaths. Hence, the post-Leap revival of birth planning came from a realization that the tempo of agricultural production was far out of sync with population growth (White 2006). At this point, population control became an undisputed aspect of development. Targets were set for curbing population growth and promoted through better access to birth control, further public education about birth planning in rural areas, and a national campaign to promote late marriage, delayed childbearing, and a two-child-per-couple ideal.

The One-Child Policy

Despite population control efforts from 1952–1969, China's crude birth rate remained high. In fact, the natural increase of population was higher in the late 1960s and early 1970s than it was during the first years of the People's Republic (Liang and Lee 2006). In addition, a wide TFR gap persisted between urban and rural areas, exposing a huge crack in Mao-era birth control policies. In 1970, the TFR for rural China was 6.38, compared to 3.27 for urban China. As a consequence, the population growth rate did not decline too much before 1974, discounting the famine-related declines of 1959–1961 (Hussain 2002). In large part, the shortcomings of pre-1970 population control policies reflected the ambiguous political status of birth planning. For example, the Third Five-Year Plan

(1966–1970) excluded birth control targets, which prevented a mandate of population control within the cadres, i.e., the grassroots channels for implementing and overseeing a concerted program of restricting TFR (White 2006). Not until January 1970 did the Politburo recognize birth control as an economic issue per se (Scharping 2003). After this barrier was crossed, birth control became a cornerstone of economic planning.

However, the decline of the rural birth rate—which is a fundamental condition for population control in an agrarian country—started with the later-longer-fewer (*wan xi shao*) campaign. This slogan referred to *later* marriage and childbirth, *longer* intervals (4–5 years) between first and second births, and *fewer* total births per couple (Liang and Lee 2006). This campaign amounted to a two-child policy, in essence, because three children were labelled too many. The success of the later-longer-fewer campaign has led some critics to interpret the controversial one-child policy as unneeded, but Merli and Smith (2002) argue that this assessment miscalculates its far-reaching demographic effects. The authors point out that the difference between the TFR (1.5) prescribed under a one-child standard and the TFR (2–3) under the later-longer-fewer campaign is huge according to the goals of economic reform. The tighter birth control policy aimed for a long-term *reduction* in the population base, not just containment of population growth. The reforms were intended to improve living standards and foster modernization, which involved reducing the "denominator" in order to increase individual wealth and national investable surpluses.

In 1979, there was still considerable skepticism about Chinese agricultural production. Deng Xiaoping expressed his pessimism about grain output being sufficient for industrialization, lamenting that population growth would smother all prospects for economic development without tighter restrictions on birth rates (Scharping 2003). The later-longer-fewer campaign appeared to be an inadequate measure for either stabilizing or reducing the population base, particularly since large cohorts of 1960s baby boomers would enter reproductive age throughout the upcoming decade (White 2006). In this context, the planners readjusted their birth control goals, setting a population growth rate of 5 per 1000 in 1985 (down from the 9 per 1000 under the later-longer-fewer initiative) and zero population growth in 2000. As noted, the overarching goal was to prevent China's population from exceeding 1.2 billion, which implied a 1.7 TFR. Based on a controversial computer model of projected population growth, the TFR target was pegged at 1.0, leading to the implementation of the one-child-per-couple regulation in 1979–1980 (Greenhalgh 2003).

China's one-child policy (OPC) represented a historic socio-demographic engineering project. Chinese officials claim that the OCP prevented 300 million births (Peng 2004). The OCP was not a uniform, national program, however, as provincial authorities were responsible for implementing it according to local circumstances. Although the OCP started with a strict one-child limit—the original demand was that 95 percent of urban and 90 percent of rural women should have no more than one child—this rule was later relaxed (Scharping 2003). Scharping (2003) identifies several phases of the OCP, which reflect modifications to the one-child rule. The initial phase (1979–1983) was a period of no concessions: one-child families were to be the norm. Deng insisted that the Four Modernizations would fail if exceptions were made. In 1984, there was a relaxation of this position, doubling rural second-child permits from their original levels. This retreat from a hard line reflected popular resistance, and the OCP would go through subsequent revisions as officials attempted to better balance their goals with the needs and preferences of the people.

The immediate jump in the birth rate after the 1984 relaxation, however, made Chinese planners nervous about giving couples greater control over their reproductive behaviours (Merli and Smith 2002). This jump in births prompted a re-tightening of the OPC in order to prevent a collapse of population control targets. The Chinese government remains concerned about latent demand for children in rural areas, which could upset population control if the OCP was terminated. That being said, the current OCP is not a rigid one-child-per couple edict. As Peng (2004) illustrates, the current OCP involves multiple levels of regulation that are intended to accommodate different social and cultural conditions and local economic needs. Of course, the core regulation is a one-child-per-couple rule (with few exceptions), which applies to all urban residents and rural residents in Jiangsu and parts of Sichuan. This regulation, however, is relaxed for rural residents of other provinces if the first child is a girl, reflecting the need for male farm labour and a son for old-age support. Most rural residents are also permitted a second child with a four-year interval between births. In addition, ethnic minorities living in rural areas are permitted 2–3 children, and there is no regulation of birth in rural Tibet.

Gu and his coauthors (2007) demonstrate that the relaxation of the hard-line in 1984—the so-called "opening of small holes"—led to the localization of the OCP. This "opening of small holes" represented a more liberal approach to second births, but aimed to clamp down on third or higher order births, a principal reason for high population growth. This policy change was a response to the economic hardship the hard-line approach posed for agrarian households and poor families, as well as the repercussions of mass sterilization and forced abortion. The localization of the OCP, therefore, reflected the political limits of an overarching national agenda that was insensitive to local needs and socio-cultural preferences. Accordingly, the OCP is not uniform across China. To be sure, an orientation toward tight population control is the common theme, but there is interregional variation in its implementation, and even between-village differences in some cases. As indicated below, this variation is responsible for inter-provincial exceptions to the one-child rule, depending on factors such as the couple's ethnic status, economic need, and gender of their first-born child.

A carrot-and-stick approach is used to enforce the one-child rule. Couples that sign the one-child certificate are entitled to state benefits, including cash bonuses, better access to public childcare and education, health care subsidies, better housing, and foodgrain allotments (Wang 1996; White 2006). The reverse applies to out-of-plan births, with economic penalties for couples in violation of the one-child rule. The most ominous penalties are, of course, enforced sterilization and abortions. There has been grassroots resistance to the one-child rule and the draconian tactics of enforcement, leading to considerable non-compliance. The one-child rule and political objective of preventing third and higher order births was impossible to enforce in absolute terms (Attané 2002). Common strategies of resistance are outright evasion (concealing pregnancies), collusion between local cadres and peasants, and cover-up of true local-level birth rates by enforcement officers (White 2006). Hence, there are doubts about the accuracy of official fertility statistics because of underreporting of births (Scharping 2007).

The socio-cultural disdain for the one-child rule is illustrated in the State's decades-long struggle to contain out-of-plan births. The frequent modifications to the one-child rule reflected the political difficulties of attempting to force a sudden change in traditional reproductive behaviors. The core objective of reducing third and higher order births was, therefore, not achieved overnight. The OCP initiated a gradual normative shift in family size preferences, with a growing acceptance of within-plan ideals (Merli and Smith 2002). In 1980, third and higher order births accounted for 35 percent of total national fertility (Attané 2002). This declined to 25 percent in 1988 and 20 percent in 1995, illustrating the persistent resistance and gradual compliance to birth control regulations. In 2002, about 95 percent of all births were within-plan births, and the percentage of third or higher order births further declined to under 2 percent in 2003 (Zhang and Cao 2007).

Although there is high compliance among urban residents, the OCP has been less successful in rural areas, where son-preference and economic circumstances tend to inflate the number of children desired (Wang 1996). For example, socioeconomic underdevelopment increased second or higher order births from 1980-1985. This suggests socioeconomic development is a significant mediator of compliance to State population control policies. As Poston (2000) observes, part of China's TFR decline (and thus demographic transition) is attributable to economic development. The growing compliance to population control objectives, then, also represents individual-level responses to improving socioeconomic conditions. In general, social acceptance of the State's message about family planning remains stronger in developed regions than in underdeveloped, isolated areas (Merli and Smith 2002).

The OCP and Demographic Transition

China's radical approach to population control has had profound demographic effects. Though the OCP focused on reducing the national birth rate and curbing population growth, its demographic effects reached a lot further, with concomitant changes in population age-structure and sex ratios. This section reviews the major demographic implications of the OCP, including fertility trends, sex ratios at birth (SRB), and population aging.

Fertility Trends

The OCP amounts to a massive political effort to achieve a rapid demographic transition. The crude birth rate declined from 33 per 1000 in 1970 to 16 per 1000 in 1998, underlining the effectiveness of post-1960s population control policies (Merli and Smith 2002). Moreover, China reached a below replacement level (a TFR of under 2.1 children per woman) of fertility in 1992 (see Figure 1), which, if it persists, will involve a potential *contraction* of China's population base in future decades (Guo and Chen 2007). For example, under the present birth control regulations China's population will peak at 1.4 billion people in 2030, and then enter a period of population decline, reducing to 894 million people in around 2080 (Zeng, 2007). Official (2000) census figures indicate a national TFR of between 1.2 and 1.4, but expert reconstructions that account for underreporting of births indicates a present TFR of about 1.6 (see Scharping 2007; Wang and Mason 2008). Although a significant portion of the reduction in TFR trailed the later-longer-fewer campaign—e.g., the TFR dropped from over 6.0 in the mid-1960s to 2.7 in 1978—the OCP generated additional declines. The OCP intersected with other influential policy changes, such as the second Marriage Law, which raised the legal age of marriage, and also a dramatic rise in the prevalence of contraception (required after first birth) and sterilization (required after second birth) (Poston 1992).

As indicated above, there is variation in OCP implementation and administration, and these differences are reflected in different birth rates across provinces, localities, and ethnic groups. For example, the TFR was under 1.0 in Beijing and Shanghai, but 3.11 in Tibet (Peng 2004). The urban–rural divide continues to be a principle source of variation, in this respect, with a national TFR of 1.13 for all urban centers and 1.49 for all rural regions (Liang and Lee 2006). Hence, Gu et al. (2007) disaggregate the OCP into several categories to represent such local variation: the strict one-child rule, which applies to all urban residents and residents of six provinces that have rural or agricultural household registration status; a 1.5-child rule in 19 provinces, which allow a second child after an interval if the first child is female; and a two-child rule in rural areas of five other provinces. Under this classification scheme, 35.4 percent of the population is subject to the one-child rule, 53.6 percent to the 1.5 rule, 9.7 to the two-child rule, and an additional 1.3 percent are unregulated. After accounting for the 1.5 rule, Gu et al. estimate that 63 percent of Chinese couples have one child, 36 percent have two children, and the remainder have three or more children. This translates into a TFR of below 1.5 for about 832 million people and a TFR of 1.5 and over for 407 million people.

Sex Ratio at Birth

The most disturbing demographic effect of the OCP is, perhaps, the increasing imbalance in the sex ratio at birth after 1979. In general, the biological SRB is stable at about 106 male births per 100 female births, which implies that most deviations from this natural standard are a result of human interventions (Zeng et al. 1993). As Figure 2 presents, this estimation of natural SRB corresponds with China's SRB from 1950–1979. After 1979, China's SRB begins to move in an unnatural direction, which most observers attribute to a convergence of the one-child rule and traditional

FIGURE 2
Sex Ratio at Birth: China, 1950–2005

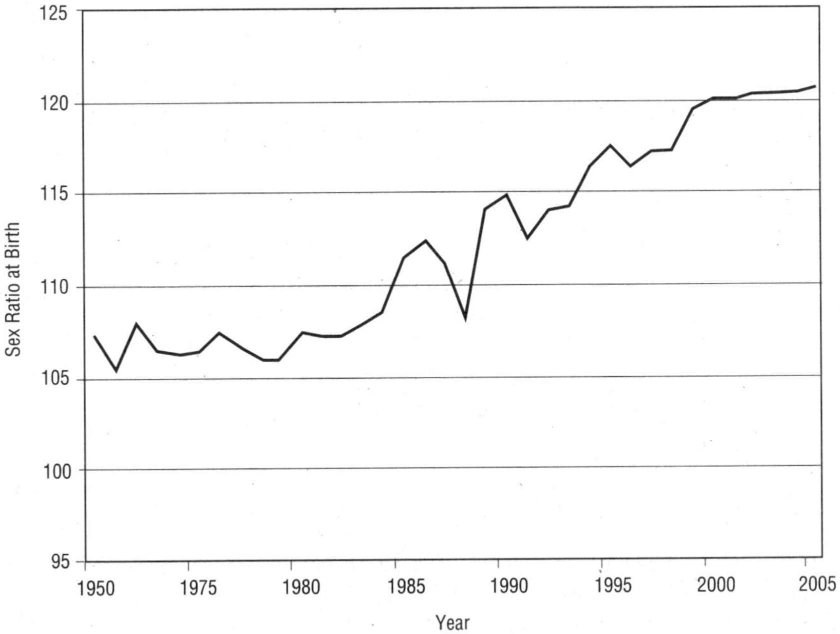

Sources: National Population and Family Planning Commission (1990); Gu and Xu (1994); *China Population Statistics Yearbook 1991*; the 1990 Census; *China Population Statistics Yearbook*; Special Tabulations of the 2000 Census; and Special Tabulations of the 2005 1 percent Population Sample Survey.

son preference. In the 1990s, the overall SRB ranged between 112 and 119, as Figure 2 shows. The super high post-1990s SRB is probably somewhat inflated because of problems with official statistics for this period (see Scharping 2003), such as underreporting of female births; but sex-selective abortion and female infanticide are serious issues (Zeng et al. 1993).

As with TFR, there is a stark urban–rural division in SRB. Li (2007) demonstrates that the 1995 SRB was 111.9 in cities, 115.6 in towns, and 117.8 in rural areas. The SRB, moreover, appears to concentrate with second and higher order births, which is opposite to natural tendencies. For example, the 1990 SRB was around normal for first births, but 121.4 for second births, 125 for third births, and 132.2 for fourth births. The literature suggests that sex-selective abortion, and to a lesser extent female infanticide, is responsible for this trend (Zeng et al. 1993). The fact that these SRB imbalances stem from the OCP is evident from inter-regional patterns, which indicate that the biggest abnormalities occur in regions where the OCP is rigid (see Attané 2002; Gu et al. 2007; Li 2007). To illustrate, the SRB for 1990 was normal only in provinces with large ethnic populations, which corresponds with a relaxation of the OCP toward minorities. In contrast, the SRB imbalance is greatest in regions where strong traditional preferences for sons intersect with a comparative hardline toward the one-child rule.

Population Aging

Population aging is a pervasive effect of the OCP, reducing the ratio of the number of working-age adults to the number of senior-age adults. Of course, improvements in life expectancies factor into the increase of older people, but the OCP is the prime factor behind the reduction of working-age adults. In short order, there will be 125 million Chinese seniors, which is about the size of Japan, the world's 10th largest nation (Wang and Mason 2007). As Figure 3 illustrates, the proportion of senior-age persons is increasing at a rapid pace. From 1950–1980, the proportion of seniors was stable, remaining under 5 percent. Their current proportion stands around 8 percent of the national population, but what is disquieting is the projected proportional increase of Chinese seniors. Under the prevailing demographic trends, the senior-aged population is expected to reach 24 percent in 2050. This projection implies a large reduction in the support ratio from 2013–2050, which could translate into serious eldercare deficits (Wang and Mason 2008). In 1975, there were just under 8 senior-age persons per 100 working age adults (United Nations 2002). This is expected to increase to 19 seniors in 2025 and 37 seniors in 2050.

In China, families are responsible for providing old-age support (*filial piety*), as state pension plans, health care, and retirement facilities are far too meagre to meet present needs, let alone future demand (Banister 1992). Though some urbanites are eligible for a state pension, rural workers are

FIGURE 3
Percent of Population Aged 65 and Over: China, 1950–2050

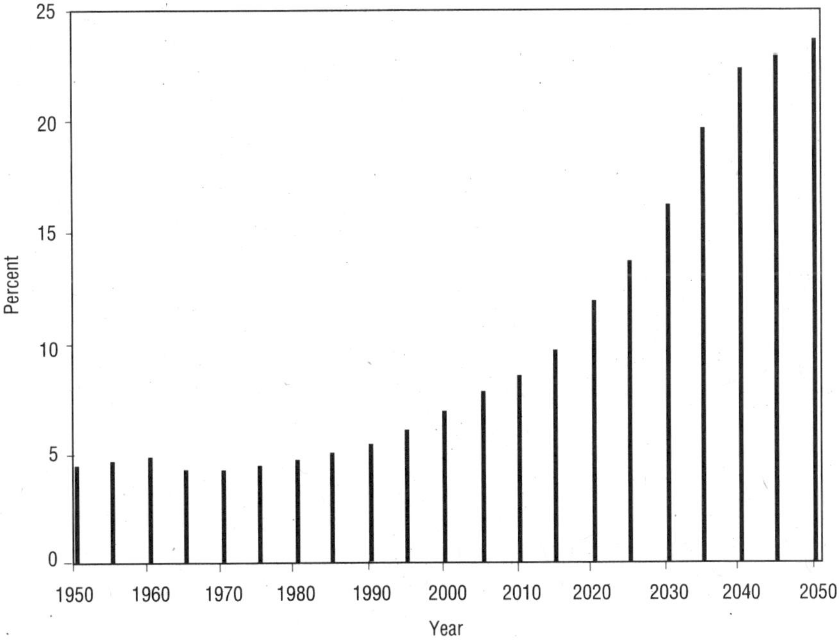

Source: United Nations (2007, pp. 316–317).

not—the government expects their children to furnish their needs in old-age, irrespective of the looming OCP-related reduction in this vital source of eldercare. In fact, the economic reforms intensified the burden on families, weakening or terminating the old-age benefits under the commune system, such as pensions, foodgrain allowances, and health care. This dilemma of population aging in China is termed the "4:2:1 paradigm"—i.e., the future family structure of 4 grandparents, 2 adult children, and 1 grandchild (Flaherty et al. 2007). This change in family structure raises a major concern about whether these two adult children can support four grandparents, especially after these individuals become seniors themselves.

Conclusion

The post-Mao leadership termed inefficacious birth control policies a "hard-to-correct, historical mistake" that was equivalent to the Great Leap in terms of its negative economic repercussions (Scharping 2003). Though mainstream economics is now critical of the neo-Malthusian perspective on the relationship between population growth and economic development, this logic guided post-1970s Chinese population control policies

(Wang and Mason 2008). The origins of a hard line against out-of-plan births is rooted in long-standing anxieties about demographic pressures on agricultural output and scarce natural resources. Their anxieties about food shortages were, in part, based on the 1959–1961 famine, which claimed millions of lives. As White (2006) observes, the pressure for birth control ebbed and flowed with the size of annual foodgrain supplies, with demands for stricter birth control increasing during poor harvests. In this regard, China arrived at a one-child-per-couple rule largely because of instable grain production.

Whether a strict one-child rule was the most appropriate response to foodgrain shortages is questionable. There is a literature outlining potential alternatives to the OCP (e.g., Bongaarts and Greenhalgh 1985; Zeng 2007), but how such softer responses to China's population question would have affected economic development is a matter of debate. The tremendous economic development since 1979, however, cannot be dislocated from population control policies. The neo-Malthusian perspective is dubious economics, to be sure, but a reduction of population growth was indeed an important economic objective for China. In particular, the one-child rule reduced the number of dependent children to adult workers, resulting in a demographic dividend (Zeng 2007). As Wang and Mason (2008) outline, the concept of a *demographic dividend* refers to an effect of a proportional increase of working-age or non-dependent adults. At prime working-age, an individual tends to produce more than he/she consumes, resulting in an investable surplus. Hence, a proportional increase of working-age people in the population generates greater investable surpluses because there is a lower proportion of non-productive dependents (e.g., children) to consume surplus production. Wang and Mason estimate that this demographic dividend contributed to 15 percent of China's economic growth from 1982-2000.

The demographic effects of China's economic reforms are impossible to understand without direct reference to the one-child policy. This institution has had a tremendous impact on China's demographic transition and reproductive behaviours, and brought much social hardship. Besides the ethical questions about mass sterilizations and forced abortions, the socio-demographic costs of an abnormal SRB are high. The one-child rule has intensified traditional son preference, and therefore produced an unnatural demographic shift. The immediate concern is how state policies have widened gender inequalities and created a shortage of marriageable women (Li 2007). The "missing female" phenomenon thus presents two major challenges. First, the sex ratio imbalance represents gender discrimination of an insidious kind—i.e., sex-selective abortion and female infanticide—which is a hindrance to women's development and concomitant economic development. Second, the acute shortage of women is creating a "marriage squeeze," and this could threaten familial institutions and create a glut of unmarried men, which are potential sources of future social problems.

In addition, though having some initial economic benefits, a continuation of a hard line towards birth control could result in future economic problems. The demographic dividend is almost spent (Wang and Mason 2008). Under the OCP, the labour force is projected to shrink in the long term and the proportion of non-productive dependents (e.g., very old seniors) will increase. This implies that future consumption rates and eldercare burdens could deplete investable surpluses, and therefore limit China's economic development, unless current birth restrictions are modified to account for potential labour shortages.

Note

The authors would like to thank Guo Zhen for research assistance.

References

Attané, I. 2002. "China's Family Planning Policy: An Overview of Its Past and Future." *Studies in Family Planning* 33:103–113.

Banister, J. 1992. "Implications of the Aging of China's Population." Pp. 463–490 in *The Population of Modern China*, edited by Dudley L. Poston, Jr. and David Yaukey. New York, NY: Plenum Press.

Bongaarts, J., and S. Greenhalgh. 1985. "An Alternative to the One-Child Policy in China." *Population and Development Review* 11:585–617.

Coale, A.J. and E.M. Hoover. 1958. *Population Growth and Economic Development in Low-Income Countries: A Case Study of India's Prospects*. Princeton, NJ: Princeton University Press.

Ehrlich, P.R. 1968. *The Population Bomb*. New York, NY: Ballantine Books.

Flaherty, J.H., M.L. Liu, L. Ding, B. Dong, Q. Ding, X, Li, and S. Xiao. 2007. "China: The Aging Giant." *Journal of the American Geriatrics Society* 55:1295–1300.

Goldstein, A. 1996. "The Many Facets of Change and Their Interrelations, 1950–1990." Pp. 3–19 in *China: The Many Facets of Demographic Change*, edited by Alice Goldstein and Wang Feng. Boulder, CO: Westview Press.

Greenhalgh, S. 2003. "Science, Modernity, and the Making of China's One-Child Policy." *Population and Development Review* 29:163–196.

Gu, B., and Y. Xu. 1994. "Sex Ratio at Birth in China." *Chinese Journal of Population Science* 3:41–48 (in Chinese).

Gu, B., W. Feng, G. Zhigang, and Z. Erli. 2007. "China's Local and National Fertility Policies at the End of the Twentieth Century." *Population and Development Review* 33:129–147.

Guo, Z., and W. Chen. 2007. "Below Replacement Fertility in Mainland China." Pp. 54-70 in *Transition and Challenge: China's Population at the Beginning of the 21st Century*, edited by Zhongwei Zhao and Fei Guo. Oxford, UK: Oxford University Press.

Hussain, A. 2002. "Demographic Transition in China and its Implications." *World Development* 30:1823–1834.

Johnson, D. G. 1999. "Population and Economic Development." *China Economic Review* 10:1–16.

Johnson, D. G., and R.D. Lee, eds. 1987. *Population Growth and Economic Development: Issues and Evidence*. Madison, WI: University of Wisconsin Press.

Li, S. 2007. "Imbalanced Sex Ratio at Birth and Comprehensive Intervention in China." Paper presented at the Asia Pacific Conference on Reproductive and Sexual Health and Rights, Hyderabad, India.

Liang, Q., and C-F. Lee. 2006. "Fertility and Population Policy: An Overview." Pp. 8-19 in *Fertility, Family Planning, and Population Policy in China*, edited by Dudley L. Poston, Jr., Che-Fu Lee, Chiung-Fang Chang, Sherry L. McKibben, and Carol S. Walther. New York, NY: Routledge.

Liu, C., and W. Ts-ang-p'ing. 1979. "The Economic Rationale for Population Control in China." *Population and Development Review* 5:559–563.

MacFarquhar, R., T. Cheek, and E. Wu, eds. 1989. *The Secret Speeches of Chairman Mao: From the Hundred Flowers to the Great Leap Forward*. Cambridge, MA: Harvard University Press.

Merli, M.G., and H.L. Smith. 2002. "Has the Chinese Family Planning Program Been Successful in Changing Fertility Preferences? Evidence from Linked Records in Four Counties in Rural Northern China." *Demography* 39:557–572.

National Population and Family Planning Commission. 1990. *Findings from the Chinese Fertility and Contraception Survey*. Beijing: Chinese Population Press (in Chinese).

——— 2006. *Findings from the Chinese Fertility and Contraception Survey*. Beijing: Chinese Population Press (in Chinese).

Peng, X. 1987. "The Demographic Consequences of the Great Leap Forward." *Population and Development Review* 13:639–670.

——— 2004. "Is it Time to Change China's Population Policy?" *China: An International Journal* 2:135–149.

Poston, D.L., Jr. 1992. "Fertility Trends in China." Pp. 277-285 in *The Population of Modern China*, edited by Dudley L. Poston, Jr. and David Yaukey. New York, NY: Plenum Press.

——— 2000. "Social and Economic Development and the Fertility Transitions in Mainland China and Taiwan." *Population and Development Review* 26:4–60.

Scharping, T. 2003. *Birth Control in China 1949-2000: Population Policy and Demographic Development*. New York, NY: RoutledgeCurzon.

——— 2007. "The Politics of Numbers: Fertility Statistics in Recent Decades." Pp. 34–53 in *Transition and Challenge: China's Population at the Beginning of the 21st Century*, edited by Zhongwei Zhao and Fei Guo. Oxford, UK: Oxford University Press.

Seltzer, J.R. 2002. *The Origins and Evolution of Family Planning Programs in Developing Countries*. Santa Monica, CA: RAND.

Sun, W., and G. Jin. 1994. "A Study on Effects of Socio-Economic Development on Fertility." *Population Research* 6:10–21 (in Chinese).

Tien, H.Y. 1973. *China's Population Struggle: Demographic Decisions of the People's Republic, 1949-1969*. Columbus, OH: Ohio State University Press.

United Nations. 2002. *World Population Ageing, 1950-2050*. New York, NY: United Nations.

——— 2007. *World Population Prospects: The 2006 Revision*. New York, NY: United Nations, pp. 316–317.

Wang, F. 1996. "A Decade of the One-Child Policy: Achievements and Implications." Pp. 97–120 in *China: The Many Facets of Demographic Change*, edited by Alice Goldstein and Wang Feng. Boulder, CO: Westview Press.

Wang, F., and A. Mason. 2007. "Population Ageing: Challenges, Opportunities, and Institutions." Pp. 177–196 in *Transition and Challenge: China's Population at the Beginning of the 21st Century*, edited by Zhongwei Zhao and Fei Guo. Oxford, UK: Oxford University Press.

——— 2008. "The Demographic Factor in China's Transition." Pp. 136–166 in *China's Great Economic Transition*, edited by Loren Brandt and Thomas G. Rawski. Cambridge, UK: Cambridge University Press.

Wang, J., Z. Wang, Y. He, and C. Duan. 2004. "An Assessment of Total Fertility Rate of Provinces in China in 2000. *Population Research* 2:20–28 (in Chinese).

White, T. 2006. *China's Longest Campaign: Birth Planning in the People's Republic, 1949-2005*. New York, NY: Cornell University Press.

Xie, Z. 2000. "Population Policy and the Family Planning Programme." Pp. 51–63 in *The Changing Population of China*, edited by Peng Xizhe and Guo Zhigang. Malden, MA: Blackwell.

Zedong, M. 1975. *Selected Works of Mao Tse-Tung*. Volume 4. Peking, CN: Foreign Languages Press.

Zeng, Y. 2007. "Options for Fertility Policy Transition in China." *Population and Development Review* 33:215–246.

Zeng, Y., T. Ping, G. Baochang, X. Yi, L. Bohua, and L. Yongpiing. 1993. "Causes and Implications of the Recent Increase in the Reported Sex Ratio at Birth in China." *Population and Development Review* 19:283–302.

Zhang, W., and X. Cao. 2007. "Family Planning During the Economic Reform Era." Pp. 18–33 in *Transition and Challenge: China's Population at the Beginning of the 21st Century*, edited by Zhongwei Zhao and Fei Guo. Oxford, UK: Oxford University Press.

Part III

Looking Forward

9

Ongoing Reform: The New Economic Policies Promoted by the 17th CCP Congress in 2007

SHUJIE YAO, STEPHEN MORGAN, AND KAILEI WEI

The 17th Chinese Communist Party Congress in October 2007 attracted attention within and outside China for its bold development agenda. After 30 years of economic reform that remarkably improved living standards and reintegrated China into the world economy, the Party unveiled a program that would push China to become a world superpower over the next 30 years. China's ambition is to achieve full industrialization and sustainable prosperity by becoming a technologically innovative "moderately prosperous" and "harmonious society" with a "scientific outlook on development." Whether China is able to achieve its objectives will depend on the Party's ability to implement new economic policies and address the social and political challenges that economic growth has created. The aim of this chapter is to examine the policies, motivations, and constraints that China faces in achieving the objectives laid out at the Party Congress.

Introduction

The Seventeenth Chinese Communist Party (CCP) Congress in October 2007 was held at a historic time, as China neared 30 years of economic reform and transformation. Unveiled at the Party Congress were policies that signalled China's drive to become a superpower over the next 30 years. By 2038, China wants to overtake the United States as the world's largest economy in absolute size (Yao 2007).

Thirty years ago, China was a very poor country, with the vast majority of its population living in poverty, malnutrition, and hunger. Today, China is a world power. Its gross domestic product (GDP), measured in nominal dollars, is the fourth largest in the world; and measured in purchasing power parity (PPP) dollars, it is the second largest, twice that of

Economic Transitions with Chinese Characteristics: Social Change During Thirty Years of Reform, eds. Arthur Sweetman and Jun Zhang. Montreal and Kingston: McGill-Queen's University Press, Queen's Policy Studies Series.

Japan and half that of the US. Per capita incomes surpassed US$2,600 in 2007, raising China from a "low income" to a "low middle income" economy as defined by the World Bank. The Chinese economy is not only large but also open—and more open than many OECD countries. In 2007, China was the second-largest exporting country in the world, generating over US$262 billion trade surplus, a total trade volume of US$2.17 trillion, and an accumulated foreign exchange reserve of US$1.53 trillion (NBS 2008). China's integration with the rest of the world is shown in its thirst for and ability to absorb foreign capital, which in 2007 was US$74.8 billion, along with an increasing capability to invest abroad.

Living conditions have improved beyond the imagination of many, including the planners of Chinese economic reforms. Most of the development targets set by China's reform architect, Deng Xiaoping, have been achieved and surpassed five to ten years before anticipated. The new target set at 2007 Party Congress is to quadruple per capita GDP in 2020 from its 2000 level, compared with a similar target set at the 16th Party Congress five years ago to quadruple China's GDP, rather than per capita GDP.

China's "economic miracle" has created new problems and challenges. The most difficult challenge is the quality of Party leadership, which has been plagued with deep-rooted and pervasive corruption, from Beijing central organizations to remote villages. Corruption is the number one enemy of the Party, the state, and the people, which, if not contained, could jeopardize the China miracle and the country's ambition to become the next superpower. Another challenge is to shift the development trajectory of the last 30 years, which has been characterized by a high demand for energy, intensive consumption of raw materials, extensive pollution, and environmental degradation, towards a more sustainable path. A third major challenge is rising inequality, which has proved difficult to contain and is multidimensional: urban–rural divisions, unbalanced regional growth, sectoral imbalances, class formation, and marginalization of urban and rural poor. If China is to become a world superpower, it must address these fundamental problems while maintaining growth momentum. The "good and fast" growth model proposed by Hu Jingtao to replace the "fast and good" growth model points to the critical need to improve the quality of economic growth in the pursuit of rapid industrialization, urbanization, and internationalization and the goal of becoming a market- and information-based economy.

Similar to the three stages of the trajectory of China's Moon Goddess I satellite launched in late 2007, China's development has progressed in three stages in terms of time path, strategies, and goals, as illustrated in Figure 1. The first stage was to eradicate hunger, malnutrition, and poverty, signified by a per capita GDP of US$800–$1,000, which Deng Xiaoping specified as *wen bao* ("warm and not hungry"). This stage ran from the late 1970s to 2000. During this stage, China passed through two phases of development. The first phase was the implementation of rural reform and the household responsibility system between 1978 and 1984. Rapid growth in agricultural productivity and output during this period laid the foundation for subsequent reform of the urban industrial sectors from the mid-1980s. The second phase, which emphasized openness and export-led growth, began in 1992 following Deng Xiaoping's southern tour. Huge amounts of foreign direct investment (FDI) flowed into China to accelerate its export-push strategy and to catch up with the advanced economies through the technological spill-over of foreign capital and technologies.

FIGURE 1
Development Time Path, Strategies, and Goals of China

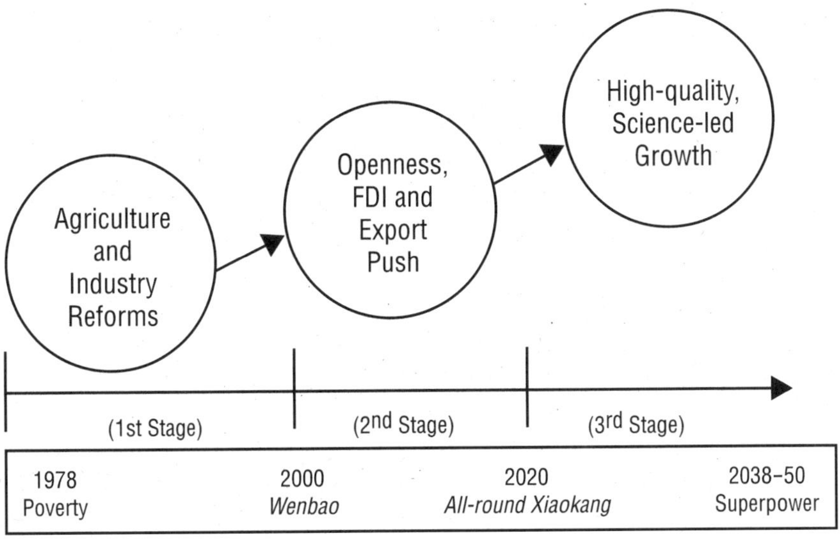

Source: Authors' own creation.

The second stage of China's strategy was to make the country a middle income economy, in which its population could enjoy a comfortable standard of living, signified by a per capita GDP target of US$4,000, as defined by Hu Jingtao as *all-round xiao kang* ("comfortable living conditions"). This stage will run from 2000 to 2020, during which China will become even more integrated with the world economy. The first step was China's accession to the World Trade Organisation (WTO) in 2001, which has seen FDI rapidly increase and the volume of trade grow even more quickly, generating a trade surplus that has propelled foreign reserves to a staggering US$1.53 trillion. China is forecast to become the world's leading exporter by 2010.

The third stage is China's quest to become the world's next superpower by the middle of the 21st century.[1] The October 2007 Party Congress adopted wide-ranging economic, political, and social policies designed to realize this quest. The remainder of this chapter will analyze the past achievements and identify the challenges, motivations, and constraints China faces in attempting to implement these policies critical for maintaining growth momentum. The next section will explore nine of the key policy initiatives, and the subsequent section will discuss the constraints the Party leadership faces in implementing these policies.

Understanding the New Policies

In China's government development literature, each policy objective must come with at least one policy instrument. The key development objectives of the 17th Party Congress and their associated policy instruments are summarized in Table 1.

TABLE 1
Development Objectives and Policy Instruments of Hu Jingtao's Report

Development Objectives	*Key Policy Instruments*
1. Building an innovative state	Medium- and long-term planning; investments in research and human capital
2. Structural change and upgrading of industries	Augmenting domestic consumption; balancing the development of agriculture, industry, and services
3. Comprehensive rural development	Improving farm incomes and rural development
4. Higher efficiency in energy and use of natural resources	Energy and materials saving technologies; better economic and industrial structure to reduce pollution and environmental degradation
5. Balancing regional development	More incentives to backward areas; establishment of cities clusters as engines of growth, particularly in the poor regions
6. Building a complete economic system and a modern market system	Ownership diversification with dominance of state-ownership; improvement of the efficiency of state economy
7. Establishing an effective regulatory system based on financial and tax reforms	Balancing central-local budgets; investments in public services; improving the efficiency of the financial sector; preventing financial crisis; compensating uses of ecosystem services
8. Improving the quality of an open economy	Continuing open policy; nurturing world-class big businesses; improving China's international competitiveness and the quality of foreign investments

Sources: Abstracted from Hu Jingtao (2007), Report to the 17th CCP Congress, 15 October 2007.

Making China an Innovative State

Making China a leader in science and technology is the most important objective of the Congress. Rapid growth in the last 30 years was based on low-level technology, extensive use of energy and raw materials, and export processing with low productivity and efficiency. Although China has become a major global exporter, many of its exports are concentrated at the lower end of the value chain. Chinese firms rely on multinational companies (MNCs) for the design and key technologies to produce export products. A large share of the value of exports is captured by the foreign MNCs and retailers in the rich, developed countries. Chinese labour and exporters share in only a fraction of the value-added of the exports. The phrase "made in China" obscures the origin of the technology. If China were able to invent all the key technologies, the manufacturing of its export goods would not have to depend on foreigners. Consequently, Chinese labour and exporters would be able to appropriate a larger share of the export value.

Were China to improve its science and innovation capability, it would raise the productivity of industries and increase the efficiency of energy and resource consumption, which would enhance its ability to maintain high growth, reduce environmental degradation, and promote sustainable growth. For this reason, building an innovative state is the most important development objective but also the most difficult to achieve. Specific policies will require huge investments in science and innovative activities. The central factor is the accumulation of human capital, including the education and nurturing of high-level scientists and the establishment of an effective and efficient research environment.

The development of science and technology in China has been based on the principle of "walking with two legs," an idea that has its roots in the Maoist development strategies of the 1950s but which today is premised on combining the import of technologies with domestic research and development.[2] Imports of foreign technologies take two forms: direct buying of foreign technologies, and embedded technological transfers through foreign direct investment (FDI). China has been a big buyer of foreign technology. In 2006 alone, China spent about US$17.6 billion on foreign technologies. FDI has also been an effective means of absorbing foreign technologies and managerial practices. Up to one-third of China's technological progress during 1979–2005 was due to FDI (Yao and Wei 2007). In other words, apart from the physical contribution, FDI has indirectly contributed about one percentage point to China's GDP growth per year in the last quarter century.

Domestic research and innovation in China are conducted in three different systems: the national and regional research network of the Chinese Academy of Sciences, universities, and large and medium-size enterprises. Chinese scientists have made tremendous progress in recent decades in many research areas, such as space technologies, as exemplified in the Moon-Goddess I satellite and the manned space craft Shenzhou VI in 2006. In manufacturing, China still depends largely on foreign technologies and processes. Domestic researchers have made advances mostly in the applications such as "utility models" and "designs."

Table 2 shows the number of patent applications with the Chinese government. The patents are divided into three categories: invention, utility model, and design. Invention is innovative technology, the most important type of patent. Although the number of patent applications by domestic researchers is greater than those by foreign researchers, the number of foreign invention patents is only a little short of the domestic patents. If we used the number of patents granted, instead of the number of applications, more invention patents have been granted to foreigners than to domestic applicants. About three quarters of domestic patent applications are non-innovative. This suggests that in the foreseeable future, China will continue to rely on foreign technologies and innovation to sustain its economic growth and upgrading of industries and services.

TABLE 2
Three Kinds of Patent Applications To The Chinese Government

Year	*Total*	*Invention Patents*		*Utility Models*		*Designs*	
	(000)	*Domestic (000)*	*Foreign (000)*	*Domestic (000)*	*Foreign (000)*	*Domestic (000)*	*Foreign (000)*
1990	41.47	5.83	4.31	27.49	0.13	3.27	0.45
1995	83.05	10.02	11.62	43.43	0.31	15.43	2.24
1996	102.74	11.47	17.05	49.34	0.26	21.40	3.22
1997	114.21	12.71	20.95	49.90	0.23	27.46	2.96
1998	121.99	13.73	22.23	51.22	0.18	31.29	3.35
1999	134.24	15.60	21.10	57.21	0.29	37.15	2.91
2000	170.68	25.35	26.40	68.46	0.35	46.53	3.59
2001	203.57	30.04	33.17	79.28	0.45	56.46	4.29
2002	252.63	39.81	40.43	92.17	0.97	73.57	5.69
2003	308.49	56.77	48.55	107.84	1.27	86.63	7.43
2004	353.81	65.79	64.35	111.58	1.24	101.58	9.27
2005	476.26	93.49	79.84	138.09	1.48	151.59	11.78

Sources: NBS (2004, 2005, 2006, 831).

Japan, the US, Germany, and other western European countries are the most important sources of foreign invention patents granted in China. This suggests that acceleration is occurring in technological diffusion from the world's most advanced industrialized nations to China (see Table 3). The three richest economies—the US, Japan, and Germany—accounted for almost 80 percent of the invention patents granted in China in 2003.

TABLE 3
Invention Patents Granted, by Country of Origin, 2003

Country	Number	%
Total	25,750	100.00
Japan	9,369	36.38
USA	5,733	22.26
Germany	2,615	10.16
Korea	2,017	7.83
France	1,038	4.03
Sweden	791	3.07
Switzerland	762	2.96
Netherlands	756	2.94
UK	572	2.22
All others	2,097	8.14

Source: NBS (2004).

Shifts in Economic Development

Past rapid growth in China has been driven by extensive investments and exports. The second policy objective of the Party Congress is to change this pattern of growth, to make significant structural change and technological upgrading of existing industries. The proposed policy instrument is a shift from reliance on FDI and exports to a more balanced pattern of consumption, investments, and exports.

Figure 2 shows that over the reform period, the share of consumption in China's GDP has declined from 67 percent in the early 1980s to about 50 percent. Meanwhile, the share of capital formation rose by more than 10 percent—from 33 percent to 43 percent. The share of net exports rose from a negative value in 1978 (-0.3 percent) to about 5.5 percent in 2005.

There are two implications of these changes to the structure of the Chinese national economy over the reform period. First, economic growth has become increasingly reliant on investments and less able to employ labour. China is a labour-abundant economy with 150–250 million unemployed and under-employed people; but the development of the past 25 years has not absorbed these people into labour-intensive industries. From 1982 to 2005, the capital/GDP efficiency declined by one-third.

Second, China's economic growth has increasingly relied on international trade. The trade/GDP ratio increased from about 10 percent in 1978 to 63 percent by 2005, generating a significant trade surplus, which was equivalent to 5.5 percent of GDP in 2005 (see Figure 3). While the increased openness means China is more integrated with the world and has been able to benefit from the international division of labour, the increased dependency on trade for economic growth has had some undesirable consequences for the domestic economy. As trade has developed

FIGURE 2
Shares of Consumption and Capital Formation in GDP, 1978–2005 (%)

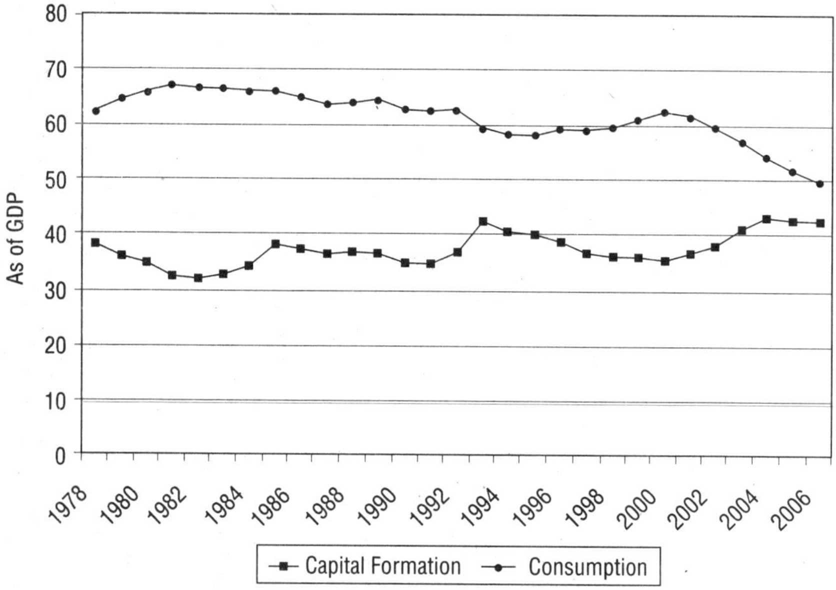

Source: NBS (2007, Table 3-15).

FIGURE 3
Trade/GDP Ratio and Contribution of Net Exports to GDP, 1978–2005 (%)

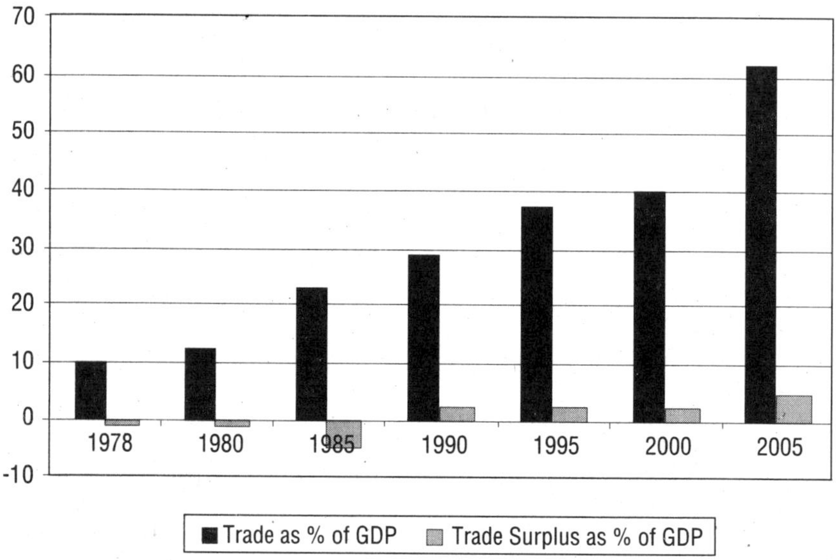

Source: NBS (2007).

unevenly across the regions, regional inequality has increased (Yao and Zhang 2001). Moreover, the diversion of resources to the trade sector has suppressed development in domestic demand, which has led to a declining share of domestic consumption in GDP. In the long term, this pattern of economic growth is undesirable for sustainable development.

Rural–Urban Development

Apart from the early reforms of 1978 to 1984, the living standards of Chinese peasants have trailed their urban counterparts. Urban–rural inequality declined between 1978 and 1984 with the success of agricultural reforms, the abolition of the communes, and the implementation of the household responsibility system. But from 1985 onward, the urban–rural gap began to widen again. Nowhere in the world is urban-rural inequality as great as in China (Riskin et al. 2001).

Figure 4 shows that the ratio of urban–rural incomes per capita was only 1.8 in 1985, but rose steadily to 3.2 by 2005, despite the government policies to reduce the tax burden on agricultural production and to stimulate farm incomes. From 2004, the government has implemented a series of pro-rural, pro-agricultural and pro-peasant policies, including the abolition of agricultural taxes in 2006, free education for rural children for nine years, and health care insurance and social security subsidies. These

FIGURE 4
Urban/Rural Per Capita Income Ratio, 1978–2005 (ratio)

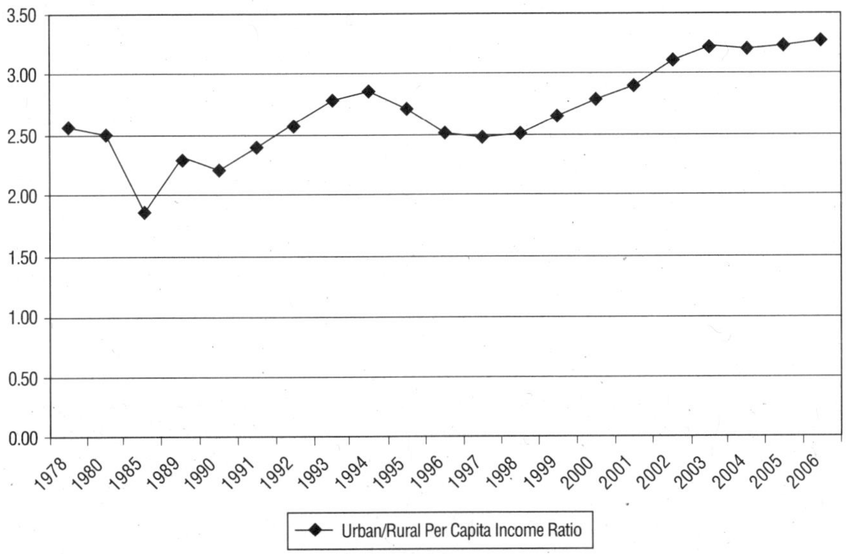

Source: NBS, *China Statistical Yearbook* (various issues, 1990–2007).

policies are good for the farmers and for rural development, but the assistance is too little and too late to arrest the upward trend in inequality because urban incomes continue to grow faster than rural incomes.

The urban–rural divide was one of the three divides that Mao Zedong wished to eliminate when the CCP came to power: the differences between urban and rural incomes, worker and peasant incomes, and intellectual and manual workers' incomes. Despite many initiatives under various party leaders, these differences persist and have widened under economic reforms. While Mao made many mistakes regarding economic and development policies, he never gave up the hope of building a prosperous and egalitarian society.

Deng Xiaoping redressed Mao's mistakes, introduced a market economy to replace a planned one, opened China to the world, and encouraged FDI and exports to promote economic growth and technological progress. Successors Jiang Zemin and Hu Jingtao have continued the reforms, without which China would not have achieved its current growth dynamics and huge improvement in living standards. An undesired consequence, however, has been increasing inequality, especially between urban and rural residents. Economists and policy-makers may argue that rising inequality is good for economic growth and is a short-term aspect of the early stage of industrialization, urbanization and market development. The persistence of urban-rural inequality in China, however, may indicate that it is a more substantive problem.

First, the increasing level of urban–rural inequality occurs despite the Party's objective to bring equality and prosperity for all. Second, based on Kuznets's rule, rising inequality is good for economic growth in the early stage of development, but it can hamper economic growth if inequality is allowed to become too extreme and introduce inefficiencies and instabilities into society (Kuznets 1955, 1963). Third, the rise in urban–rural inequality stems in part from poor policies and corruption in China. Inequality could have been reduced with stronger and more pro-poor policies. Such a policy shift, however, would impinge on vested interests, especially those of party and state officials, managers of state-owned enterprises, private entrepreneurs, employees of monopolistic industries, and many professionals. Without more radical reform of the economic system and a stronger willingness to challenge vested interests, efforts to promote more balanced urban–rural development will be in vain.

Urban–rural inequality can be reduced in two ways: by accelerating the pace of urbanization to transform peasants into urban citizens and by raising rural incomes through comprehensive rural development. China has become more urbanized over the last 30 years, the share of urban population increased from 18 percent in 1978 to 44 percent in 2006, while the share of employment in agriculture has declined from 71 percent to 43 percent. Agriculture's share of GDP, however, has declined faster, from 28 percent to less than 12 percent. As a result, agricultural productivity and rural incomes have been left behind, which explains the difficulty in trying to arrest the growing urban–rural inequality. Further industrialization and urbanization may not improve peasant incomes because the rapid growth in urban population has produced alarming effects on the quality of living in the crowded urban environment. More effective ways to raise rural incomes and the living standards of the peasantry are now sought through comprehensive rural development, or in Hu Jingtao's words, to build "socialist new villages," where farmers would have access to non-farm employment while enjoying living amenities similar to those of urban residents.[3]

Constructing socialist new villages will require government investments in rural infrastructure—such as roads, schools, hospitals and water projects—and help villagers to build a social safety net to look after the vulnerable, the old, the sick, and other dependents. This is difficult. China has failed many times over the past six decades in its attempts to promote equality between the urban and rural population. Comprehensive rural development and socialist new villages are attractive concepts, but they may yet again be another false promise for the peasantry.

Sustainable Development

Economic growth in China has relied not only on high investments but also on high consumption of energy and non-renewable resources. In Mao's period, China's modernization and socialist construction were narrowly based on two important economic indicators: the output of grain and the output of steel. Grain was important to ensure basic staple sustenance for the people. Steel was important for development and regarded as a symbol of industrialization. In the late 1970s, China's target for steel production by the end of 2000 was set at 80 million tonnes, compared with 32 million tonnes in 1978. Yet steel production in 2000 was 60 percent greater than this target, reaching 129 million tonnes. From 2000 to 2006, steel production grew rapidly. By 2006, steel output was 420 million tonnes, more than three times the 2000 level. China's steel output is greater than the combined production of the world's two largest economies, Japan and the US. China is also a large net importer of steel. In 2005, for example, China exported 20 million tonnes of steel but imported 26 million tonnes (Gao and Hu 2007).

Strong and rapid growth in steel production has two contradictory implications. On the one hand, it is a measure of the success of China's economic reforms and its ability to increase industrial production. On the other hand, it implies that China has had to use too much steel and its related industrial products, such as coal and electricity, to sustain its fast economic growth. Figure 5 shows that in 2005 China's share in the world total GDP was only 14 percent (measured in PPP terms, and about

FIGURE 5
China's Shares of Steel, Coal, and GDP, in World's Total, 1950–2005

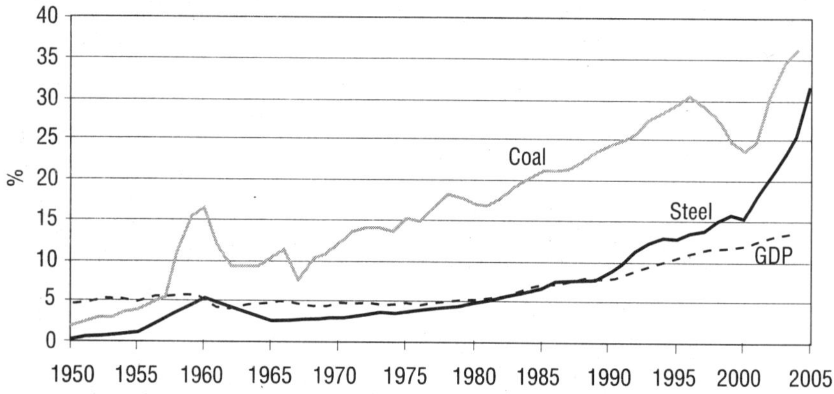

Sources: NBS (1999a); Maddison (2003); International Iron & Steel Institute (2005); Gao and Hu (2007).

5 percent in nominal dollars), but it produced more than one-third of the world's total steel output and almost 40 percent of the world's total coal output.

Apart from steel and coal, China is also the largest producer and consumer of cement and chemical fertilizers in the world. The output of cement increased 20 fold from 65 million tons in 1978 to 1.24 billion tons in 2006 (an annual growth rate of 12 percent). The output of chemical fertilizers increased more than six fold from 8.7 million tonnes to 53.5 tonnes over the same period. As grain production increased 62 percent, the grain/fertilizer output ratio declined from 35 to 9.3. In other words, for every tonne of grain production, the input of fertilizers increased 3.7 times from 1978 to 2006 (see Table 4).[4]

TABLE 4
Key Agricultural and Industrial Products, 1952–2006

Products	*Unit*	*1952*	*1978*	*2006*
Grain	million tonnes	164.0	305.0	497.0
Meat products	million tonnes	3.4	8.6	80.5
Fish	million tonnes	1.7	4.7	52.9
Coal	million tonnes	66.0	620.0	2,373.0
Electricity	billion KWH	7.3	256.6	2,865.7
Steel	million tonnes	1.4	31.8	419.2
Cement	million tonnes	2.9	65.2	1,236.8
Fertilizer	million tonnes	0.0	8.7	53.5
Vehicles	1,000 units	0.0	149.1	7,278.9

Source: NBS, *China Statistical Yearbook* (various years, 1980–2007).

Apart from steel, coal, cement and chemical fertilizer, the production of electricity and vehicles also experienced an enormous growth during the reform period. These increases reflect China's ability to sustain extraordinary level of growth, but they also have serious implications for its long-term ability to maintain such a growth momentum, since there is obvious evidence that the economy has been driven by excessive consumption of products, a pattern which is hostile to the environment and over-dependent on non-renewable energy and natural resources. According to Martin Wolf, "the increase in China's energy demand between 2002 and 2005 was equivalent to Japan's current annual energy use"; by the end of 2007, China would become the world's largest CO_2 emitter, and by 2010, the world's largest energy consumer (Wolf 2007). If China were able to achieve the same energy- and material-intensity per unit of GDP as the US and Japan, the current level of consumption of coal, cement, steel and electricity would be sufficient to double or even quadruple its GDP. Unless China shifts from its current pattern of dependency on these energy-intensive products, by 2020 China would have required the equivalent of, or more than, today's world total outputs of steel, coal, and cement to achieve its growth objective.

This scenario suggests that China cannot continue to follow the pattern of past rapid growth without severely damaging natural environment and depleting the reserves of certain non-renewable resources. Hence, it is imperative that China change its mode of development. First, China has to reduce its dependency on the manufacturing sector to sustain its economic growth rate. A more balanced industrial structure should be developed that encourages the services sector, which is less dependent on energy and raw materials. Second, China should use more science and technology to improve the efficiency of industrial use of energy and materials. Third, China should focus more on the development of labour-intensive, capital- and material-efficient, and environmentally-friendly industries.

Balanced Regional Development

One major problem with China's economic growth during the past 30 years is the widening of income inequality in different dimensions, of which regional inequality accounts for about one-third of total inequality. Among China's three large geo-economic regions, the East is the richest region, the West is the poorest, and the Central region is somewhat in between.

Figure 6 shows that per capita real GDP in the East was higher than that in the other two regions at the start of economic reforms, though the gaps were relatively small. Economic theory suggests that regional incomes will converge over time because of the law of diminishing returns, which implies that capital will gradually move from the rich to the poor regions such that the poorer regions catch up with the richer ones. In China, unfortunately, the opposite seems to have taken place: the gaps in

FIGURE 6
Real Per Capita GDP in Comparison, 1979–2005 (yuan)

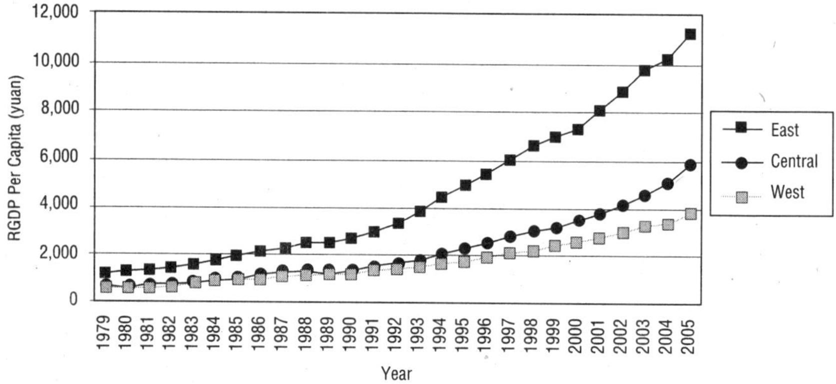

Note: Per capita GDP is measured in 1990 prices.
Sources: NBS (1999b); NBS, *Statistical Yearbook of China* (1998–2006, various issues).

per capita incomes between the three regions have steadily widened. The ratio of East-Central-West per capita real GDP was 1.71/1.23 to 1 in 1979, 2.03/1.15 to 1 in 1992, rising to 2.98/1.56 to 1 in 2005.

This increasing regional inequality has two important consequences and policy implications for the Chinese economy. First, regional inequality has led to large inter-regional migration, putting economic, social, and environmental pressure on the coastal areas. These regions have become densely populated, and the cities are struggling to provide adequate public services for migrants and their families, resulting in a significant increase in urban poverty, crime, and prostitution. On the other hand, the poor regions have suffered from a shortage of educated, able, and young people to develop the local economies, worsening the coastal–inland income disparities. Some researchers and policy-makers argue that migration reduces inter-regional inequality as migrants remit their incomes back home. The remittances, however, may not compensate for the negative effect of emigration on the development of the local economies. In addition, migrants in the cities and the coastal areas are employed in low-paid and arduous jobs, unwanted by the urban residents or the coastal peasants. Moreover, some migrant workers become unemployed, and their children live in poverty without access to education.

Second, regional inequality can also result in social instability and low efficiency of the national economy, leading to unsustainable development. At any one time, there is a large floating (transitory) population, a significant proportion of which does not have a regular home or income and often endures harsh living conditions. Poor young men without jobs or incomes may resort to crime, while the young women are vulnerable to entrapment in the sex industry. Increasing income inequality means that some urban elites can afford to consume such services as "massages" and "baths" that recruit poor country girls. The unhealthy consumption by the rich of such services occurs as investments in education, health care, and infrastructure in the poor regions are neglected. Furthermore, the commercial sex industry in China, driven by income inequality and rural–urban migration, has public health implications, such as the spread of HIV/AIDs and other sexually transmitted diseases (Sutherland 2006).

To reduce regional inequality, a more balanced regional development strategy is required, focused more on developing the western and central regions and revitalizing the northeast region, while maintaining the prosperity in the eastern region. Development in the less advantaged regions will enable people to stay at home or commute to work in the nearby cities, which will reduce the pressure for the long-distance movement of labour and the level of crime and prostitution and will improve the overall level of economic efficiency.

Regional development also requires specific strategies. Development can be evenly spread out to cover every corner of a region (carpet-style development), or it can be focused on a few centres of growth to lead the development of their surrounding areas (growth centres–led development). Development experiences in East China have proven that the growth centres–led development model works effectively (Yao and Zhang 2001). The same strategy should be adopted in the development of the inland regions. The government should facilitate the development of city clusters (growth centres) in these areas to enable them to lead the growth of surrounding townships and countryside. For example, the West region may focus its efforts on developing a few large and medium-size cities, such as Chongqing, Chengdu, Xi'an, Lanzhou, Urumqi, Kunming, and Nanning as the growth centres which, during the next 10–15 years, can lead the entire West region toward the next phase of growth and prosperity.

Modern Market Economy

One of the most important policy objectives is to build a comprehensive economic system and a modern market economy. According to Hu Jingtao's report to the Party Congress, the Party will continue to uphold its policy of building a market economy, but the Chinese market economy will differ from that of advanced western countries by retaining state-ownership, in which the central and regional governments will continue to control the majority ownership of many large commercial corporations.

Because state-owned enterprises are renowned for their low efficiency, reforms should focus on how to make them more efficient and profitable without relinquishing state control. In other words, as China avoids wholesale privatization, it should encourage private and other forms of ownerships to compete with the state economy. After almost 30 years of reforms, it is believed that joint-stock ownership can be used to reform the state economy to enable large state firms, such as the state commercial banks, insurance companies, and enterprises in the energy, transportation, communication, media, metallurgic, and other monopolistic industries. These industries can be listed on stock exchanges to attract private investments. Public listing of these state-owned companies will improve corporate governance, efficiency, and competitiveness.[5] China also aims to develop many large big businesses to compete in the international market. By 2007, China had already produced five of the world's largest ten companies in market values (see Table 5). The profitability and productivity of these giant companies, however, are well below those of their counterparts in the advanced industrialized countries.

The top five Chinese giants are PetroChina, China Mobile, Industrial and Commercial Bank of China (ICBC), Sinopec, and China Life. PetroChina moved its listing from the Hong Kong Stock Exchange to the Shanghai Stock Exchange on 5 November 2007, and its share value soared 161 percent on the same day to reach 43.6 RMB per share, compared with only HK$1.8 when it was listed in 2000. Although PetroChina was over twice the size of EXXON in market value and the only company in the world to exceed US$1 trillion, its revenue or profit was only one-third as large as that of EXXON, and its labour force 10 times as large as that of EXXON. This means that labour productivity of PetroChina, is about one-

TABLE 5
The World's 10 Largest Companies in Market Values, November 2007

Company	*Market Capital 5 Nov 2007 (US$ billion)*	*Revenue 2006 (US$ million)*	*Profit 2006 (US$ million)*	*Labour 2006 (persons)*
PetroChina	1,079.40	110,520	13,265	1,086,966
EXXON	484.69	347,254	39,500	106,400
GE	412.92	168,307	20,829	319,000
China Mobile	378.79	35,914	6,260	130,637
ICBC	371.49	36,832	6,179	351,448
MICROSOFT	344.84	12,542	8,922	79,000
Gazprom	307.79	81,115	20,321	432,230
Sinopec	301.97	131,636	3,703	681,900
SHELL	268.30	318,845	25,442	108,000
CLI	257.78	33,712	174	77,660
China 5	2,389.42	348,613	29,581	2,328,611
China 5/EXXON	4.93	1.00	0.75	21.89

Notes: Market capital is calculated based on share values on 5/11/07.
Revenue, profits and labour are for 2006. 1$=7.4538 RMB.
ICBC = Industrial and Commercial Bank of China, GE = General Electric, CLI = China Life Insurance.
China 5 = PetroChina, China Mobile, ICBC, Sinopec and CLI.

Sources: Yahoo Finance (date: 05/11/2007); cnnmoney (31/12/2006).

30th of its US counterpart. Together, the market value of the top five Chinese companies was US$2.4 trillion, or 4.9 times the market value of EXXON. Their combined profit in 2006 was only three quarters of that of EXXON, however, while their workforce was 22 times that of EXXON. Measured by labour productivity, the Chinese companies are overvalued by 30 times compared to EXXON. Measured by the price/earning ratio, the Chinese companies are overvalued by six to seven times. Although China has produced super-large companies by market value, the quality of these companies pales before their US counterparts. Were the Chinese stock markets to crash, the market values of these Chinese giants would be reduced many times, leading to an unforeseeable suffering among shareholders.[6] High volatility of share prices implies a great degree of speculation in the Chinese stock markets, signifying potential bubbles and risks in the financial system.

Effective and Efficient Regulatory Systems

The role of the state in the economic development of China is more than the control of large corporations. As the market economic system becomes more mature and complex, the state has to establish an effective regulatory system based on the deepening of financial and tax reforms. Financial reform over the past few years has been characterized by the reform of the state-owned commercial banks, state-owned insurance companies, and the Shanghai and Shenzhen Stock Exchanges. From 2005, nine commercial banks and one insurance company have been listed on the stock markets. These are among the world's largest listed banks in market value. The ICBC has surpassed Citigroup to become the world's largest commercial bank.

As financial reform deepens, it is important that the central government develops an effective regulatory mechanism to provide an environment conducive for market competition and to guard against market failure, especially large-scale financial crisis.

China has 31 provinces, each with its own interests in local economic development. To protect regional interests and to ensure that national economic and social policies are implemented to maximize the welfare of all people, it is important to establish a fair tax system, a fair and efficient central–regional budgetary allocation model, and a fair and effective compensation system for the use of ecosystem services. A fair tax system is necessary for establishing a level playing field for competition and for enhancing the state's ability to improve income equality through the "second round" distribution of national production. A fair central–regional budgetary allocation model is important for enhancing regional development incentives as well as helping the less developed regions. A fair compensation system is necessary for the state to build a harmonious society and to protect the most vulnerable groups of the population from exploitation by the advanced regions and elite groups.

Improving the Quality of an Open Economy

China's latest stage of economic growth has been driven by massive inflows of foreign capital and international trade. Most people believe that China has been producing low-quality and cheap products to serve the world markets. The expression "made in China" does not mean "made *by* China" and is often regarded as the synonym for "cheap and low-technology." To change this image, along with the strategy to transform science and technology, additional policies are needed.

First, exports need to become high-value and high-technology products, instead of mass-produced low-value products. Second, "made in China" should increasingly depend on domestic technology and innovations rather than on foreign technologies, to enable Chinese exporters and labour to win a larger share of the value chain for exported goods and services. Third, China should encourage more domestic consumption to reduce the dependence on exports and investments for economic growth, which would enlarge the opportunity for quality upgrading and international competitiveness and reduce the risks from fluctuation in international business cycles. Finally, foreign investments need to be directed towards the less advantaged regions and towards the more high-technology sectors in the advanced regions of China.

Constraints and Challenges on Chinese New Economic Policies

We have discussed the eight key economic policies outlined in Hu Jingtao's report to the October Party Congress. Party leaders are aware of what needs to be done and in what way things can be done better to achieve China's development goals and objectives.

If these policies are implemented effectively and successfully, China will achieve its medium-term objective of quadrupling per capita GDP from 2000 to 2020. By 2020, per capita GDP will reach US$4,000, and China will become an innovation-oriented state possessing a stronger capability in research and scientific innovations. In addition, China will lay a foundation for further economic growth and prosperity beyond 2020. By 2038, China's nominal GDP will be as large as that of the US and, in PPP terms, much larger.

This is an achievable target given the present growth momentum and past achievements. China, however, can also fail. There are many significant constraints and challenges that have emerged and that will emerge as China moves up the ladder of industrialization, urbanization and internationalization.

The most important challenge is the capacity of the Party to lead another 30 years of high economic growth and development that will deliver prosperity for all. The Party Congress selected many new people to fill the most powerful policy-making bodies: the Politburo of the CCP and its Standing Committee. These policy-makers are younger and more educated than their predecessors. They represent the hope for continuity in the Party's leadership, which many perceive as a necessary condition for China's social and political stability, and in turn, economic growth and prosperity.

Strong and stable Party leadership, however, is not a sufficient condition for China's ultimate success, which also depends on the ability of the leadership to devise good policies and make these policies work. In other words, strong leadership is different from good policies, and good policies are different from successful implementation. The Chinese leadership has claimed that the Party and the government do an excellent job, but more often than not, their promises fail to deliver the desired results.

For instance, Mao Zedong wanted to reduce the three differences of rural–urban, worker–peasant and mental–manual incomes, but these persist. In the early 1980s, and again in recent years, the government has emphasized year after year that farm incomes should rise and the livelihood of peasants improve, yet the gap between urban and rural incomes continue to widen. Chinese media is full of reports about efforts to crush central and regional corruption. Hu's speech to the Party Congress emphasized that prevention of corruption bears "on the popular support for the Party and its very survival," but official efforts seem inadequate. Corrupt officials and state employees flee the country or are protected covertly by those who sit in the most powerful decision-making bodies of the Party and the state.

Despite the use of the death penalty and lengthy imprisonment for convicted corrupt government officials, the scale of corruption has been growing faster than China's GDP. The Party disciplinary machine is ineffective. People are unhappy and feel let down. Open demonstrations are prohibited; but nonetheless, tens of thousands of small-scale anti-government uprisings occur every year, triggered by grass-root anger over the misconduct of local government officials, property developers, and the like.

In academic circles, scholars debate the link between corruption and economic development.[7] Some argue that corruption cannot be eliminated within a one-party system. Theory aside, the CCP has not found an effective way to fight corruption, despite the implementation of many legal and control organizations at all levels of governments. Frequently, these legislative and enforcement organs are found to be more corrupt than other party or governmental organizations.

In the last 15 years, as reforms in the financial, real estate, education and health care sectors deepen, opportunities for party and state corruption have exploded. Large state-owned industrial companies with monopolistic power are controlled by party and state officials and/or their relatives. Private firms are also linked with party and state officials (Dickson 2003, 2007). New emerging classes combine power with money and business. Their quickly accumulated wealth is often based on exploitation of ordinary workers, rural migrants, and peasants. For example, many of the richest Chinese in recent years are property developers. They are clever and hard-working, building successful businesses, but many have colluded with politicians, village leaders, bankers, and other powerful people to obtain loans, sell land, and evade taxes. The profits of these property developers are shared among these powerful groups, while ordinary people lose their land without compensation and struggle with high house prices.

The banking sector is dominated by the four large state-owned banks, whose revenues are guaranteed through state-fixed interest charges. The government fixes deposit and lending rates to allow a high interest spread (at least 3 percentage points) to ensure that these banks receive interest income. In addition, the government intervenes to protect banks: for example, 2.7 trillion RMB of non-performing loans were stripped off the four banks before three of them were listed on the stock exchange. In effect, tax-payers and depositors have subsidized these banks, which, in turn, have supported a small proportion of the population in becoming super rich and evading social responsibilities.

Malpractices in business, abuses of political and administrative power, and collusion between powerful officials and new capital-rich classes are responsible for many of the social, economic and political problems, and constraints and challenges in China today. For example, some of the rising inequality can be attributed to officials and business people who enrich themselves through easy access to capital, land, and state assets. Peasants, state employees, migrant workers, and urban poor do not share in the new wealth that is created. This process of class formation and social polarization has taken place despite the Party's ideology that workers and peasants are the masters of the country.

The "three large mountains" that Mao Zedong wished to destroy were imperialism, semi-feudalism and semi-colonialism, and bureaucratic capitalism. In theory, the first two "mountains" were destroyed when the People's Republic was established in 1949. The bureaucratic capitalists, rural landlords, and rich peasants were ruthlessly suppressed in the 1950s. The suppression of the industrial and commercial entrepreneurs, rural rich classes, and intellectuals had a detrimental effect on China's economic growth during Mao's leadership. Under Deng Xiaoping and his successors, free markets have been encouraged and capitalism re-emerged as "socialism with Chinese characteristics" or "the early stage of socialist construction."

Corruption and poor governance are to some extent responsible for China's present industrial structure and environmental degradation. China's 31 provinces resemble 31 states that compete, city against city, province against province, to set up steel factories or vehicle plants, because increasing the local economy and profits is the performance standard by which local governments are judged. As a result, China has been able to quickly expand production of many industrial products, such as steel and vehicles, but often by duplicating factories, with detrimental consequences for efficiency and the natural environment. Much of China's water, soil, and air pollution can be attributed to local government competition. Corruption has also exacerbated environment effects due to inappropriate or semi-illegal approval of polluting factories (Economy 2004, 2007).

In short, economic reform and free market policies have produced remarkable achievements and made China more prosperous; but the rebirth of the "mountain" of bureaucratic capitalism has led to many undesirable social, economic, and political problems. The new rich class of bureaucratic capitalists in China comprise the following groups: party and state officials, especially corrupt officials; former party or state officials who have been assigned to run state-owned enterprises; property developers and bankers; owners of large and medium-size private enterprises; stock brokers and fund managers; and a small proportion of intellectuals and professionals in the universities, research institutes, schools, hospitals, and law firms. Some of these new rich have made fortunes through their own efforts and creative activities, but many are rent-seekers whose gains have come from illegal or semi-illegal activities, market imperfections, tax evasion, abuses of power, and so on.

The newly rich are either in power or have the loudest voice in Chinese politics, while the most marginalised groups are isolated. The wealthy risk frustrating the vision for harmony and common prosperity presented in Hu Jingtao's speech. Consequently, if the government is to fundamentally change Chinese society, radical political reforms are required. Corruption must be dealt with severely, and the Party must broach no tolerance of power abuses and collusion between officials and business. Tax reforms must be implemented so that the state is able to tax the rich far more aggressively and transparently. Tax incomes should be used to support development of the poor regions and to create better employment opportunities for the poor. The job market should be made fairer and more competitive to give better access to the rural and urban poor.

Another critical challenge for China's new economic policies is to raise the efficiency of growth. China's GDP growth, which has been as high as 10 percent per year, has not translated into an equivalent improvement in living standards. Excessive inputs of energy and raw materials, high level of pollution and environmental damage, wasteful investments, and slow rates of technological progress and efficiency improvement suggest that further high growth cannot be maintained without social and environmental consequences.

From 1978 to 1985, China's GDP and personal incomes grew in tandem. Real per capita GDP increased 67 percent, real per capita urban income rose 52 percent, and real per capita rural income increased 169 percent (see Figure 7a). Economic growth significantly improved living standards, especially for the rural population. Meanwhile, the long-term urban-rural income inequality was greatly reduced, and over 75 percent of the rural poor were lifted out of poverty (Yao 2000). The urban–rural income ratio declined from 2.6 to 1.8 over the period (see Figure 4). This period was the best example of rapid growth with high quality in China's post-1949 modern economic history, as GDP growth was reflected immediately in improved living conditions, reduced income inequality and poverty, and increased employment.

Yet the quality of economic growth deteriorated after 1985 as the focus of reforms shifted from the rural economy to the industrial urban sector, marked by heavy investments, foreign capital, increased exports, and above-all, high consumption of energy and materials. GDP grew faster, but the growth of personal incomes slowed, especially rural incomes. Over the 20-year period from 1985 to 2005, real per capita GDP increased by 400 percent and real urban per capita income by 270 percent, but real rural per capita income rose by a mere 132 percent (see Figure 7b). The increase in rural income over 20 years was significantly less than during the first years of reforms. In addition, high investment and consumption of energy and resources have been accompanied by losses in economic efficiency and environmental degradation, along with rising income inequality. Without improving the quality of growth, China will be unable to build a harmonious society with sustainable prosperity.

FIGURE 7a
Real Per Capita GDP, Urban and Rural Incomes, 1978–1985 (1978=100)

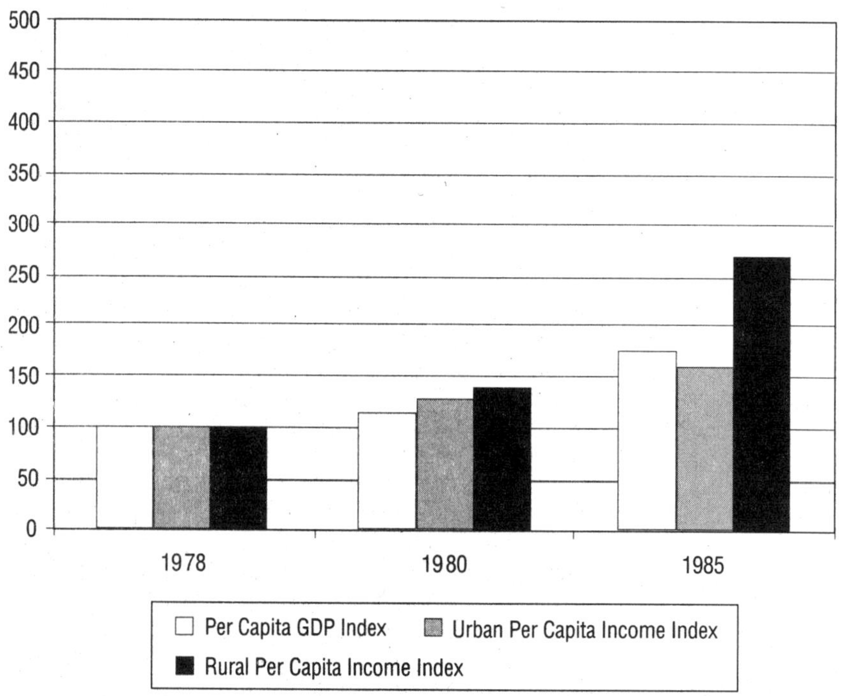

FIGURE 7B
Real Per Capita GDP, Urban and Rural Incomes, 1985–2005 (1985=100)

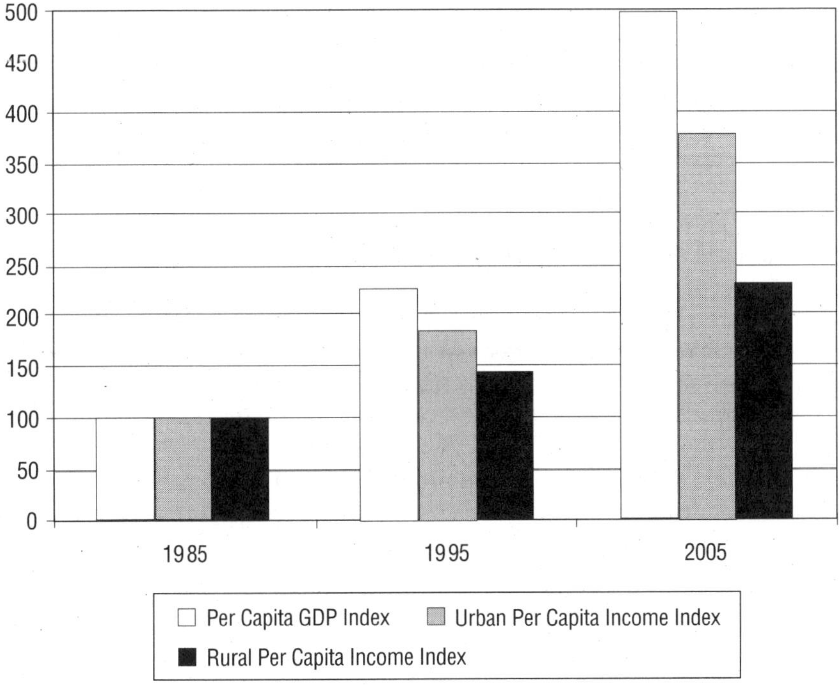

Source: NBS (2006).

Conclusions

The eight key economic policies of the 17th Party Congress discussed in this chapter outline the CCP's intention to resolve the problems and reduce the constraints that will affect future growth and prosperity. These policies can be summarized in two phrases as mentioned in Hu Jingtao's report: "building a harmonious society" with a "scientific approach."

Building a harmonious society is a long-term goal. Harmony means that all people are to share fairly in economic growth and prosperity, which means that income inequality has to be reduced, regional development to become more balanced, and party and state officials to abandon rent-seeking and corrupt activities. If the Party can build a harmonious society, it may retain power with popular support. Otherwise, the Party may lose power. As a result, building a harmonious society is central to the survival of the CCP.

To build a harmonious society, Hu Jingtao argued that a scientific approach was required. This comprises the following: China needs to rely on science and innovation to improve production efficiency, reduce its dependency on non-renewal energy, and create a better economic and market system to enable the country to become more competitive internationally, improve the current industrial structure, and reduce its dependency on manufacturing as the basis of high economic growth. By these means, China will be able to improve the quality of industrialization and urbanization, reduce pollution and environmental degradation, find alternative sources of energy and materials, improve the quality of living for all people in education, health care and other public services, and make China a superpower able to influence world affairs.

China has moved from the first to the second stage of its development program to become a world superpower. The next 13 years from 2007 to 2020 is a critical period to realize the goals of the second stage. If China achieves its growth objective of quadrupling per capita GDP by 2020 and stems the rising trend of personal income inequality and regional disparities, it will lay a solid foundation for its last stage of development towards to the middle of the 21st century. China's success, however, will largely depend on whether the new policies unveiled at the Party Congress can be effectively implemented. These new policies discussed in Hu Jingtao's report signal China's push towards attaining sustainable growth, common prosperity for all, and a world superpower status.

Notes

1. David Miliband, Britain's foreign secretary, suggested that the EU must be a model power but not a superstate or superpower. He said that the only superpower of the world is the USA. Any possible candidate of the next superpower must be China and/or India, but not the EU (16 November 2007, the Independent), http://news.independent.co.uk/europe/article3166411.ece.
2. The original idea of "walking on two legs" was the simultaneous development of agriculture and industry, the linking of rural and urban strategies, that would achieve balanced growth that delivered welfare benefits for both farmers and urban workers. One of the spectacular failures of this strategy was the small backyard steel furnaces during the Great Leap Forward that resulted in huge losses of scarce iron resources. See Carl Riskin (1986) for a concise summary of these ideas.
3. The socialist new villages program is an evolution of the ideas that informed the promotion of township and village enterprises in the 1980s, as encapsulated in the slogan "leave the soil, but not the village; expand industries but not cities" (*li tu, bu li xiang; kuo ye, bu kuo cheng*) (Morgan 1994).
4. Some fertilizers are used for non-grain production. We assume the same proportion of fertilizer was used for non-grain production in 1978 as in 2006 in the calculation.
5. The policy to encourage listing of part of the state-owned sector was unveiled at the 15th Party Congress 10 years ago by Jiang Zemin, who told the congress that joint stock form of ownership was suitable not only for western capitalism but also for firms in socialist market economies.

6. On 19 November 2007, the share prices of the top five Chinese giants had plummeted by 28 percent from their peak reached two weeks earlier, and China Life was forced out of the world's top-10 list.
7. The literature on corruption in China is huge. The World Bank and other international agencies have published papers on measures to combat it. See, among others, Lü (2000) and Dickson (2003).

References

Economy, E. 2004. *The River Runs Black: The Environmental Challenge to China's Future.* Ithaca, NY; London: Cornell University Press.

——— 2007. "The Great Leap Backward? The Costs of China's Environmental Crisis." *Foreign Affairs* 86(5) (Sept-Oct):38–59.

Dickson, B.J. 2003. *Red Capitalists in China: The Party, Private Entrepreneurs, and Prospects for Political Change.* Cambridge: Cambridge University Press.

——— 2007. "Integrating Wealth and Power in China: The Communist Party's Embrace of the Private Sector." *The China Quarterly* 192 (December):827–854.

Gao, Y., and A. Hu. 2007. "Development of China's Steel Industry." Paper presented to the 18th Annual Conference of CEA (UK), April 2007, University of Nottingham.

International Iron and Steel Institute. 2005. *World Steel in Figures 2005.* Available at http://www.iisi.org.

Kuznets, S.S. 1955. "Economic Growth and Income Inequality." *American Economic Review* 45(1):1–28.

——— 1963. "Quantitative Aspects of the Economic Growth of Nations." *Economic Development and Cultural Change* 11(2):1–80.

Lü, X. 2000. *Cadres and Corruption: The Organizational Involution of the Chinese Communist Party.* Stanford, CA: Stanford University Press.

Maddison, A. 2003. *The World Economy: Historical Statistics.* Paris: OECD.

Morgan, S.L. 1994. "The Impact of the Growth of Township Enterprises on Rural-Urban Transformation in China, 1978-1991." Pp. 213–236 in *Asian City: Processes of Development, Characteristics and Planning,* edited by A.K. Dutt, F.J. Costa, S. Aggarwal, and A.G. Nobel. Norwell, MA: Kluwer Academic.

National Bureau of Statistics (NBS). 1999a. *Comprehensive Statistical Data and Material on 50 Years of New China.* Beijing: China Statistics Press.

___ 1999b. *China Statistical Data for 50 Years 1949–98.* Beijing: China Statistics Press.

___ 2004. *China Science and Technology Statistical Yearbook.* Beijing: China Statistics Press.

___ 2005. *China Science and Technology Statistical Yearbook.* Beijing: China Statistics Press.

___ 2006. *China Statistical Yearbook 2006.* Beijing: Statistical Press.

___ 2007. *China Statistical Yearbook.* Beijing: China Statistics Press.

___ 2008. *Statistical Communiqué of the People's Republic of China on the 2007.* 28 February 2008. Available at http://www.stats.gov.cn/english/newsandcomingevents/t20080228_402465066.htm.

Riskin, C. 1988. *China's Political Economy.* Oxford: Oxford University Press.

Riskin, C., Z. Renwei, and L. Shi (Eds). 2001. *China's Retreat from Equality: Income Distribution and Economic Transition.* Armonk, NY; London: M.E. Sharpe.

Smil, V. 1984. *The Bad Earth: Environmental Degradation in China.* New York: M.E. Sharpe; London: Zed Press.

___ 2004. *China's Past, China's Future: Energy, Food, Environment.* New York; London: RoutledgeCurzon.

Sutherland, D. 2006. "Applying the scientific concept of development to HIV / AIDS in China." In *Scientific Development Concept and China's New Industrialization: Theory, Problem and Policy* (in Chinese), edited by C. Qilin. Xiamen: Xiamen University Publishing House.

Wolf, M. 2007. "Welcome to the New World of Runaway Energy Demand." *Financial Times.* November 14, 2007. Available at http: / / www.ft.com / cms / s / 0 / ba8b0d6a-9254-11dc-8981-0000779fd2ac.html.

Yao, S. 2007. "Can China Really Become the Next Superpower?" Professorial inaugural lecture, University of Nottingham, 1 March 2007.

Yao, S., and K. Wei. 2007. "Economic Growth in the Present of FDI From A Newly Industrializing Economy's Perspective." *Journal of Comparative Economics* 35(1): 211–234.

Yao, S., and Z. Zongyi. 2001. "On Regional Inequality and Diverging Clubs: A Case Study of Contemporary China." *Journal of Comparative Economics* 29(3):466–484.

About the Authors

GORDON BETCHERMAN is Sector Manager and Lead Economist in the Europe and Central Asia region of the World Bank. He specializes in labour markets and social protection. His recent research includes the implications of population aging, informal sectors, labour taxes, and youth unemployment. He is a Visiting Fellow at the School of Policy Studies at Queen's University, Canada.

JOHN CAI, PhD, is Professor of Economics, and Chair of Department of Public Economics at Fudan University in Shanghai. His recent research includes the reform of Chinese health care system, international comparison of health care systems, and public economics. He also serves as a senior health policy analyst with the Massachusetts State Government.

JIE CHEN, PhD, is Associate Professor of Industrial Economy in the School of Management at Fudan University, as well as Adjunct Faculty of Institution for Housing and Urban Research at Uppsala University in Sweden. His research interests focus on housing economics, urban economics, and real estate finance. His publications have appeared in the *Journal of Housing Economics*, *Urban Studies*, and *Housing Studies*, among others.

ZHAO CHEN, PhD, is Professor of Economics, as well as the deputy director of the China Center for Economic Studies (CCES) at Fudan University in Shanghai, and Director of the Fudan Institute for Industrial Development Studies. His research interests include urban and rural development, economic transition and political economy. His publications have appeared in the *Journal of Comparative Economics*, *Review of Income and Wealth*, and *Journal of the Asia Pacific Economy*, among others.

WEILI DING is an Assistant Professor at the School of Policy Studies and Department of Economics at Queen's University, Canada. Her research focuses on topics within the economics of education as well as the causes and consequences of recent rural developments and urban transitions in China. She holds a PhD in Economics from the University of Pittsburgh.

Steven F. Lehrer is an Assistant Professor at the School of Policy Studies and Department of Economics at Queen's University, Canada, and a faculty research fellow at the National Bureau of Economic Research (NBER). His research focuses on health economics, economics of education, causal inference, and experimental economics.

Shuzhuo Li is a Professor of Demography and Director of the Institute for Population and Development Studies at Xi'an Jiaotong University in China.

Xiaofeng Liu is a master's student at the China Center for Economic Studies (CCES) at Fudan University in Shanghai. He is currently researching urban–rural migration policy in China and the happiness of internal migrants in Shanghai.

Stephen Morgan is Associate Professor in Chinese Studies in the School of Contemporary Chinese Studies at the University of Nottingham. He has been involved with China for more than 30 years as a student, academic, and foreign correspondent. His primary research is in the fields of economic and business history of 19th- and 20th-century China, but he has mostly taught graduate and undergraduate programs in international business and strategic management. At Nottingham, he is involved in developing the new graduate programs in Chinese business and management. He has worked extensively as a journalist on newspapers in Australia and Hong Kong.

Naoki Murakami, PhD, is the Professor of Economics at Advanced Research Institute for the Sciences and Humanities (ARISH) at Nihon University in Japan. His research interests are rural industrialization and industrial organization in China. Since 2008, he has been a member of the Board of Directors of Japanese Research Association for Chinese Economy.

Ana Revenga is the Director of the Poverty Reduction and Development Effectiveness Group at the World Bank. Between 2005 and 2008, she was Lead Economist for Human Development and Manager for Labour and Social Protection in the East Asia and the Pacific region. She has published extensively on poverty, labour, and trade issues.

Christoph M. Schimmele is a PhD candidate in Sociology at the University of Victoria in Canada.

Arthur Sweetman, PhD, is Professor and the Director of the School of Policy Studies at Queen's University in Canada, where he holds the Stauffer-Dunning Chair in policy studies. He also holds appointments in the Department of Economics, and the Department of Community Health and Epidemiology. Most of his research focuses on economic issues regarding labour markets and health policy.

MINNA HAHN TONG is a World Bank consultant specializing in social protection in the East Asia region. Her current work focuses on labour market issues, social assistance programs, and social insurance policies in China and Vietnam. She has also worked extensively on social protection issues in Southeast Asia.

KAILEI WEI is currently Associate Professor of Economics at Hainan University in China. She obtained her PhD in economics from Middlesex University in 2008 and has published several journal articles on Chinese economic growth and FDI, including articles in the *Journal of Comparative Economics* and *Applied Economics Letter*.

GUANZHONG JAMES WEN, PhD, holds joint appointments in the Department of Economics and the International Studies Program at Trinity College, USA. He is also a specially appointed Professor and Director of the Center for Agriculture and Coordinated Rural–Urban Development in the Advanced Research Institute at the Shanghai University of Finance and Economics, in addition to sitting on the editorial board of several publications including the *China Economic Quarterly* and the *China Economic Review*. His research interests are China's farming sector, the Great Leap Famine, and land issues related to urbanization, globalization, and modernization, and is among the first to use an economic geographical perspective to study the Needham Puzzle.

ZHENG WU is Professor of Sociology, and Chair of the Department of Sociology at the University of Victoria in Canada.

SHUJIE YAO is Professor of Economics and Chinese Sustainable Development, Head of the School of Contemporary Chinese Studies, and Coordinator of the China and the World Economy Programme at the Leverhulme Trust Centre of Globalisation and Economic Policy (GEP), University of Nottingham. He is also Special Chair Professor of Economics in Xi'an Jiaotong University in China. He is an expert on economic development in China, has published six research monographs, and has edited books as well as over 70 refereed journal articles. His current research projects include "Reforms of the state commercial banks in China," funded by the Leverhulme Trust.

JUN ZHANG, PhD, is the Cheung Kong Professor of Economics and the Director of the China Center for Economic Studies (CCES) at Fudan University in Shanghai. His recent research includes productivity, growth accounting, and the political economy of growth in post-reform China. Since 2001, he has served as editor-in-chief for the *Journal of World Economic Papers*.

Yuan Zhang, PhD in Economics, is Associate Professor at the China Center for Economic Studies (CCES) at Fudan University in Shanghai. His recent research focuses on micro finance, rural poverty and social network in rural China. Since 2004, he has served as editor for the *Journal of World Economic Papers*.

Queen's Policy Studies
Recent Publications

The Queen's Policy Studies Series is dedicated to the exploration of major public policy issues that confront governments and society in Canada and other nations.

Our books are available from good bookstores everywhere, including the Queen's University bookstore (http://www.campusbookstore.com/). McGill-Queen's University Press is the exclusive world representative and distributor of books in the series. A full catalogue and ordering information may be found on their web site (http://mqup.mcgill.ca/).

School of Policy Studies

Politics of Purpose, 40th Anniversary Edition, Elizabeth McIninch and Arthur Milnes (eds.), 2009 Paper ISBN 978-1-55339-227-9 Cloth ISBN 978-1-55339-224-8

Dear Gladys: Letters from Over There, Gladys Osmond (Gilbert Penney ed.), 2009 ISBN 978-1-55339-223-1

Bridging the Divide: Religious Dialogue and Universal Ethics, Papers for The InterAction Council, Thomas S. Axworthy (ed.), 2008
Paper ISBN 978-1-55339-219-4 Cloth ISBN 978-1-55339-220-0

Immigration and Integration in Canada in the Twenty-first Century, John Biles, Meyer Burstein, and James Frideres (eds.), 2008
Paper ISBN 978-1-55339-216-3 Cloth ISBN 978-1-55339-217-0

Robert Stanfield's Canada, Richard Clippingdale, 2008 ISBN 978-1-55339-218-7

Exploring Social Insurance: Can a Dose of Europe Cure Canadian Health Care Finance? Colleen Flood, Mark Stabile, and Carolyn Tuohy (eds.), 2008
Paper ISBN 978-1-55339-136-4 Cloth ISBN 978-1-55339-213-2

Canada in NORAD, 1957–2007: A History, Joseph T. Jockel, 2007
Paper ISBN 978-1-55339-134-0 Cloth ISBN 978-1-55339-135-7

Canadian Public-Sector Financial Management, Andrew Graham, 2007
Paper ISBN 978-1-55339-120-3 Cloth ISBN 978-1-55339-121-0

Emerging Approaches to Chronic Disease Management in Primary Health Care, John Dorland and Mary Ann McColl (eds.), 2007
Paper ISBN 978-1-55339-130-2 Cloth ISBN 978-1-55339-131-9

Fulfilling Potential, Creating Success: Perspectives on Human Capital Development, Garnett Picot, Ron Saunders and Arthur Sweetman (eds.), 2007
Paper ISBN 978-1-55339-127-2 Cloth ISBN 978-1-55339-128-9

Reinventing Canadian Defence Procurement: A View from the Inside, Alan S. Williams, 2006
Paper ISBN 0-9781693-0-1 (Published in association with Breakout Educational Network)

SARS in Context: Memory, History, Policy, Jacalyn Duffin and Arthur Sweetman (eds.), 2006
Paper ISBN 978-0-7735-3194-9 Cloth ISBN 978-0-7735-3193-2
(Published in association with McGill-Queen's University Press)

Dreamland: How Canada's Pretend Foreign Policy has Undermined Sovereignty, Roy Rempel, 2006
Paper ISBN 1-55339-118-7 Cloth ISBN 1-55339-119-5
(Published in association with Breakout Educational Network)

Canadian and Mexican Security in the New North America: Challenges and Prospects, Jordi Díez (ed.), 2006 Paper ISBN 978-1-55339-123-4 Cloth ISBN 978-1-55339-122-7

Global Networks and Local Linkages: The Paradox of Cluster Development in an Open Economy, David A. Wolfe and Matthew Lucas (eds.), 2005
Paper ISBN 1-55339-047-4 Cloth ISBN 1-55339-048-2

Choice of Force: Special Operations for Canada, David Last and Bernd Horn (eds.), 2005
Paper ISBN 1-55339-044-X Cloth ISBN 1-55339-045-8

Force of Choice: Perspectives on Special Operations, Bernd Horn, J. Paul de B. Taillon, and David Last (eds.), 2004 Paper ISBN 1-55339-042-3 Cloth 1-55339-043-1

New Missions, Old Problems, Douglas L. Bland, David Last, Franklin Pinch, and Alan Okros (eds.), 2004 Paper ISBN 1-55339-034-2 Cloth 1-55339-035-0

The North American Democratic Peace: Absence of War and Security Institution-Building in Canada-US Relations, 1867-1958, Stéphane Roussel, 2004
Paper ISBN 0-88911-937-6 Cloth 0-88911-932-2

Implementing Primary Care Reform: Barriers and Facilitators, Ruth Wilson, S.E.D. Shortt and John Dorland (eds.), 2004 Paper ISBN 1-55339-040-7 Cloth 1-55339-041-5

Social and Cultural Change, David Last, Franklin Pinch, Douglas L. Bland, and Alan Okros (eds.), 2004 Paper ISBN 1-55339-032-6 Cloth 1-55339-033-4

Clusters in a Cold Climate: Innovation Dynamics in a Diverse Economy, David A. Wolfe and Matthew Lucas (eds.), 2004 Paper ISBN 1-55339-038-5 Cloth 1-55339-039-3

Canada Without Armed Forces? Douglas L. Bland (ed.), 2004
Paper ISBN 1-55339-036-9 Cloth 1-55339-037-7

Campaigns for International Security: Canada's Defence Policy at the Turn of the Century, Douglas L. Bland and Sean M. Maloney, 2004
Paper ISBN 0-88911-962-7 Cloth 0-88911-964-3

Understanding Innovation in Canadian Industry, Fred Gault (ed.), 2003
Paper ISBN 1-55339-030-X Cloth 1-55339-031-8

Delicate Dances: Public Policy and the Nonprofit Sector, Kathy L. Brock (ed.), 2003
Paper ISBN 0-88911-953-8 Cloth 0-88911-955-4

Beyond the National Divide: Regional Dimensions of Industrial Relations, Mark Thompson, Joseph B. Rose and Anthony E. Smith (eds.), 2003
Paper ISBN 0-88911-963-5 Cloth 0-88911-965-1

The Nonprofit Sector in Interesting Times: Case Studies in a Changing Sector, Kathy L. Brock and Keith G. Banting (eds.), 2003
Paper ISBN 0-88911-941-4 Cloth 0-88911-943-0

Clusters Old and New: The Transition to a Knowledge Economy in Canada's Regions, David A. Wolfe (ed.), 2003 Paper ISBN 0-88911-959-7 Cloth 0-88911-961-9

The e-Connected World: Risks and Opportunities, Stephen Coleman (ed.), 2003
Paper ISBN 0-88911-945-7 Cloth 0-88911-947-3

Knowledge Clusters and Regional Innovation: Economic Development in Canada, J. Adam Holbrook and David A. Wolfe (eds.), 2002
Paper ISBN 0-88911-919-8 Cloth 0-88911-917-1

Lessons of Everyday Law/Le droit du quotidien, Roderick Alexander Macdonald, 2002
Paper ISBN 0-88911-915-5 Cloth 0-88911-913-9

Improving Connections Between Governments and Nonprofit and Voluntary Organizations: Public Policy and the Third Sector, Kathy L. Brock (ed.), 2002
Paper ISBN 0-88911-899-X Cloth 0-88911-907-4

Governing Food: Science, Safety and Trade, Peter W.B. Phillips and Robert Wolfe (eds.), 2001
Paper ISBN 0-88911-897-3 Cloth 0-88911-903-1

The Nonprofit Sector and Government in a New Century, Kathy L. Brock and Keith G. Banting (eds.), 2001 Paper ISBN 0-88911-901-5 Cloth 0-88911-905-8

The Dynamics of Decentralization: Canadian Federalism and British Devolution, Trevor C. Salmon and Michael Keating (eds.), 2001 ISBN 0-88911-895-7

Institute of Intergovernmental Relations

Canada: The State of the Federation 2006/07: Transitions – Fiscal and Political Federalism in an Era of Change, vol. 20, John R. Allan, Thomas J. Courchene, and Christian Leuprecht (eds.), 2009 Paper ISBN 978-1-55339-189-0 Cloth ISBN 978-1-55339-191-3

Comparing Federal Systems, Third Edition, Ronald L. Watts, 2008 ISBN 978-1-55339-188-3

Canada: The State of the Federation 2005: Quebec and Canada in the New Century – New Dynamics, New Opportunities, vol. 19, Michael Murphy (ed.), 2007
Paper ISBN 978-1-55339-018-3 Cloth ISBN 978-1-55339-017-6

Spheres of Governance: Comparative Studies of Cities in Multilevel Governance Systems, Harvey Lazar and Christian Leuprecht (eds.), 2007
Paper ISBN 978-1-55339-019-0 Cloth ISBN 978-1-55339-129-6

Canada: The State of the Federation 2004, vol. 18, *Municipal-Federal-Provincial Relations in Canada*, Robert Young and Christian Leuprecht (eds.), 2006
Paper ISBN 1-55339-015-6 Cloth ISBN 1-55339-016-4

Canadian Fiscal Arrangements: What Works, What Might Work Better, Harvey Lazar (ed.), 2005
Paper ISBN 1-55339-012-1 Cloth ISBN 1-55339-013-X

Canada: The State of the Federation 2003, vol. 17, *Reconfiguring Aboriginal-State Relations*, Michael Murphy (ed.), 2005 Paper ISBN 1-55339-010-5 Cloth ISBN 1-55339-011-3

Canada: The State of the Federation 2002, vol. 16, *Reconsidering the Institutions of Canadian Federalism*, J. Peter Meekison, Hamish Telford and Harvey Lazar (eds.), 2004
Paper ISBN 1-55339-009-1 Cloth ISBN 1-55339-008-3

Federalism and Labour Market Policy: Comparing Different Governance and Employment Strategies, Alain Noël (ed.), 2004 Paper ISBN 1-55339-006-7 Cloth ISBN 1-55339-007-5

The Impact of Global and Regional Integration on Federal Systems: A Comparative Analysis, Harvey Lazar, Hamish Telford and Ronald L. Watts (eds.), 2003
Paper ISBN 1-55339-002-4 Cloth ISBN 1-55339-003-2

Canada: The State of the Federation 2001, vol. 15, *Canadian Political Culture(s) in Transition*, Hamish Telford and Harvey Lazar (eds.), 2002
Paper ISBN 0-88911-863-9 Cloth ISBN 0-88911-851-5

Federalism, Democracy and Disability Policy in Canada, Alan Puttee (ed.), 2002
Paper ISBN 0-88911-855-8 Cloth ISBN 1-55339-001-6, ISBN 0-88911-845-0 (set)

Comparaison des régimes fédéraux, 2e éd., Ronald L. Watts, 2002 ISBN 1-55339-005-9

Health Policy and Federalism: A Comparative Perspective on Multi-Level Governance, Keith G. Banting and Stan Corbett (eds.), 2001
Paper ISBN 0-88911-859-0 Cloth ISBN 1-55339-000-8, ISBN 0-88911-845-0 (set)

Disability and Federalism: Comparing Different Approaches to Full Participation, David Cameron and Fraser Valentine (eds.), 2001
Paper ISBN 0-88911-857-4 Cloth ISBN 0-88911-867-1, ISBN 0-88911-845-0 (set)

Federalism, Democracy and Health Policy in Canada, Duane Adams (ed.), 2001
Paper ISBN 0-88911-853-1 Cloth ISBN 0-88911-865-5, ISBN 0-88911-845-0 (set)

John Deutsch Institute for the Study of Economic Policy

The 2006 Federal Budget: Rethinking Fiscal Priorities, Charles M. Beach, Michael Smart and Thomas A. Wilson (eds.), 2007
Paper ISBN 978-1-55339-125-8 Cloth ISBN 978-1-55339-126-6

Health Services Restructuring in Canada: New Evidence and New Directions, Charles M. Beach, Richard P. Chaykowksi, Sam Shortt, France St-Hilaire and Arthur Sweetman (eds.), 2006 Paper ISBN 978-1-55339-076-3 Cloth ISBN 978-1-55339-075-6

A Challenge for Higher Education in Ontario, Charles M. Beach (ed.), 2005
Paper ISBN 1-55339-074-1 Cloth ISBN 1-55339-073-3

Current Directions in Financial Regulation, Frank Milne and Edwin H. Neave (eds.), Policy Forum Series no. 40, 2005 Paper ISBN 1-55339-072-5 Cloth ISBN 1-55339-071-7

Higher Education in Canada, Charles M. Beach, Robin W. Boadway and R. Marvin McInnis (eds.), 2005 Paper ISBN 1-55339-070-9 Cloth ISBN 1-55339-069-5

Financial Services and Public Policy, Christopher Waddell (ed.), 2004
Paper ISBN 1-55339-068-7 Cloth ISBN 1-55339-067-9

The 2003 Federal Budget: Conflicting Tensions, Charles M. Beach and Thomas A. Wilson (eds.), Policy Forum Series no. 39, 2004
Paper ISBN 0-88911-958-9 Cloth ISBN 0-88911-956-2

Canadian Immigration Policy for the 21st Century, Charles M. Beach, Alan G. Green and Jeffrey G. Reitz (eds.), 2003 Paper ISBN 0-88911-954-6 Cloth ISBN 0-88911-952-X

Framing Financial Structure in an Information Environment, Thomas J. Courchene and Edwin H. Neave (eds.), Policy Forum Series no. 38, 2003
Paper ISBN 0-88911-950-3 Cloth ISBN 0-88911-948-1

Towards Evidence-Based Policy for Canadian Education/Vers des politiques canadiennes d'éducation fondées sur la recherche, Patrice de Broucker and/et Arthur Sweetman (eds./dirs.), 2002 Paper ISBN 0-88911-946-5 Cloth ISBN 0-88911-944-9

Money, Markets and Mobility: Celebrating the Ideas of Robert A. Mundell, Nobel Laureate in Economic Sciences, Thomas J. Courchene (ed.), 2002
Paper ISBN 0-88911-820-5 Cloth ISBN 0-88911-818-3

The State of Economics in Canada: Festschrift in Honour of David Slater, Patrick Grady and Andrew Sharpe (eds.), 2001 Paper ISBN 0-88911-942-2 Cloth ISBN 0-88911-940-6

The 2000 Federal Budget: Retrospect and Prospect, Paul A.R. Hobson and Thomas A. Wilson (eds.), 2001 Policy Forum Series no. 37, 2001
Paper ISBN 0-88911-816-7 Cloth ISBN 0-88911-814-0

Our publications may be purchased at leading bookstores, including the Queen's University Bookstore
(http://www.campusbookstore.com/), or can be ordered online from: McGill-Queen's University Press, at
http://mqup.mcgill.ca/ordering.php

For more information about new and backlist titles from Queen's Policy Studies, visit the McGill-Queen's
University Press web site at:
http://mqup.mcgill.ca/